Letters from Saints to Sinners

Letters from Saints to Sinners

Edited and selected by
JOHN CUMMING

A Crossroad Book
The Crossroad Publishing Company
New York

1996

First published in the U.S.A. 1996 by
THE CROSSROAD PUBLISHING COMPANY
370 Lexington Avenue
New York, NY 10017

First published in Great Britain 1996 by
BURNS & OATES
Wellwood, North Farm Road,
Tunbridge Wells, Kent TN2 3DR

Library of Congress Cataloging-in-Publication Data

Letters from saints to sinners / edited and selected by John Cumming.
    p. cm.
  Includes bibliographical references.
  ISBN 0-8245-1560-9 (pb)
    1. Christian saints—Correspondence. 2. Christian biography. 3. Christian life.
4. Meditations. I. Cumming, John. 1937–   .
BX4657.L456   1996
248.4—dc20   95–43599
                                                                              CIP

*The picture on the front cover is adapted by Penelope Burns
from a French thirteenth-century MS.*

Typeset by Search Press Limited
Printed in Finland by Werner Söderström Oy

Contents

9. RELIGIOUS LIFE AND CHURCH BEHAVIOUR   167

10. TRUE BELIEF AND TRUE RELIGION   205

Introduction

"The greatest saints and sinners have been made / The proselytes of one another's trade." I hope that this book will provide only slight, if entertaining, evidence of one aspect of Samuel Butler's remark yet amply demonstrate the truth of the other. It contains letters from saints beatified or canonized by the Catholic Church but also from other men and women whose lives are acknowledged as exemplary. In its own way each letter discloses the holiness of the writer. Of course this does not exclude humour, severity, testiness, gossipiness, anecdotal verve, historical and intellectual perception, and even rebelliousness.

Each letter is a revealing or instructional work in its own right, and offers matter for meditation, therapeutic reflection and sheer enjoyment of a person's individuality. The letters are grouped thematically but can be read from start to finish as a conspectus of the Church across the ages and of the vagaries of human experience.

The saints' correspondents are "sinners" in the sense that anyone other than a saint may be taken to be a sinner, although in many cases the writer makes it very plain that he or she considers the recipient to be in a parlous condition of soul, for, says Kierkegaard: "God creates out of nothing. Yes, to be sure, but he does what is still more wonderful: he makes saints out of sinners." Some, indeed, of those addressed and charitably reproved or improved were eventually recognized as saints in their own right. The recipients include popes, close members of the saint's family, religious superiors and inferiors, monarchs and politicians, and the humble as well as the eminent. Sometimes the saint fiercely corrects pope or king, parent, brother or sister. Sometimes the letters pour out the trials but as often the joys of holiness, divulge the conditions of the age, or relate amazing and exciting even if distressing events of the saint's life. They may also describe

9

and analyze the character and inspiring or trying behaviour of various individuals. Occasionally the letters refer to major historical events, to private affairs of the heart, or to forthcoming martyrdom.

The variety of these documents not only provides a source for exploration of the nature of saintliness, showing it to be something far from mawkish or sentimental, but brings out the sheer humanity of holy men and women. They range from major actors on the stage of history and leading intellectuals and writers to simple but brave workers and peasants. Their courage, compassion, hope, determination, faith and apostolic spirit, but above all their enduring love and concern for truth, speak powerfully to us across the centuries. After all, our moral choices are essentially the same as those which prompted these men and women to speak and write their words of truth.

Truth to self is an essential mark of the saint as letter-writer. "Our letters are our selves," wrote John Donne. But the accuracy of this statement is difficult to grasp in the second half of the twentieth century. The importance of any kind of letter-writing has dwindled and it can scarcely be spoken of as an art. After the at first gradual then galloping erosion by the telegraph, the telephone and the fax of leisurely and even of literary written communication, only the unpredictable communitarianism of the Internet promises something like a revival of correspondence. In this form, however, it is often anonymous in origin, increasingly public in appearance, and infinitely adaptable or reconstructible on reception.

Yet almost from the start of the Christian era until fairly recently, letters comprised a major category of documentary records of religious life and thought. Just as in the various branches of secular life the letter was a vital instrument of communication public and private, so all sorts of churchpeople, from the eminent to the reclusive, used letters to testify, inform, inquire, argue, instruct, commission, advise, influence, motivate, praise, coax, nag, incite, irritate, blame, rebuke and condemn.

Of course the more subtle mentors among holy letter-writers judiciously combined these and other purposes and effects, and worked, say, a morale-boosting phrase or two into a memorable reproof. Such mixed intentions and corresponding stylistic devices often appear in the letters that we now find most beguiling, moving or convincing. This is not strange, for in this century of progress and degradation, the literature, art, music and philosophy, but also the religious writing, that we find most "authentic" have to do more than one thing. The most important documents, indeed, are thought to be those which have much more to say to us than their formal statements intend. We are most interested in those which offer beneath the surface, in asides, and "in the gaps"—in what is not said—revelations about the writers and their circumstances that we have been taught to detect by the duplicities and reversals of history, the knowledge of human behaviour proffered by the psychological sciences, and the refined irony we prize so greatly. This approach, we feel, is true to the condition of our times, when investigations of particular personalities are as wary, tender and sophisticated as the injustices meted out to whole classes and nations are crude, gross, and barbaric.

Even though letters with these characteristics are very much to present-day taste, those in more straightforward, traditional categories remain important and effective. A major distinction has often been made (especially in biblical criticism) between "letters" from person to person, or to a specific group, when we have to know something about sender and recipient and why specifically the letter was sent, and "epistles," or only relatively short essays or pronouncements addressed to the general public, or to the Church or a church as a whole. The thirteen Pauline letters and letters 2-3 of John are now generally accepted as "letters" in this sense, in which letters are sometimes thought of as less formal and, incorporating as they may do all sorts of occasional references to everything possible from mood to food, even as more wayward than "epistles" (the remaining New Testament letters, for instance). Epistles of course are, or seem to be, letters only because of the literary convention that sets them out in that form. Still, these categories are often more fluid than they seem. The very convention means that all through its reading the general epistle has to be thought of as a letter to a definite correspondent or body of correspondents. This supposition, even though acknowledged as such, is a necessary condition of the desired effect. Neither the epistles of Paul nor the "Provincial Letters" of Pascal could easily forgo their literary form. Because of that, and beyond that, the epistolary convention allows the writer in the course of a letter skilfully to focus the message on a (possibly named) individual or sub-group within the group addressed. The personal letter, in its turn, can broaden out so that the recipient becomes an example of a whole class of people—whom, sometimes, it is hoped the letter will reach in copies and reports.

Other letters from the devout share one or more of the themes and devices characteristic of religious autobiographies or "confessions." They may be accounts of revelations or experiences of conversion, expressions of sorrow for regrettable or sinful acts, and declarations of thanks to God for his saving grace, and are intended to awaken or confirm an appropriately similar attitude in the addressee.

In 2 Corinthians and Galatians 1 St Paul looks back on his life thus, and over the centuries writers of general and particular epistles have followed him in describing their spiritual development under divine inspiration and guidance. The emphasis may be on the inward stages of this evolution, on vast struggles to reach certain positions within, to order and define them, and even to abandon or negate them in a more advanced state of spiritual achievement. Equally, such letters may chronicle or describe the events of an outward progress, when the writer has survived very real battles and physical persecution on the way to a calm that could be interrupted at any time, or one that precedes death, promising imminent access to a greater peace.

Confessional letters of this kind tend to reflect dominant contemporary emphases arising from changing movements of thought and corresponding theological and devotional innovations. Throughout the Christian ages, however, singular individuals have written in a heightened form, sometimes reaching the level of elated or jubilant narrative, in order to affect their correspondents by conveying, as only letters can, the special intensity of their experience.

John Donne began one letter thus: "I make account that this writing of letters, when it is with any seriousness, is a kind of ecstasy, and a departure and secession and suspension of the soul, which doth then communicate itself to two bodies. And as I would every day provide for my soul's last convoy, though I know not when I shall die, and perchance I shall never die; so for these ecstasies in letters, I oftentimes deliver myself over in writing when I know not when those letters shall be sent to you, and many times they never are, for I have a little satisfaction in seeing a letter written to you upon my table, though I meet no opportunity of sending it." This collection contains several examples from different eras of such letters that successfully impart the extraordinariness of the author, and are as important to writer as to recipient. Others, of course, follow established conventions yet depart subtly from them.

Though the epistle-writers of the New Testament have always provided important models, many religious letter-writers from the Fathers of the Church until the present century have followed instead the patterns of classical antiquity. For the most part these were the letters of Marcus Tullius Cicero, of Seneca and of Pliny the Consul on formal topics and to their several friends, but also the "epistles" of Horace and others. The styles of these major writers were distinctive and personal and marked the practice of many later writers, not only in Latin but in modern European languages. The best instances of classical letter-writing among the more than 140,000 examples that have come down to us from ancient Greece and Rome became models of propriety, commonsense, elegance, ease and good taste. The beautifully ordered qualifications of Cicero's architecture, in which each device modifies the whole, but also the artful amplifications of Seneca's prose, marked not only the letters of many of the Fathers of the Church but, even if variously, the letters of ecclesiastics in later centuries, which have often equalled the balance and subtlety of their predecessors.

Most classical models were highly formal. This was partly because almost all of them were dictated to scribes, but also because the subject-matter was formal, being concerned with legal or political affairs or, even when apparently personal in nature, intended for circulation among statesmen or in intellectual circles of influence. The scribe was often almost equally responsible for the finished letter, and sometimes for everything beyond the basic outline. The New Testament epistles were also dictated, and range from the simple and direct to the magisterially elaborate. Such carefully re-worked and re-handled letters, in which the basic thought is expanded and qualified by a number of rhetorical devices, are often among the most influential Christian documents, and I have included some letters from different ages that stand in this tradition.

The medieval mystics, however, when they cast their devotional treatises as letters, looked back to somewhat different, much later, philosophical and mystical forebears, such as the Pseudo-Dionysus. The quasi-mystical letter is an important form, and the present selection contains a few examples (from, say, the author of the *Letter of Private Direction*, or St John of the Cross).

But formality in church letter-writing has always remained a necessity and a temptation. As the organization of the Church became monarchical and imperial, so popes and patriarchs in their letters of decree, appointment and correction became appropriately regal. Episcopal briefs and papal encyclicals are certainly letters of a kind, but they have had an unfortunate influence on less exalted ecclesiastical correspondence. For the most part, this anthology avoids this kind of formal missive.

As the centuries passed, of course, new models were established. Above all, the Fathers themselves, hortatory, argumentative, definitive and urgent in controversy and crisis, defined the topics and forms of much religious letter-writing. Their magisterial tone, and their high serious-ness—stated as well as implied—in settling controversy, but also their often fascinating individuality of tone, expression and anecdote, were imitated well into our own century by churchmen and churchwomen intent on correcting heretics, schismatics and the ill-informed.

Some letters of correction avoid formal devices in order to administer a short sharp reproof to the wayward, licentious or downright evil, whether individuals or governments. Occasionally, however, when an appeal to social conscience is in question, they must deftly modulate their corrective tone if not content. I have included many examples of such letters in various styles, from St Bernard to Elizabeth Fry. Sometimes, as with Fénelon's appeal to his monarch, Pascal's *Provincial Letters*, and Wesley's longer letter-treatises, the letter form is a literary device. The hard-hitting "letter" is intended for wide circulation, and first appears in "open" form in a journal or magazine, or as a book, or—as in the case of the pieces by Kierkegaard in this selection—is even attributed to a fictional character. A few examples of the different types of letter in this important category appear here.

Another major tendency in saintly letter-writing is that of what might be called modified introspection. The best examples of this tradition from the eighteenth century onwards draw on the great models of personal narrative and example already referred to, but show the influence of the international to-and-fro of Romanticism, the cultivation of the sensibilities, Pietism, and the Anglo-Scottish literary and philosophic cult of individualism. This kind of emphasis has remained marked in our own century, but with the additional effects of an interest in disparate, conscious and even unconscious impulses. This has affected not only modern religious letter-writing but our reading of letters from the devout of past ages.

Nevertheless, in the agonizing crises of our own time, Christians have had to face much the same choices as in past centuries. Under persecution and expecting martyrdom for their beliefs they have written final letters as resolute and inspiring as their predecessors'. These range from Dietrich Bonhoeffer's measured testimony to Christians of the future to perhaps the simplest and most moving of all—Maximilian Kolbe's few pencilled lines from the hell of Auschwitz, written in an alien tongue on a thin mean card.

Many, of course, of the most revealing, entertaining and spiritually profitable letters in this book belong to none of the foregoing categories. They are plain though often masterly descriptions of personal experiences. In them, missionaries, priests, monks, nuns and lay-people relate not merely their own misfortunes and achievements to warn or encourage others, but the everyday events of their lives in foreign countries, in the convent or at school or home. They may contain admonitions but as often admissions, mundane requests such as those of the great mystic Teresa of

Avila for fish or orange-flower water, poignantly ordinary descriptions of everyday joys and anxieties, and, of course, jokes—"God deliver us," said St Teresa, "from sullen saints!" Some readers, to be sure, may also find this an unusually cross-denominational and ideologically generous selection. Of course, most of the letters in this collection are from, or are reliably ascribed to, saints in the sense of men and women beatified and canonized, formally or by tradition and repute, by the Catholic Church. Nevertheless, a number of those that appeal most acutely to a modern sensibility are from persons uncanonized though recognized as saintly in various ways, and some of these were certainly—twisting the phrase slightly—"*ni saint, ni romain.*" A few of them, like Blaise Pascal or George Macdonald, opposed certain aspects of their own churches and were even condemned by them, and yet their very opposition to authority remains part of their saintliness. Some, like Gerard Manley Hopkins or Charles de Foucauld, may be found wanting because of some quirkiness of character, yet their obscure struggle or quaint obduracy, as with many of their canonized predecessors, makes them especially attractive to people today. Some, such as John Henry Newman, were acknowledged as saintly in their own lifetimes—as indeed were many canonized saints—but would never have characterized themselves thus. In a letter of 1850, Newman wrote: "You must undeceive Miss A.B. about me, though I suppose she uses words in a general sense. I have nothing of a saint about me as every one knows, and it is a severe (and salutary) mortification to be thought next door to one. I may have a high view of many things, but it is the consequence of education and a peculiar cast of intellect—but this is very different from being what I admire. I have no tendency to be a saint—it is a sad thing to say so. Saints are not literary men, they do not love the classics, they do not write Tales." In this very disclaimer we sense the particular quality of Newman that declares his saintliness but has made him and others unappealing to higher ecclesiastics, and has discouraged any formal elevation to sainthood.

In recent years, to be sure, the Roman Catholic Church has stepped up the rate at which it declares Catholics blessed or saints, yet an even greater number of Christian people, Catholics and others, are still pronounced saintly by, as it were, the reputation of their lives and achievements. And there is no longer any need to apologize for bringing together great Christians, even when they cannot be reconciled in the doctrinal lines of their own times. Furthermore, no church of the Reformation, apart from the Church of England, has formally declared any of its members saints. The sole exception is King Charles the Martyr. For nearly three hundred years the Book of Common Prayer contained a service of commemoration for Charles I which was removed in the reign of Queen Victoria. Unfortunately his surviving letters are rather tedious.

But there are many men and women, whether Roman Catholics or from other denominations, whose undoubted holiness makes their letters fascinating or is clearly apparent in them. A number of them are listed in the calendar of the Alternative Service Book of the Church of England. The spiritually, morally and socially committed lives of some of them, such as Elizabeth Fry and John Wesley, speak directly from even the few letters by them included here. Others, such as George Fox, Charles Wesley and John Keble, are outstanding but largely unproblematical figures. Yet others are great, if often inwardly tortured, divines, such as John Donne and Søren Kierkegaard, whose letters reveal something of their exemplary personal conflicts, and point up their fine representation or salutary contradiction of the often tragic ethos of their times. Some of them, like Corrie ten Boom, are humble people, and others theologians of the stature of Dietrich Bonhoeffer—who is undeniably to be ranked with Thomas More and other spiritual forebears of noble intellect and saintly courage. These men and women declared their convictions in the face of predominant evils of the twentieth century that continually re-echo in the public catastrophes and private neuroses of our own days.

Inevitably, some readers will ask why there are so many letters from certain individuals; why some classic letters and not instead obscure, hitherto unpublished or even atypical pieces by their famous authors were included; why this or that saint or devout person does not appear here; and why there are so few letters or even only a single letter from their favourite saint.

First, this is only a selection from a vast range of possibilities. Some saints, such as Bernard of Clairvaux and Teresa of Avila, wrote so many superbly individual letters on important topics, that a generous representation of their richly varied minds and spirits more than compensates for avoiding the "beginner's stamp-catalogue" approach of choosing one letter from each of as many different saints as possible. Similarly, although I have included a number of reasonably unfamiliar letters, and some that show the calcified great in a perhaps oddly revealing and all-too-human light, this book is like a verse anthology in that it also draws on a basic stock of "classic" pieces. It has to include letters well-known or relatively familiar in the past, which, by judicious pruning, editing or re-translation, I have tried to make available to a new readership. Some of these central texts have appeared in a different form in previous, now generally unavailable selections, or in multi-volume collections usually accessible only in libraries. I am grateful for the help provided by these often scholarly sources, and for permission to reprint extracts from a few copyright works. These are acknowledged at the end of this book.

Second, I have not included some of the great letter-writing Fathers of the Church, and certain other major saints are represented only minimally. The main reason for this is that an off-putting apparatus of notes and even essays would be needed to explain the general setting and local references of so many historically important documents and personal exchanges. This applies to many figures from St Basil to Karl Barth, and to fine letter-writers from contexts as diverse as, say, those of the first century of the Reformation, sixteenth-seventeenth century French spirituality, German Pietism or the establishment of the churches in the New World and in colonial territories, and their development in the Third World. For similar reasons this selection is largely restricted to Western Christianity, to whose particular history, problems, and ethos these letters speak in ways still relevant.

In view of that restriction, this Introduction does not attempt anything like a potted survey of the lives and times of the letter-writers in which diverse personalities over the centuries are mutually accommodated in a miniature history of the Church. Nor have I tried to establish anything like a typology or to distil an essence of saintliness. This is something that each reader must do for himself or herself. All these letters speak for themselves and their writers. Nevertheless, each is prefaced with a short note containing the minimal information needed to grasp the circum-stances of a letter, of its writer and possibly of its recipient. These remarks are amplified by short biographies at the end of the book, and are complemented by basic reading lists of, above all, collections of letters (wherever possible in the original language and in translation), but also of recommended biographies and a few amenable commentaries. These should enable the interested reader to follow up writers whom he or she finds especially appealing.

John Cumming

CHAPTER 1

Childhood and Youth

A Big Fat Kiss

St Thérèse of Lisieux   1877

When four years of age; to her sister's friend

Few letters from the saints at so early an age have been preserved. The unassuming innocence and charm of this one are still apparent in the "Autobiography" of its writer, who died at the age of twenty-four.

Dear Louise,

   I've never met you but I love you very much indeed all the same. Pauline said write to you. She has got me on her knee because I can't use a real pen all on my own. She wants me to say I'm lazy. But that isn't true. I work hard all day long playing tricks on my sisters, poor things! I'm a little villain who never stops laughing. Bye-bye, Louise darling! Here's a big fat kiss for you! Give Sister Marie Aloysia and Sister Louise de Gonzaga a good hug for me because I don't know the others....

Thérèse

Educating Paula

St Jerome   403

To Paula's mother

In this delightful letter to Laeta on the training and education of a daughter, one of the most learned Fathers of the Church, and one of the most intransigent, even vituperative critics of the morals of his times, shows himself as a relaxed and sympathetic correspondent. Though most people today would find his attitude to the education of girls somewhat strict, his very concern that it should be done proficiently was "liberal" in the fourth century.

Dear Lady,

You come from a mixed marriage but little Paula's parents are you yourself and dear Toxentius. It seems incredible that a mother's promise should have been answered by granting Albinus, a pagan high-priest, a Christian granddaughter, and that her grandfather should be delighted with his little granddaughter babbling the Alleluia of Christ, and in his old age cradle on his breast a child vowed to God?...

I shall do what you ask and teach you, her mother, how to bring up our precious little Paula. This is the way to raise a soul that will be God's own temple. During her upbringing, only that which is based on the holy fear of God must reach her ears or cross her lips. She must have unworldly nurses and governesses, not worldly women who would pick up vile habits and, much worse, teach them to the child. Give her an alphabet of boxwood or ivory and make sure that each letter has its correct name. These must be her toys so that she learns something even from games. She must not only learn the correct order of the letters and get them by heart in a singsong rhyme, but you must always be shuffling them, putting the last letters in the middle and the middle ones at the start, so that she recognizes them by sight as well as by sound.

As soon as she begins to move her pencil over the paper, guide those tiny fingers while the hand is still uncertain by putting your own hand over hers, and make sure that she keeps to the lines that have already been ruled and does not stray outside them. Promise her a reward for good spelling and encourage her with little gifts of the kind that children of her age love. Make sure that she has some little friends to keep her up to scratch and spur her to greater efforts when she is rather slow to respond. But persuade her to remain lively by praising her. Then she will be proud of her achievements when she does better than others, and blush when they do better than she. Above all take care that she does not begin to hate her lessons, otherwise the dislike of infancy will remain with her in later years.

The words she learns to put together so slowly must not be chosen at random, but selected and assembled with deliberation, so that while she is practising something else her memory benefits too.

And take care that no silly woman teaches her to use baby-talk or to waste time in expensive finery. The one will ruin her conversation and the other her character. She must not learn when a child what she will have to unlearn later. Much of the Gracchi's eloquence is due to the way their mother talked to them from early childhood. Hortensius became an orator when he was still in his father's arms. Early impressions are difficult to erase from the mind. Once you have dyed wool purple it is impossible to get it back to its original colour. For a long time a spit-new jar keeps the taste and smell of what was poured into it orignally. We learn from the Greek historians that Alexander, the greatest of kings and lord of the world, never managed to free himself from the bad manners and gait that he picked up from his tutor Leonides when he was a little boy. Evil is easily copied and if you cannot imitate people's virtues, you will copy their inadequacies soon enough.

When Paula visits her grandfather she may climb on his knee, put her arms around him and sing Alleluia in his ear whether he likes it or not. Her grandmother will kiss and caress her; her smiles will show that she recognizes her father; and she will be such a pet that the whole family will be glad that they possess such a perfect rosebud. Tell her immediately who her other grandmother is, and who her aunt is. Tell her about her true Sovereign in whose army she is a little recruit already being trained for service.

Of course you may say: How can I do all this when I am a woman of the world, living in Rome among all these vast crowds of people? Well, don't do anything you can't manage. When little Paula can do without you, send her to her grandmother. Give up this little jewel for Mary's room and put her in the cradle where the infant Jesus cried. Let her be raised in the monastery and join the nuns' choirs. If you send your little Paula, I promise that I shall be both her teacher and her foster-father. I am old but I shall give her piggy-backs and train her faltering speech. My work will be even more glorious than that of the worldly philosopher, for I shall not be teaching a Macedonian monarch how to die one day of Babylonian poison, but a handmaid and bride of Christ to prepare for the kingdom of heaven.

Yours affectionately,

Jerome

Learned Women

St Thomas More   May 22nd 1518

To the tutor of his children

In some of the intervals between his lectures at Cambridge, Erasmus visited the Gonnell family at Landbeach, and later recommended the schoolmaster and copyist William Gonnell to Sir Thomas More as a tutor for his household. Here More outlines the principles he is to follow. They are remarkable in many ways, not least for the insistence that the tutor must make no distinction between the education of More's daughters and his son—recalling the description of equal opportunities for learning in "Utopia".

My dear Gonnell,

Thank you for your letter, elegant and affectionate as ever.

I can see how devoted you are to my children. Their own letters tell me how hard you work. I was pleased with all their letters, but I was especially gratified to see that Elizabeth is more gentle and self-controlled in her mother's absence than some children would be were she present. Elizabeth should know that this good conduct delights me more than a collection of all the letters I could receive.

Although I prefer learning and virtue to all the treasures of kings, a reputation for learning without a good life is no more than the glitter and notoriety of ill-fame, especially in a woman. An erudite woman is a novelty and shows up men's laziness, so many people tend to attack her and infer that scholarship is really responsible for what nature has caused, hoping that the vices of the learned will persuade people to think that their own ignorance is virtuous. On the other hand, if a woman (and I hope, with you as their teacher, that this will be true of all my daughters) adds even slight intellectual powers to great virtue, I believe that she will find that more profitable than all the riches of Croesus and the beauty of Helen. This is not because she will win glory in this way, though glory is to virtue as a shadow to a body, but because the reward of wisdom is substantial; it is not lost like riches and does not fade like beauty, for it depends on an inward awareness of what is right and not on human gossip, the most foolish and unprofitable of things.

The chief benefit which people gain from learning is that in studying we are taught to look not for praise but for a useful end. Most learned men, especially the philosophers, who are our guides in this life, have taught this. So, dear Gonnell, since this is the road we have to take, I have often begged not only you, who care so much for my children that you would do so anyway, and not only my wife, whose mother's love prompts her enough in that regard anyway, but all my friends to warn my children to avoid the dangers of pride and haughtiness, and to walk in the pleasant fields of modesty; not to be dazzled by the sight of gold, not to be saddened by a lack of what they wrongly admire in others; not to think the more of themselves because of any cheap finery, or less because they have none; neither to neglect the beauty nature has given them and thus distort it, nor try to increase it by artificial means; to put virtue first and learning second;

and when studying to think most of whatever teaches them piety to God, love to all, and Christian humility for themselves. In this way God will give them the reward of an innocent life, and they may look forward without fear to certain death.

Meanwhile, with their undoubted joy, they will neither be carried away by the empty praise of human beings nor depressed by what silly people have to say. I would say that these are the true fruits of learning. Admittedly not all men of learning have them, but I would say that anyone who devotes himself or herself to study with these goals in view will easily get what he or she wants and become perfect.

I do not think it will affect the harvest much whether a man or a woman sows the crop. They both have the same human nature which reason tells us is different from that of animals. So both are equally suited for studies which cultivate the intellect and, like well-ploughed land, give a good crop once the seed of good principles has been planted. If it were true that the soil of a woman's brain was poor and tended to bear bracken rather than corn (and by saying just that many people stop women from studying), I think, that, on the contrary, a woman's mind would then need all the more careful cultivation, so that industry could repair nature's deficiencies. This was the opinion of the ancient authors, of the most prudent and the holiest. Not to speak of the rest, St Jerome and St Augustine not only advised excellent matrons and most noble virgins to study, but, to help them, also carefully explained the difficult parts of the Bible, and for tender girls wrote letters so very erudite that nowadays old men who claim to be professors of theology can scarcely read them correctly, let alone understand them. My dear and learned Gonnell, kindly make sure that my daughters learn the works of these holy men thoroughly. Then they will discover above all what to aim at when studying, and the fruit of their labours: the testimony of God and a good conscience. Then peace and calm will govern their hearts and they will be troubled neither by exaggerated praise not by the stupidity of the unlearned who despise erudition.

Of course you will object that these things, though advisable, are beyond my young daughters' capacity, for you will scarcely find a man, however old and however learned, whose mind is so assured and unyielding as not to be affected to some degree by a longing for glory. But, dear Gonnell, do make sure that my children are completely spared this plague of vainglory. I must ask you and their mother and all their friends to sing this song to them, to carry on singing it, and to drive into their heads the assurance that vainglory is vile and contemptible, and that there is nothing so sublime as the humble modesty which Christ so often praises. There is nothing more helpful to this end that to read them the lessons of the ancient Fathers who, they will know, cannot be angry with them. When they honour them because of their holiness, they must also be greatly moved by their authority. If, in addition to their reading Sallust, you read something of this kind to Margaret and Elizabeth, as more advanced than John and Cecily, I and they will treasure you all the more. Then you will make my children who are dear to me first of all by nature, even dearer by learning and virtue, and dearest of all because they gain in wisdom and advance in a virtuous life.

Farewell,
> *Thomas More*

Grace and Wit

St Thomas More   September 3rd 1522

To his children

Sir Thomas More's children by his first wife Jane were Margaret, born 1505, Elizabeth, born 1506, Cecily, born 1507, and John, born 1509. More was always concerned that they should be educated with equal care. Much of his advice on letter-writing remains valid today.

My dear Children,

The Bristol merchant brought me your letters the day after leaving you—a great delight. Anything from your workshop, however rough and unfinished, gives me more pleasure than anyone else's perfect composition. I found all your letters very pleasing. Nevertheless, I must admit— somewhat ingenuously—-that my son John's letter gave me most pleasure, because it was the longest, and because he seems to have spent more labour and study on it. He not only sets out what he has to say attractively, in a quite polished style, but plays beguilingly and cleverly with me, and wittily turns my jokes against me. He does so entertainingly but moderately, for he never forgets that he is joking with his father. He carefully avoids all offence and gives only delight.

I expect each of you to send me a letter almost every day. No excuses (John makes none), such as a lack of time, the messenger leaving early, or nothing to say! No one stops you from writing; everyone encourages you to do so. If you don't want to keep the messenger waiting, why not prepare for him, and have the letters written and sealed, ready for anyone to take?

And there is no need to hunt for a subject when you write to me: I am pleased to hear about your studies or your games. I am most pleased when, if there's nothing to write about, you write about that nothing at great length. Nothing is easier. After all, you are girls, and therefore naturally have much to say about nothing at all.

Whether you write about serious or quite unimportant things, I want you to write carefully and conscientiously. It won't do you any harm to write it all in English first; then it will be much less difficult to put into Latin. You won't have to think what you are going to say, but only how to say it. But that is really up to you. Nevertheless I insist on your scrutinizing whatever you say before making the final version. First study the entire sentence, then each part of it. Find any mistakes in your first thoughts, correct them, write out the whole letter once more, and examine it again. Sometimes, when you rewrite something, errors you thought you had got rid of, creep in again. If you take all this care, the unimportant things will become serious matters. It is true that silly and thoughtless verbiage can make anything precise and witty seem dull. But there is nothing so dull in itself that, with a little thought, you cannot bring to life gracefully and wittily.

Your loving father

Margaret's Gold

St Thomas More

September 11th 1522

To his daughter

Margaret, born in 1505 was the eldest of More's four children (three daughters and a son), all by his first wife Jane Colet, who died in 1511. More was a great advocate of the education of women and is said to have instructed the seventeen-year-old Jane in literature, music and theology, though she resisted his attempt to make her summarize sermons she had heard; Margaret is said to have been similarly firm-minded. Nevertheless More was concerned to ensure that his daughters had the same opportunities for learning as his son, but this tender and affectionate letter shows that he was far from heavy-handed in his approach.

Dear Margaret,

You have asked me for money far too shyly and timidly, for your father is only too willing to give, and you have written so fine a letter that I am not only inclined to pay for each line of it with a golden philippine, as

Alexander paid for the verses of Cherilos, but if my funds were as great as my desire I would answer each syllable with two gold ounces. But I have sent what you asked. I would have sent more but just as I am keen to give so I am eager to be asked and persuaded. The sooner you spend this money well and the sooner you ask me for more, the more you can be sure of pleasing me.

This evening I was with the Lord Bishop of Exeter. John Exeter is a profoundly learned man with a considerable reputation for holiness. While we were talking I took from my desk a paper that had to do with our business and by chance your letter also came to light. He picked it up with pleasure and examined it. When the signature showed him that it was a letter from a lady the novelty of such a thing made him read it with all the greater interest. When he was done, he said he would never have believed that it was your work unless I had assured him that it was so. He began to praise it most fulsomely (why should I hide this?) for its excellent Latin, correctness, learning and tenderness. Since he was so pleased with your letter I showed him your speech. He read it and your poems, but although he praised you most warmly his face showed that his words were not strong enough to express his feelings. Immediately he took from his pocket a Portuguese gold coin which you will find in this letter. I tried every way to refuse the gift but found I could not reject it as a pledge and token of his good will to you. This stopped me from showing him your sisters' letters, for I was afraid that it would seem that I had taken them out only to get for them too something that I was troubled to accept for you. But he is so good a man that I am happy to be able to please him. Write to thank him with great care and delicacy. One day you will be glad to have pleased such a man.

Farewell,

Your father

Do What The Teachers Say

St Théophane Vénard   1847

To his little brother

The future martyr of Indo-China was one of five children of a French village school-teacher. He was not ordained a subdeacon until 1850. This delightful letter was written when he was an eighteen-year-old student.

Dear Brother,

What do you think of school? Are the lessons too hard? Make you sick, do they? Don't worry. You're still at the bottom of the ladder. In a short time you'll be several rungs up and you can look back on what you've achieved. Have you met any friendly boys? Are you really having a good time? Write to tell me about everything. Poor chap, I think about you a great deal and wish I could be there with you, especially during the first few weeks.

It's half past six in the evening here and the wind is whistling through the cracks. The weather is really nasty. Is it the same there? I really feel for you. I bet your paws and toes are covered in chilblains. Mine used to be. I'm sure that the end of your nose is as blue as mine was. Right? Well, that's school. I suppose we go to school in order to learn how to put up with things in life. But I won't say anything more about wintry things. Let's wish each other a very, very happy New Year and Heaven some day— though not just yet, I sincerely hope! I certainly don't long for my brother to be whisked off there so soon. I remember how you used to long for New Year because of all the presents and sweets—only school: awful! Never mind, one of these days you'll be glad that you did learn your lessons. They'll help you to do better what God wants you to do: to get to heaven at the very end of it all. Work hard, work steadily, not for praise, or honour, or prizes—but just to please God. Say your prayers. Do what the teachers say because God has put them there. Be kind and friendly to your school fellows, then everyone will like you and you'll be as happy as you can be.

Théophane

Schooldays

St John Bosco

May 10th 1884
To the Salesian Fathers

St John Bosco, one of the most sympathetic of the great nineteenth-century educators, especially of the abandoned, orphaned and neglected, states with the dramatic verve of a good teacher the basic principles of the work that earned him great love and respect from the Salesian teachers he trained and from the boys themselves.

My dear Brothers in Turin,

However far away you are I never cease to keep you in mind. All I wish is to see you happy in this world and the next. This thought and this longing make me write to you now. The distance between us is distressing. I am immeasurably sad not to have you within sight of my eyes or near me. If it had been possible I would have written this letter earlier.... These are the words of someone who loves you tenderly in Christ Jesus and is entitled to speak to you with the freedom proper to a father. Let me do so, give me all your attention, and do what I recommend ....

One evening recently I went up to my room and was preparing to sleep. I was praying as my dear little mother taught me when suddenly—I do not know whether I fell asleep or was distracted—I seemed to see two former pupils of the Oratory before me. One of them greeted me affectionately and said:

"Don Bosco! Do you recognize me?"

"Yes, of course I know you," I replied.

"Do you still remember me?" the other asked.

"Yes, and all your contemporaries. You are Valfré, who was at the Oratory."

"Well," said Valfré, "shall I show you the youngsters who were at the Oratory in my day?"

"If you could, I should be greatly pleased."

And he showed me all the young people looking just as they did at that date, the same height and age. I seemed to be present in the old Oratory at recreation time. The scene was full of life, movement and joy... It was quite clear that between boys and masters there was a balanced feeling of complete cordiality and trust...

Another of my former pupils asked if I would like to see the boys of the Oratory today. It was Joseph Buzzetti.

"Yes," I said, "for it is a month and more since I saw them last."

He showed me them. I saw the Oratory and the pupils at recreation. There were no peals of merriment and bursts of singing. There was none of the former bustle and liveliness. The manner and looks of many pupils revealed only boredom and tedium, sulkiness and distrust, and my heart was rent. Of course I did see some of them running and playing, rushing about carelessly and happily, but more than a few were standing alone leaning against pillars, looking uneasy. Some were on the staircases, in the corridors and on the balconies overlooking the gardens, where they could get away from the general recreation. Others were in groups walking slowly about, speaking *sotto voce* and darting sly, sharp looks at this and that. Even though they smiled it was in a way that I am sure would have made St Aloysius blush. Even the boys who were playing showed that their hearts weren't in the game....

Joseph said: "In the old days at the Oratory, surely the masters were among the boys, especially during recreation? You must remember those happy years. Weren't they unbelievably good? We always look back to those days with joy because the masters ruled by love and we hid nothing from them."

"Yes, it was pure joy. The boys would crowd round me eagerly, listening to every word and anxious to follow my advice and put it into practice. But now you must understand how endless interviews, all sorts of business, and the state of my health make that impossible."

"All right, but if you can't do it yourself, why don't your Salesian sons follow your example? Why don't you demand, insist indeed, that they treat the boys as you treated them?"

"I do. I'm always saying they should. But these days far too many of them seem to have no idea of really giving themselves as once we did."

"They neglect the little things and in that way lose the big ones, and even the reward their work deserves. If the masters accept what appeals to the boys, the boys will accept what appeals to the Superiors. Then their task will be made all the easier. This change in the Oratory means that many boys no longer trust those in authority. In days gone by, all hearts were open to the Superiors that the boys loved and obeyed immediately. But now the Superiors are looked on as no more than Superiors. They are no longer fathers, brothers and friends. Thus you find more fear than love. If you want to create one mind and one heart, for the love of God you must overthrow that fatal barrier of distrust and open the door to friendly confidence. Then obedience will guide the pupils as a mother guides her infants and the peace and joy we knew then will prevail throughout the Oratory."

"Yes, but what can we do to destroy those barriers?"

"We have to build up a close family spirit with the boys, especially at recreation. If there is no sense of family, then there will be no affection, and without affection there will be no mutual understanding. Anyone who wants to be loved has to show love. Jesus Christ made himself little with the little ones and shared our weakness. Study the perfect Pattern of a family spirit. If a master is seen only in the teacher's desk he will always be a master and nothing else, but if he shares the boys' recreation he will become a brother. A priest in the pulpit is doing no more and no less than his duty, but if he speaks at recreation he is a friend. Many changes of heart are the result of a few words spoken by chance at play. Anyone who is aware of affection will return it. Anyone who is loved can get all he needs in return, especially from boys. Mutual trust is like an electric current between boys and those put in charge of them. Hearts are opened, their needs are revealed, and their faults are laid bare. Affection persuades them to go to their Superiors with their attempts, trials, bruised feelings, troubles, failings and things undone. Our Lord did not crush the bruised reed or quench the smoking flax. He is your model. Imitate Jesus and none of you will do things out of vainglory or punish others merely to do justice to his injured love of self. No one will try to get out of supervision because he is jealous and thinks someone else will do better than him. No one will grumble about others because he wants to win the affection and respect of the boys over and above all the other Superiors. (All he will get for his trouble is in fact empty homage and actual contempt.) No one will concentrate on a favourite and neglect the rest of the class for his sake. No one will put his own comfort first and treat the major duty of supervision as unimportant. No one will try to avoid unpopularity by omitting to correct those who need it. If true love guides you will desire only the glory of God and the salvation of souls. When this love is weak things begin to go wrong. Why do people want to put cold order in place of warm affection? Why do those in authority neglect the observance they were given by Don Bosco? Why do they gradually drop their habit of forestalling trouble by the exercise of wise vigilance, and instead promote rules which are more convenient for officials and less exacting? Rules like that, when enforced by the rod, only evoke hatred and encourage resentment. If they are permitted to go by default they awaken disrespect for authority and give rise to serious problems. Restore love and constraint will disappear and along with it all the fatal burden of secrets. The Superiors need be absolutely firm only in the case of immorality."

... "How, then, " I asked him, "can we really make sure that the family spirit, mutual love, and complete trust prevail?"

"Observe the rules of the house to the letter."

"Nothing else?"

"The best dish at any meal is good cheer."...

Shall I tell you what this poor old man who has spent his whole life on his beloved boys asks of you? Only this: as far as you can, restore the happy days of the first Oratory. They were days of sympathy and Christian trust between the boys and those in authority, days of friendliness and forbearance towards one another for love of our Lord, days of openness, simplicity and straightforwardness, days of love and true joy for all.

...Priests, clerics, dearest boys, Farewell!

Don Bosco

Studying

St Thomas Aquinas 1270

To a student

The golden advice of the Angelic Doctor, one of the greatest philosophers in the history of the Church, remains valid in our own day.

My dear John,

You have asked me how to assemble a rich storehouse of knowledge. This is my advice.

1. Do not dive straight into the sea of knowledge but make your way to it by minor streams. It is wise to work upwards, from the easier to the more difficult. This is my advice, and you would do well to follow it.

2. Be slow to speak and be slow in entering the parlour.

3. Prize a pure conscience very highly.

4. Never neglect your times of prayer.

5. Stay willingly in your own cell if you want to enter God's wine-cellar.

6. Show a cheerful face to everyone.

7. Never pry into others' business.

8. Don't be too familiar with anyone, because familiarity breeds contempt and offers a pretext for neglecting serious work.

9. Be careful not to interfere in outsiders' words and actions.

10. Don't waste time in pointless chatter.

11. Take care to follow in the footsteps of good and holy men.

12. Don't concentrate on the speaker's personality but store up in your mind anything useful he may say.

13. Make sure that you thoroughly grasp whatever you read and hear.

14. Look up doubtful points.

15. Try your best to hoard whatever you can in that little book-case of a mind. You must try to fill it as full as possible.

16. Don't concern yourself with things outside your competence.

If you do all this you will sprout leaves and bear useful fruit in the vineyard of the Lord of Hosts all the days of your life. If you follow my advice to the letter you will reach your desired goal.

Farewell,

Thomas Aquinas

Chapter 2

Prayer and the Spiritual Life

Prayer

St Augustine   411

St Augustine offers a masterly summary of the nature and purpose of prayer.

Madam,

You asked me to say something about prayer....

For us human beings, words are a necessity, not because they tell God what we want or change his intentions, but because they help us to see into our own selves and to face our needs. When we say "Hallowed be thy name," we arouse in ourselves the desire that God's name, essentially holy in itself, may also be thought holy by people and not despised; for it brings profit not to God but to human beings. And when we say: "Thy kingdom come," although it is bound to come whether we wish it or not, we arouse a longing in our own souls for that kingdom, that it may come within ourselves, and that we may be found worthy to reign in it....

Whatever other words we use, if we pray correctly and appropriately, we say no more than what is already to be found in the Lord's prayer. Anyone who asks for anything that cannot find a place in that prayer from the Gospel makes not exactly an unlawful but an unspiritual prayer. If you examine the petitions of all holy prayers, I am sure that you will find nothing that is not summed up and included in the Lord's prayer. In praying, therefore, we are free to use any words we please, but we must ask for the same things. We have no choice here. Faith, hope and charity lead the soul that prays towards God; that is, they guide the soul that believes, hopes, desires and looks for guidance about what to ask God by studying the Lord's prayer. Whoever begs from God that "one thing," and looks for it, does so in perfect confidence, because that one thing is the only true and happy life in which, with bodies and souls that are immortal and incorruptible, we shall contemplate the joy of the Lord for ever and ever. We desire and quite correctly demand all other things with a view to this single end. There is the fountain of life for which we now thirst in prayer as long as we live in hope, not as yet perceiving the things we hope for, trusting under the spreading wings of God before whom is all desire, to be satisfied with the plenteousness of his house, and to be given to drink from the river of his pleasures. For with him is the well of life and in his light shall we see light (Ps. 35:8-10).

Farewell,

Augustine of Hippo

Gwen's Packing

Friedrich von Hügel   September 1st 1919

To his niece, Gwendolen Greene

The Baron possessed the rare gift of conveying profound truths through simple metaphors drawn from everyday experience.

Dear Gwen,

I want this scribble to reach you on your starting your packing-fortnight, my very dear Niece. I want to put very shortly, what has helped myself, so greatly, for now a generation.

Well—you are going to pack, pack and unpack, unpack for a fortnight. What is it that I would have you quietly set your mind and heart on, during that in itself lonesome and dreary bit of your road, Child? Why this, Dear! You see, all we do has a double-relatedness. It is a link or links of a chain that stretches back to our birth and on to our death. It is part of a long train of cause and effect, of effect and cause, in your own chain of life—this chain variously intertwisted with, variously affecting, and affected by, numerous other chains and other lives. It is certainly your duty to do quietly your best, that these links may help on your own chain and those other chains, by packing well, by being a skilful packer.

Yes, but there is also, all the time, another, a far deeper, a more daring and inspiring relation. Here, you have no slow succession, but you have each single act, each single moment joined directly to GOD—himself not a chain, but one Great Simultaneity. True, certain other acts, at other moments, will be wanted, of a kind more intrinsically near to God—Prayer, Quiet, Holy Communion. Yet not even those other acts could unite you as closely to God as can do this packing, if and when the packing is the duty of certain moments, and if, and as often as, the little old daughter does this her packing with her heart and intention turned to God her Home, if she offers her packing as her service, that service which is perfect liberty.

Not even a soul already in heaven, not even an angel or archangel, can take your place there; for what GOD wants, what GOD will love to accept, in these Herst rooms, in those packing days, and from your packing hands, will be just this little packing performed by the little niece in those little rooms. Certainly it has been mainly through my poor little self-exercising in it, that I have got on a bit, and Gwen will get on faster than I have done with it. You understand, Dear? At one moment packing; at another, silent adoration in church; at another, dreariness and unwilling drift; at another, the joys of human affections given and received; at another, keen, keen suffering of soul, of mind, in an apparent utter loneliness; at another, external acts of religion; at another, death itself. All these occupations, every one, can, ought, and will be, each when and where, duty, reason, conscience, necessity—GOD calls for it—it will all become the means and instruments of loving, of transfiguration, of growth for your soul, and of its beatitude. But it is for GOD to choose these things, their degrees, combinations, successions; and it is for Gwen, just simply, very humbly, very gently and peacefully, to follow that leading.

Through the Cross to Light.

Loving old Uncle,

H.

What Does God Ask?

St Théophane Vénard

August 3rd 1851
To his brother

The future martyr of Indo-China was ordained priest in 1852. In this letter of advice to his younger brother he summarizes the principles that guided his own choice of vocation from an early age.

My dear Eusebius,

Now you are old enough to choose a career for yourself. You are at an age when people start thinking for themselves and when they form certain convictions which affect their behaviour. When you meet people you will come across a lot of prejudice, many odd notions and perversions of truth, for European society has become quite corrupt. Of course there were many bad people in the past just as there are now, for people are always the same. But in the past there were certain social rules and conventions that only really dissolute people ignored. Religion was the accepted basis of society, and God breathes life into nations as well as into individuals. Now all these safeguards have disappeared or are ignored, as you will see when you grow older.

Of course you are wondering what to do. Pray simply, humbly and devoutly to find out the will of God, and the way you must go will be revealed to you. Then you must follow the inspiration that the mercy of God will instil in your heart....

You want to know what God asks of you. Humility, prayer, obedience to his divine commands, and to the voice of our holy mother Church, and complete obedience to his divine providence. You say that your hopes, tastes and the secret inspiration of grace strongly attract you to the priesthood. May God's holy Name be praised! If our Lord summons you, you must answer. One day the infant Samuel heard a voice crying aloud: "Samuel, Samuel!" "Here I am, Lord," he said. If you think that our Lord has summoned you, then like Samuel you must reply: "Here I am, Lord. What do you want me to do? With the help of your grace I shall do everything you decide, for I know that I shall never be without your grace." You are the child of our divine Lord and of his blessed Mother, the child of his love and the sheep of his pasture. Trust in God. Never forget that God is in everything, whether great or small. He must be the single motive of your thoughts, words and deeds. There is a great future before you, a noble vocation. Anchored in God's infinite mercy you must repeat humbly yet quite trustingly St Paul's words: "I go straight for the goal— my reward is the honour of my high calling in Christ Jesus" (Phil. 3:14).

Eusebius, you have reached the most noble moment in your life. I shall tell you why. You are at an age when you are assailed by fierce passions, hard struggles and great victories. Our Lord "looks" on a young man and "loves" him. You are that young man. Be courageous and worthy of your Master. Perhaps you and I will find that we are soldiers in the same regiment, travelling along the same road, bound for the same destination. May his holy will, not ours, be done. Entrust your future to him, to the heart of Jesus made man. Remember that he too was once a young man, for Jesus Christ is the God-child, God-youth, God-man and God of all ages.

Try to do each day's work steadily and joyfully. Be happy, and truly joyous. A Christian's life should be a perpetual jubilee, a prelude to the feasts of eternity....

Yours affectionately,

Théophane

We Are Made for Love

George Macdonald   1848

To Miss Louisa Powell

In spring 1848 Macdonald, growing ever more doubtful of received doctrine but still hoping to become a theological student, resigned his tutorship. The subject on which he writes to Miss Powell is close to his heart: for him love divine and love mundane are closely connected, for she is his future wife, though he has yet to ask her father's permission to refer to her thus.

Dear Louisa,

... The difficulties with which I told you I was surrounded are not the results of my situation. However ill I may bear them at times, I regard my trials here as helps, not as hindrances. But my difficulties are those which a heart far from God must feel, even when the hand of the Heavenly Father is leading it back to himself. It seems a wonder that he can bear with me.

What is it that is the principal cause of everyone's unhappiness who is not a Christian? It is the want of enough to love. We are made for love— and in vain we strive to pour forth the streams of our affection by the narrow channels which the world can give—and well is it if, stagnated in our hearts, they turn not to bitterness. The religion of Jesus Christ is intended to bring us back to our real natural condition: for all the world is in an unnatural state. This will give us that to love which alone can satisfy our loving—which alone, as we climb each successive height, can show us yet another higher and farther off—so that, as our powers of loving expand, the object of loving grows in all those glories which excite our love and yet make it long for more.

George

Love

Charles de Foucauld

November 29th 1896

To Fr Jérome

Many of Charles de Foucauld's letters combine spiritual and practical instruction with a particularly intense form of communication that reveals something of the extraordinary personality that so impressed everyone who has recorded meeting him. The following (from Rome) is an example of many such letters from the extensive correspondence he conducted with a Trappist whom he had met at a monastery in Algiers.

May Jesus always be with you, dearest Father,

Thank you, Father, for your two excellent letters. How right you are to talk to me at length about our Lord. It is certainly about him that we should talk, as two children talk of their father, or their brother, or their beloved, or whoever is their mutual all-in-all. And what are we if not two children? And how natural that we should be united as we have only one thought, one intention, one desire, one love! Our two hearts are but one for we both want to breathe only for our Lord Jesus. And then, if two beings exist on earth who should speak only of God, surely they are you and me whose friendship had nothing earthly about it? We met briefly, we shall probably never meet again in this life, and yet we love one another, we love one another very tenderly in Jesus our saviour, we love as angels love one another in heaven insofar as this is possible for poor human beings. So, dearest brother, let our conversation be the conversation of angels, let us speak only of God under whose eye we both have our being: by talking together, by writing to each other, may the earth disappear and may we live already in the radiance of the other world, probably the only one where we shall meet again. But whereas angels have tongues of gold and hearts of fire, we stammer and are lukewarm; let us do what we can and this is a reason for helping each other, for praying for each other, for loving each other all the more as we are weak and need to lean on each other from afar so as to follow our Lord Jesus along the painful way he has mapped out for us: "Take up your cross and follow me."

I am enclosing a little flower I picked for you, while praying for you, in the catacomb of St Cecilia, beside her tomb, on her feast-day: may this martyr's flower remind you, as it does me (I picked one for myself too), of what the saints suffered and what we ought to wish to suffer ourselves. That's our advantage over the angels! If they were not in a state of bliss they would surely envy us our happiness at being able to suffer with and for our

Lord Jesus! We have the best of it from this point of view. At least we have our tears, we have sorrows perhaps, please God, and blood to offer our Lord in union with his tears, his sorrows and his blood. When I pray to my guardian angel I often ask him to make me do what he would do in my place. And how he would throw himself into suffering were he in my place. When I'm holding our cross and your medal in my hand, I often pray to our guardian angels for both of us, that they may make us follow our Lord as they themselves would follow him were they on earth, and make us fulfil everything that our Beloved expects of us.

Thank you for the benefits you are bringing me by your prayers, and thank you for your affection and letters: God sees that I need help so he inspires you to do this: I praise him and thank you. Pray a lot: when we love we want to talk endlessly to the being we love, or at least look at him endlessly. This is what prayer is, endless converse with our Beloved. We look at him, we tell him we love him, we rejoice at being at his feet, we tell him that this is where we want to live and die.

I hope you are making progress with your Latin. I want this very much for you. It will enable you to drink at the pure source of the early Fathers of the Church, a source fragrant with the perfume of Jesus. Those early fathers, St Athanasius, St John Chrysostom, St Augustine, St Jerome and all the rest, are shining lights, burning flames, and I long to see you alight and aflame with their contact! Holy communion, reading and meditation on the holy gospels, prayer, reading the Fathers, this is nourishment I want for you, dearest Father, nourishment that the world does not know, but it carries it us to the mountain of God like Elijah's bread, to eternal life like the Samaritan woman's water.

And, added to that, manual labour—inevitably relegated to second place at the moment because you, like me, are in your infancy. We are not old enough yet to work with St Joseph, we are still learning to read with the child Jesus at the blessed Virgin's knee, but manual labour, humble, lowly, despised, will have its place after a while; it's a large place, and then, with holy communion, the holy books, prayer, humble manual work, humiliation, suffering, and, to end up with, if it were pleasing to God, the death of a St Cecilia and so many others—if we have all this we shall lead the life of our Lord and beloved master Jesus Christ.

Now I want to give you some advice, though I haven't the faintest authority to give you even a shred of it as I am neither a priest nor a scholar but only a sinner, indeed one thing alone authorizes me, and that is my brotherly love for you in the Lord. My advice is to consult your spiritual director in everything, on everything, even the smallest matters ... the habit of asking what we should do even on the smallest matters has a thousand good results: it brings peace (for we are never in doubt); it forms a habit of self-conquest in everything (because in everything we renounce our own will); it encourages indifference to earthly things (because we are equally ready to do one thing as much as another); it causes us to perform a host of acts of love (to obey our confessor is to obey God, and to obey is to love, it is the act of love that is the purest, the most perfect, the highest, the most disinterested, the most adorative, if I may so put it); it fosters, especially at first, quite a few acts of mortification (after a while we see things in their proper perspective, we are detached from everything, we don't experience mortifications any more, or only rarely, but simply the joy of obeying); it causes all our actions without exception to be agreeable to our Lord Jesus and even the most agreeable that we can perform, so they are the most perfect actions possible (for, after all, our confessors do not always make us do the thing that is in itself most perfect, but the love, humility and goodwill that form the essence of our obedience would render our action done through obedience much more agreeable to God, much more perfect in itself; and when God sees this perfect obedience in his children, he always gives special illumination to confessors and causes them to know his special will regarding those who truly love, those who truly obey: St Theresa experienced this a hundred times and more).

After such a long sermon I can but beat my breast and ask your forgiveness for inflicting it on you. Forgive me, dear Father, dear brother, in consideration of my great fondness for you. St Theresa wrote that the more she loved someone the more she pestered them with interminable letters and sermons. I certainly have that in common with her. Thus the length of my letter has shown you how united I am with you in our Lord, you, my companion of eternity, for it is not in the temporal sphere that we are united, but by talking together we already have one foot in the life everlasting. Pray for your unworthy brother so that he may meet you there one day.

Your brother who loves you in the heart of Jesus,

Br Marie Albéric
(Charles de Foucauld)

What We Least Want to Give

François Fénelon   November 17th 1694

To Countess Elizabeth de Grammont

The Comtesse de Grammont (née Hamilton) was one of Fénelon's company of long-term correspondents. He was her spiritual director for twenty-four years. He was not her confessor, but acted rather as an eminent psychotherapist might nowadays for ladies of station and leisure. In that sense, a letter might act as a versatile therapeutic tool in addition to consultations. The following is a typical example of Fénelon's concern for individual peculiarities while insisting on his central conviction that "religion as a whole consists merely in abandoning oneself and one's self-love in order to concern oneself with God."

Dear Madam,

I think you ought to try, though without undue effort, to think of God whenever you feel a desire for solitary meditation and a simultaneous regret that you cannot satisfy it. It is not sufficient to leave these thoughts until you have some time for yourself and can be on your own with the door closed and with no obligation to anyone. The very moment when we regret that we cannot devote our thoughts to God is the time that must be turned to advantage. Then you should open your heart to God familiarly, straightforwardly and in absolute confidence. Any moment you can snatch will be enough, not just in a carriage or a sedan chair, but when you are getting dressed, doing your hair, or even when eating and in the middle of general conversation. Then you will find that ineffably long and boring tales will not tire you but rather cheer you by supplying you with useful intervals and, by affording you time for thought, will enable you to avoid indulging your delight in ridicule. Thus all things work together for good to those who seek God. Another prime rule is to avoid committing any fault which you know is about to tempt you. If you realize that you have already committed it, take the blame resolutely. If you become aware in advance of any danger of this kind, be careful not to shun God's voice within you or you will run the risk of stifling it entirely. This voice can be quashed all too easily, for it is faint and jealous. Nevertheless it demands to be heeded and obeyed. If it is slighted, it vanishes. If you resist its demands in the least way, it is insulted. You must obey it immediately whenever it speaks. Impulsive faults or those caused by weakness are nothing compared to those done in defiance of the Holy Spirit when he speaks within us. Then there are those we acknowledge only once we have committed them: in such cases sheer irritation and bruised self-esteem are not enough for restitution. Such feelings are mere signs of the impatience of wounded pride. The only thing to do in such instances is to suffer humiliation quietly. Quietly, I say, for humiliation accepted with anger and reluctance is really no humiliation at all. Condemn the fault, try not to excuse yourself, and come before God in humility, but without bitterness or feeling discouraged, and be prepared to suffer the necessary humiliation quietly. Then you can use the venom of the snake's bite as a cure. The very feeling of humiliation because you have done something wrong can be curative if you accept it patiently. True humility is never to be found in protests against humiliation.

Trying to detect the presence of God when you are at table, particularly when meals take a long time and tediousness sets in, will help to make sure that you indulge yourself only moderately, and will also make you less prone to extreme delicacy. Often, when beginning a meal, talk ceases and the satisfaction of hunger's pangs takes over. Then, while you are eating, you can think of God. But all this is a matter of inclination and individual behaviour, and something over which you should exercise due caution.

There is another matter about which I am rather worried. We did not discuss it today and it will have to wait until we next meet. I am sure you know what I mean. I think that you must be especially severe with yourself and be careful not to let even your best intentions take over. You could even be blocking all the grace God is preparing to give you. Often what we offer to God is not what he wants. What he really wants of us is exactly what we least want to give him, and what we are most afraid we will ask of us. He asks for Isaac, our precious only son, as a sacrifice that we must surrender without mercy. The rest is nothing in his eyes, and can do little good, for God's blessing is not given to the work of a divided mind. He wants everything and will not let us rest until we have given all. As Scripture says: "Who has resisted him and has had peace?" Do you want to be at peace and God to bless everything you do? Then keep nothing. Cut down to the quick. Burn, and spare nothing, then you will be granted the peace of God. How consoling, how liberating, how strengthening! What enrichment of the heart and increased graces will result when nothing remains between God and the soul, and the ultimate sacrifice has been made! I shall pray each day to our Lord, and ask him to give you the courage needed to make that sacrifice.

Fénelon

Offer Yourself to God

Unknown English Mystic   c. 1380

To a pupil in the spirit

An anonymous spiritual director decries subtlety and over-investigative reasoning as a means of access to God and recommends a simple, direct method of contemplation.

Dear spiritual friend in God,

All I want you to do is to think, without any subtle delving into the question, that you are as you are. It doesn't matter how foul or wretched you may be, as long as you have been forgiven (as I take for granted) all your particular and general sins in the right way—as the Church requires. (If that isn't the case, then neither you nor I nor anyone else may dare to start this exercise. At any rate, I wouldn't agree to any such person beginning it). If you really feel that you have done everything you can to confess and get absolution, then you can start the exercise. Even if you still think that you are quite vile and disgusting, and you are convinced that your very own self is a ghastly nuisance, and this feeling has so got hold of you that you hardly know what to do with yourself, you must still do what I tell you exactly as I tell you.

This is what you must do. Take God, good gracious God, just as he is, without any qualification, and stick him like a plaster on your own wounded self, just as you are. Or, if you like, lift your sick self up, just as you are, and use all your desire and all your longing and try to touch God who is so good and gracious, just as he is. Touching God means good health for ever, as we know from the woman in the Gospel: "All I have to do to be safe is to touch the hem of his clothes." What you really need to get rid of your sickness is the extraordinary heavenly touch of God's own being, of his own dear self. So go right ahead and try this miraculous medicine. Raise your sick self, just as you are, until you get to God, good and gracious, just as he is. Don't speculate and don't try to look hard and meticulously in any special way at any particular aspect of your self as it is, or at any of God's characteristics or qualities, healthy or unhealthy, given by grace or nature, divine or human. All you have to do at this moment is to make absolutely sure that you are looking at the very essence of your very own being yourself, and then to lift that looking right down inside yourself right up. Take it up and up until it rises in gladness and loving desire to be united and made one in grace and spirit with the precious being of God, just as he is in himself, and no more than that.

Of course your wayward, inquisitive reason may tell you that this is a futile exercise and start nagging you all the time, suggesting that the sensible course is to give it all up and do something really practical and worthwhile. If your rational mind gets at you in this subtle, prying way (don't forget that it thinks what you're doing is useless merely because it knows nothing about it), this is a good sign. It means that what you're doing is much more valuable than anything your analytical mind can do. The course I have recommended is preferable because nothing I could do, and nothing that my investigative reason could achieve, inside or outside me, could get me as close to God and take me as far from the world, as this simple, almost imperceptible experience of offering up the very essence of my own very being myself.

Even though your rational mind finds the exercise useless and even unhealthy, and would like to cut it short, don't stop trying. Tell your critical mind to get lost. Don't just give up, and return to where you started, in spite of all the interference from reasonable objections. Of course your rational mind flourishes when you allow it room for speculation and begin to investigate the various aspects of your own psychology. That kind of cool, measured introspection can be valuable, even profitable, in its own right, but if undertaken to the detriment of the hidden contemplation and offering up of your being that I have recommended, it will only split and divide the perfect unity which ought to persist between God and your soul. So don't stop. Carry on with the exercise at the lowest rung of your spirit or being. Don't turn round and go back for any reason, no matter how good or holy the course that your rational mind advises you to follow may seem to be.

Your spiritual adviser

Remain in Quietness
St John of the Cross
October 12th 1589

To one living in the world

St John was able to reassure and encourage his correspondents not by means of any elaborate argument or by outlining an effective spiritual strategy but, as here, by the stark lyrical power of his vision and the sheer energy with which he described their condition.

Dear Daughter in the Lord,

May Jesus be in your soul. I have done anything but forget you. Just think, how could I forget one who is in my soul, as you are? While you are walking in that darkness and in those empty places of spiritual poverty you think that everyone and everything are failing you; but that is not surprising, for at these times it seems to you that God is failing you too. But nothing is failing you, nor have you any need to consult me about anything, nor have you any reason to do so, nor do you know one, nor will you find one: all that is merely suspicion without cause. She that seeks nothing but God walks not in darkness, in whatever darkness and poverty she may find himself; and she that harbours no presumptuousness and desires not her own satisfaction, either as to God or as to the creatures, and works not her own will in any way whatsoever has no need to stumble or to worry about anything.

You are progressing well; remain in quietness and rejoice. Who are you to be anxious about yourself? A fine state you would get into if you did that!

What do you think is meant by serving God, but abstaining from evil, keeping his commandments, and walking in his ways as best we can? If this be done what need is there of other apprehensions, or of any other illumination or sweetness whether from one source or from another? In these things as a rule the soul is never free from stumbling-blocks and perils, and is deceived and fascinated by the objects of its understanding and desire, and its very faculties cause it to stray. And this God is granting the soul a great favour when he darkens the faculties and impoverishes the soul so that it may not be led astray by them; and how can it walk aright and not stray, save by following the straight road of the law of God and of the Church, and living only in true and dark faith and certain hope and perfect charity, and awaiting its blessings in the life to come, living here below as pilgrims, exiles and orphans, poor and desolate, with no road to follow and with no possessions, expecting to receive everything in heaven?

Rejoice and put your trust in God, for he has given you signs that you can quite well do so, and indeed that you ought to do so. Should you do otherwise, it will not be surprising if he is angry at seeing you so foolish when he is leading you by the road that is best for you and has set you in so sure a place. Desire no way of progress but this and be tranquil in your soul, for all is well with it, and communicate as usual. Confess when you have something definite to say; there is no need to talk. When you have anything to say you will write about it to me, and write to me quickly and more frequently.

Commend me to God,
my daughter in the Lord.

Carrying out Good Desires

St Teresa of Avila   January 2nd 1577

To her brother

In this typical multi-purpose letter from one of the busiest yet most subtle correspond-
ents in the history of the Church, St Teresa, writing from Toledo to Avila, mixes
practical and spiritual advice. She tells Don Lorenzo de Cepeda (who had placed
himself under his sister's spiritual direction) not to read letters to Salcedo enclosed in
those to Don Lorenzo, because she knows that Salcedo's depression makes him
suspicious, and that any signs of interference would reduce the trust needed for a frank
correspondence between them. She discusses house purchase, offers advice on prayer
and spiritual discipline, and on safe despatch of papers, warns Don Lorenzo against
business relations with the livestock dealer Antonio Ruiz (her friend) and mentions
the scarcity of fish. Serna was Teresa'a brother's servant, Doña Quiteria a nun who
had accompanied her to the Salamanca foundation, and young Francisco her
nephew.

My dear Brother,

Jesus be with you. Serna is giving me so little time that I don't want to
write at length, but when I begin to write to you I never know how to stop,
and Serna comes so seldom that, when he does come, I need time.

Never read the letters I write to Francisco, for I am afraid he is beginning
to develop melancholy and it is a great help to him to write to me quite
freely. Perhaps God is sending him these scruples in order to take his mind
off other things; but the best thing he can do for himself is to believe what
I tell him.

I think you will have received a letter which I sent you by way of Madrid,
but, in case it has gone astray, I had better repeat what I said in it, though
it is very troublesome for me to get mixed up in the matter. First of all you
should bear in mind that one of the rooms in that house which you took
from Hernán Alvárez de Peralta has a wall which is very unsafe, or so I
heard, so you should look into that very carefully. Secondly, I want you
to send me the little box, and, if there were any more papers of mine in the
parcels—I think there was a bag containing papers—they should be done
up very securely. If Doña Quiteria sends me the parcel which she has for
me by Serna, they can come inside that. And send my seal: I cannot bear
sealing my letters with this death's head—I want to use the one with the
letters which I wish were written on my heart, as they were on St Ignatius'.
Let no one open the little box but yourself, for I think that paper about
prayer is in it, and if you happen to get a glimpse of it, you must not speak

of it to anyone else. Remember that you have not my leave to do so, nor is it well that you should, for although you may think that it would be doing God service, there are other grave objections which make it inadvisable: I will merely say that, if ever I hear you have been talking about it, I shall be careful never to let you see anything of mine again.

The Nuncio has sent to tell me to forward him a copy of the patents by which I have made these foundations, and to state how many of them there are, and where they are, and how many nuns are in them, and where the nuns come from, and their ages, and how many of them I think would make prioresses; and all the papers about this are in that little box, or perhaps in the bag. So I need everything that is there. I am told he is asking for this because he wants to make us into a province. Personally, I am afraid he wants to send our nuns to carry out reforms elsewhere; there has been talk about this before and it is not well that we should do it—there is quite enough for us to do in the convents of our own Order. Please tell the Sub-Prioress that, and ask her to send me the names of those who belong to the community at Avila, and the names of those who are there now, and how long they have been professed. She should write all this in a clear hand on a large sheet of paper and sign it with her name. No—it has just occurred to me that, as I am Prioress here, I can do that, so she need not sign, but can just send me the particulars, in her own hand, and I will copy them. There is no reason why the sisters should be told about it. Please be careful about the way the parcel is sent, so that the papers do not get wet, and send me the key.

What I said was in the book is in the one about the Our Father. You will find a great deal there about your kind of prayer, though it is not described as fully as in the other book. I think it is in the chapter on "Thy kingdom come." You should read the book again, or at least the chapters on the Our Father, and you may perhaps find something which will satisfy you.

Before I forget, why do you make vows without telling me? A pretty kind of obedience that is! I was glad to hear about the decision you had made, and yet it worried me, as I think it is very risky. You should ask about it, for it may be that the fact you have made a vow might change a venial sin into a mortal one. I will ask my confessor as well, as he is a very learned man; but it seems to me that it was very foolish of you to make such a vow at all: the one I made contained some modifications, which are not in yours. I should not have dared to make a vow like yours, for I know the Apostles committed venial sins—Our Lady alone was free from them. I feel quite sure God will have accepted your intention, but I think you would be doing quite well if you changed the nature of the vow and undertook something quite different. If you can do this by getting a Bull, get one at once. In the jubilee year it would have been easier. Venial sins are so easy to commit that one can be guilty of them almost without realizing it. May God deliver us from them. He would have attached more guilt to such sins if he had not so profound a knowledge of our nature. My view is that the matter should be put right at once— and don't make any more vows. They are very risky. I don't think it is a bad idea to talk to your confessors about your prayer now and again, for they are near at hand and will be the best people to advise you about everything, and you lose nothing by consulting them.

It is the devil who is responsible for your regret at having bought La Serna: he wants you to cease thanking God for the great favour He showed you in that matter. Do understand once and for all that it was by far the best thing to do and it has given your sons more than property—it has given them prestige. Praise God for what you did and don't imagine that, if you had a great deal of time, you would spend more of it in prayer. Get rid of that idea. It is no hindrance to prayer to spend your time well, as you are doing when you are looking after the property which you will hand on to your sons. Again and again God gives more in a moment than in a long period of time, for his actions are not measured by time at all.

So, when the Christmas holidays are over, try to get hold of someone and go through the deeds with him and put them into proper shape. Jacob did not cease to be a saint because he had to attend to his flocks, nor did Abraham, nor St Joachim. Everything seems a trouble to us when we want to get out of doing some task; at least it is to me, which is why it is God's will that I should know no peace. Discuss all these things with Francisco de Salcedo, whom I hereby appoint to fill my place as regards temporal matters.

It is a great favour from God that what other people would consider a pleasure is wearisome to you. But that must not make you give it up, for we have to serve God in his way, not in ours. What I think you might avoid is going in for livestock dealing as a business; and that is one reason why I am glad you are not doing any more with Antonio Ruiz, as far as business is concerned. Even from the worldly standpoint you stand to lose slightly, and I think you will do better to moderate your generosity a little. God has given you enough to live on, and also enough to give some of it away, but not to give as freely as you do. I don't call what you are thinking of doing at La Serna business at all—that is perfectly proper: what I have in mind is making regular profits. But, as I say, follow the opinion of Francisco de Salcedo in all these things, and then you will not be troubled by such ideas any more. Remember me to him continually, and to anyone else you like; also to Pedro de Ahumada—I wish I had time to write to him, and also to get letters from him, for I love his letters.

You can tell Teresa that there is no fear that I shall love anyone else as much as I love her, and also that she must divide the pictures, not including those I put aside for myself, and give some of them to her brothers. I am longing to see her. I was very touched to read what you wrote to Seville about her, for they sent me the letters here, and our nuns were not a little delighted to hear them—I read them in recreation and enjoyed doing so too. No one will ever stop my brother from being a ladies' man—it would be the death of him if anyone did—but as the ladies in this case are saints, he thinks it all quite safe. I think these nuns really are saints too. They are always making me feel quite ashamed.

We had a great festival yesterday. It was the Name of Jesus. God reward you for your kindness. I don't know what I can send you in return for all the things you send me except these carols which I made up. My confessor had told me to amuse the sisters, so I spent several evenings with them, and I could think of no other way of entertaining them than this. They have a nice tune, if young Francisco could manage to sing it. You can see what progress I am making. Altogether the Lord has shown me the greatest favours of late.

I am amazed at the favours he shows you. May he be blessed for ever. I realize now why you desire devotion for yourself and it is a good thing to do so. But it is one thing to desire it and another to ask for it. You may be sure that what you are doing is best: leaving it all to the will of God and committing your ways to his hands.

If, when you wake up at any time with these surging desires for God, you sit up in bed for a while, there can be no harm in your doing so, as long as you take care to get all the sleep your brain needs, for otherwise, without being aware of it, you might reach a point at which you are unable to pray at all. See, too, that you try not to get too cold, for that is bad for the trouble in your side. I don't know why you want those terrors and fears, since God is leading you by the way of love. At one time, of course, you did need them. Don't suppose it is always the devil who hinders prayer: sometimes the ability to pray is taken from us by the mercy of God; and, for many reasons which I have not time to tell you I would say that it is almost as great a mercy when He takes it away as when He gives it in abundant measure. The prayer he gives you is incomparably greater than meditations about hell. Not that you would be capable of meditating on hell even if you tried to; but don't try, for you have no reason to.

The scarcity of fish in this town is so bad that our nuns find it very troublesome. So I was delighted to get this sea-bream. I think in this weather it could be sent without the bread [*fish was packed in large slices of bread to keep it fresh*]. If there should happen to be any, or any fresh sardines, when Serna comes, give them to the Sub-Prioress, so that she can send them to us, as she packed them so well before. This is a terrible place when you are not eating meat, for you can never get so much as a fresh egg. Still, I was thinking today that it is years since I felt as well as I do now, and I keep all the fasts just like everyone else, which is a great comfort to me.

Today is the second day of the year,

Your unworthy servant,

Teresa of Jesus

Raptures Again

St Teresa of Avila   January 17th 1577

To her brother

Teresa thanks Don Lorenzo de Cepeda for sardines and sweets and offers him more advice on obedience to her in spiritual matters, and on prayer and mortification. She reports but deprecates her public raptures.

Jesus be with you.

I said in the letter that went by the Alba courier that the sardines had arrived in good condition and that the sweets had duly arrived too, though I would rather you had kept the best ones. May God reward you. Don't send me anything else: when I want anything I will ask for it.

Your confessor had already told me that your vow is not valid, and I was extremely glad, for I was worried about it. Then, with regard to the obedience you had promised to pay me, I told him there seemed to be no point in it. He says it is all right so long as it does not take the form of a promise made to me or to anybody; so I don't want any promise from you, and in any case I don't like such things myself. However, if it is any comfort to you, I will overlook that, provided you make no promise of obedience to anybody.

What great things our Lord is doing! He seems to be pleased to show forth his greatness in raising up wretched creatures and doing us all these favours—and I know of none more wretched than you and I. I must tell you that for over a week I have been in such a condition that, if it were to go on, I should hardly be able to attend to all my business. Since before I wrote to you I have had raptures again, and they have been most distressing. Several times, I have had them in public—during Matins, for example. It is useless to resist them and they are impossible to conceal. I get so dreadfully ashamed that I feel I want to hide away somewhere. I pray God earnestly not to let them happen to me in public. Will you make this prayer for me too, for it is an extremely awkward thing and I don't believe my prayer is any the better for it? Latterly I have been going about almost as if I were drunk. But at least it is clear that the soul is well employed, for, as the faculties are not free, it is a grievous thing for the soul to have to occupy itself with anything save the object of its desire.

Previously, for nearly a week, I had been in such a state that I could hardly think a single good thought, so severely was I suffering from aridity. In one way I was really very glad that this was so, as for some time before that I had been as I am now, and it is a great satisfaction to realize so clearly how little we can do of ourselves. Amen. I have said quite enough.

With regard to the experience you tell me about, I do not know what to say, for it is certainly a greater thing than you realize, and may be the beginning of much blessing if you do not lose this through your own fault. I have already experienced that kind of prayer. As a rule, after it is over, the soul remains in a state of peace, and then it sometimes engages in certain forms of penance. In particular, if the impulse has been very strong, the soul feels it cannot bear to be doing something for God, for this is a touch of love which he bestows on the soul, and if it grows stronger you will understand that it is deep grief and pain, which one experiences without knowing whence it comes, and yet it is most delectable. And although it is in fact a wound inflicted upon the soul by God, we do not know whence it comes, nor even if it comes from a wound at all, or what it is: we only feel a delectable pain, which makes us cry out.

When God takes possession of the soul, he gives it more and more dominion over created things, and even if his presence is withdrawn and the satisfaction which the soul was enjoying disappears, he does not withdraw himself from the soul, nor does it fail to grow very rich in graces, and, as time goes on, that becomes evident in the affections.

Pay no attention to those evil feelings which come to you afterwards. I have never suffered from them myself, since God of his goodness has always delivered me from such passions, but I think that the explanation of them must be that the soul's joy is so keen that it makes itself felt in the body. With God's help it will calm down if you take no notice of it.

These trembling fits will stop too. As the experience is a new one the soul takes fright, and with good reason; but after several repetitions it will become used to receiving favours. Resist the trembling fits, and any other outward manifestations, as far as you can, or they may become habitual, and that would be more of a hindrance than a help.

The heat which you say you experience will neither help nor hinder your prayer, but it might well do some harm to your health, if it occurred often. It may perhaps gradually stop, like the trembling. These things, as I understand it, have to do with one's constitution: as yours is sanguine, they may be caused by the violent working of the spirit, together with the body's natural heat; you concentrate on higher things and the intensity of your concentration is felt in the heart. But, as I say, this adds nothing to the value of your prayer.

I think I answered your question about feeling as though nothing had happened after the experience was over. I cannot recall if it is St Augustine who says: "The Spirit of God passes without leaving a trace, just as the arrow leaves no trace in the air." There are other occasions when the condition of the soul is such that for a long time it cannot return to itself; it is like the sun, whose rays give out heat even when it cannot itself be seen. The soul seems to belong to some other place, and to animate the body without being in the body, because one of the faculties is suspended.

I was once told by a very learned person that a man had come to him in great trouble, because whenever he communicated a very evil thought came to him—much worse than the things you tell me about—and so he had been ordered not to receive communion, except once a year when it is of obligation. Although not a man of much spiritual experience, this learned man saw the weakness of this, and told him to take no notice of his thoughts, but to communicate every week. He did so and lost his fear of the thoughts, whereupon they left him. So take no notice of yours either.

You are doing very well. Glory be to God, as regards the kind of meditation you are making—I mean when you are not experiencing a state of quiet. I do not know if I have answered all your questions, for, though I always re-read your letters, I have not had time today. You must not give yourself the trouble of re-reading the letters you write me. I never re-read mine. If a word here or there should have a letter missing, just put it in, and I will do the same for you, for your meaning is quite clear, and re-reading your letters would be a waste of time for you and all to no purpose.

I send you this hairshirt to use when you find it difficult to recollect yourself at times of prayer, or when you are anxious to do something for the Lord. It is good for awakening love, but you are on no account to put it on after you are dressed, or to sleep in it. It can be worn on any part of the body, and put on in any way so long as it feels uncomfortable. Even a mere nothing like this makes one so happy when it is done for God out of a love for him with the love you are feeling now, that I don't want us to omit giving it a trial. Write and tell me how you get on with this trifle. For I assure you, the more faithfully we deal with ourselves, remembering our Lord's sufferings, the more of a trifle it seems to us. It makes me laugh to think how you send me sweets and presents and money, and I send you hairshirts. You must use the discipline only for short periods, too, for in that way you feel it all the more, and at the same time it will do you less harm. Do not punish yourself with it too severely, for it is of no great importance, though you will think it very imperfect of you not to. And remember, if it affects the kidneys, you must neither wear the hairshirt nor take the discipline, or it will do you great harm. God prefers your health and your obedience to your penances.

Remember that we middle-aged people need to treat our bodies well so as not to wreck the spirit, which is a terrible trial. So do as you are ordered. That is the way to do your duty to God.

My confessor, Dr Velázquez, was here today. I discussed with him what you said about wanting to give up using the carpets and silver, as I should not like you to cease making progress in God's service because I was not helping you, but there are things in which I do not trust my own opinion. In this, however, he agreed with me. He says it is of no importance one way or the other; what matters is that you try to see how unimportant such things are and not become attached to them. It is right that you should have a suitably appointed house, as you will have to marry your sons one day. So just be patient for now. God always gives us opportunities to carry out our good desires, and he will give you a chance to carry out yours. May God watch over you for me and make you very holy.

Today is the seventeenth of January,

Your unworthy servant,

Teresa

Remembering

Blaise and Jacqueline Pascal

November 5th 1648

To Madame Périer

Pascal and his sister Jacqueline write to their married sister, Gilberte, on constancy of spiritual effort.

Dear Sister,

It is not sufficient to have grasped on one occasion the things of which you speak and to have understood them correctly: that is, having been moved by God. That is not the way to retain them. Of course it is possible to remember them. You can learn a letter of St Paul's by heart just as proficiently as a book of Virgil. The acquisition of knowledge in that way is only a feat of memory. To understand intimately that secret language which is alien to those who do not know the things of God, it is necessary for the same grace that provided the first insight to help it forwards, to keep it always before us, and to renew it constantly in the hearts of the faithful.

It soon becomes apparent that we have to renew our efforts ever and again, if we are to retain this everlasting freshness of spirit. We cannot obtain the new wine without unceasing renewal.

We should never refuse to read or to hear the sacred texts, even if we think we know them intimately, or all too well. Knowledge stored in the memory is soulless if it is not constantly re-enlivened by the spirit. It often happens that God makes more use of outward than of inward means, to ensure that people receive his grace, declare his intentions, and give as little room as possible to human vanity.

Even if a book or sermon is rather banal, it may prove more fruitful than fine speeches for those who readily make themselves open, for fine orations in general serve more to please than to instruct. Sometimes we can see that those who listen in the right way are moved by the name of God and nothing else, and experience something that has nothing to do with an increase of knowledge.

Yours ever,

Blaise and Jacqueline

Our Only Hope

Baron Friedrich von Hügel   19—

To his niece

In his conversations with and letters to Gwendolen Greene, the Baron achieved
something of that equilibrium between tenderness and austerity that he found in its
fulness in our Lord.

Dearie ...

I wait for the breath of God, for God's breath. Perhaps he will call me today—tonight. Don't let us be niggardly towards God. He is never a niggard towards us.—Let us try to be generous and accept.—My illness is so little! I have no pain—my brain is clear—why should I not accept this generously? I would like to finish my book—but if not, I shall live it out in the Beyond.—I love the angels, they stand for something we cannot otherwise express....

Plant yourself on foundations that are secure—God—Christ—Suffering—the Cross. They are secure. How I love the Sacraments! I am as certain of the real presence of Christ in the Eucharist as of anything there is. Our great hope is in Christianity—our only hope. Christ recreates. Christianity has taught us to care. Caring is the greatest thing—caring matters most. My faith is not enough—it comes and goes. I have it about some things and not about others. So we make up and supplement each other. We give and others give to us. Keep your life a life of prayer, dearie.—Keep it like that: it's the only thing, and remember, no joy without suffering—no patience without trial—no humility without humiliation—no life without death....

Your devoted old Uncle,

Friedrich von Hügel

CHAPTER 3

Self-Examination and Good Conduct

Be Faithful

St Bernadette of Lourdes

July 1st 1876

To her brother

Three years before her death, the retiring Bernadette writes from her convent at Nevers to advise her brother Jean-Marie with the simple directness for which she was noted.

My dear Jean-Marie,

In her letter our cousin Nicholau tells me that you will probably be discharged from the army this year. Let me know what you are going to do. I am sure that you realize, although I live at such a distance, that I am as interested in all you do as if I were on the spot. Rest assured that I do not ask any questions out of idle curiosity. Since our dear father and mother are dead it is my duty as the eldest sister to watch over you.

I must say that just now I am very anxious about your future and Pierre's. Every day I pray that our Lord and our blessed Lady will guide you. Above all, I firmly advise you to remember your Christian duty. Then you will take strength in all your troubles and problems. I know that soldiers have a lot to put up with, and have to do so without protest. If when they got up they were to say to our Lord every morning this short sentence: "My God, I wish to do and to endure everything today for love of you," they would store up immeasurable treasure in heaven! If a soldier did that and performed his Christian duties as faithfully as possible, he would earn the same reward as any monk in a cloister!

Your sister,

Bernadette

He Shall Exalt You

Charles Wesley   Newcastle, December 11th 1746

To Ebenezer Blackwell

Charles Wesley's letters are often fervent essays in evangelism, similar in tone and expression to his revivalist sermons. This one, to a banker living at Lewisham, then in the South London countryside, is typical of Charles's treatment of his followers and supporters as neophytes undergoing a continuous process of conversion in the midst of dangers, and needing both warning and encouragement, but also assurance that they are helping to convert others in a common endeavour of fellowship and increasing godliness.

My dear Friend,

This is the victory that overcometh the world, even our faith; and I *shall* hear my dear friend Blackwell say, "Thanks be to God, who giveth *me* the victory through *my* Lord Jesus Christ." God has undoubtedly begun his gracious work in your soul, and is ready (but waits for your hearty concurrence) to carry it on, and perform it. Cannot you hear him say this moment, "Zaccheus, make haste and come down; for today I must abide at thy house?" O receive, receive him gladly, while he comes to be guest with a man that is a sinner! You are not indeed worthy that he should come under your roof; neither can you ever prepare your own heart to admit him. All you can do, is not to hinder; not to keep him out, by willingly harbouring any of his enemies, such as worldly, proud, or angry thoughts or designs. My dear brother, whenever any such arise, do not justify yourself, or say, "I do well to be angry, peevish, stubborn," &c. Judge yourself, and you shall not be judged of the Lord. Humble yourself under his mighty hand, and he shall exalt you in due time. He that humbleth himself shall be exalted; and God has promised you this preparation of the heart, which is of him. His work is before him. Every valley shall be exalted (all the abjectness of your believing heart), and every mountain and hill made low (all the haughtiness and pride of your spirit), and the crooked shall be made straight (your crooked, perverse will), and the rough places plain (your rugged, uneven temper), and *then* the glory of the Lord shall be revealed, and we all shall see it together; for the mouth of the Lord hath spoken it. Mr P— joins in hearty love and thanks for your kind concern for him. He grows apace, is bold as a lion, meek as a lamb, and begins to speak in this Name to the heart of sinners. Poor Mrs R— has got an hook within him, which shall bring him at last to land. Meantime, I believe, with you, even his struggling in the net shall work together for good, and spread the Gospel. I shall hope for another line from Change-Alley before I leave this place. The Lord be the strength of your life, and your portion for ever! ... Farewell!

Charles Wesley

A Ciceronian ...

St Jerome   c. 384

To Eustochium

The famous self-sufficient dream section from a long letter to the now widowed St Paula's daughter, who eventually succeeded her mother as head of a convent at Bethlehem. This minor treatise may be seen as a series of letters on various aspects of choosing a life of virginity. The present section stresses the importance of discriminating between priorities. Of course, this wryly humorous account of a dream-pledge is not to be taken literally; even if that were the case, it would not mean that Jerome expunged all classical learning from his memory, wholly ceased to refer to pagan authors, or rejected everything they said.

Dear Daughter,

Don't be too keen to admire your own eloquence or to improvise your own humorous poems. Don't fastidiously copy certain married women who purse their lips then loosen them and go around lisping so stylishly that they destroy their speech, believing that everything natural is vulgar. After all, they take a similar delight in adultery, even with the tongue. For what has light to do with darkness? And what does Christ have in common with Belial? What has Horace to do with the Psalms or Vergil with the Gospels or Cicero with Paul? Surely you can lead someone astray if he or she sees you sitting at table in an idolator's temple? Even though all things are clean to the clean and nothing is to be rejected that is received with thanksgiving, we should not drink Christ's chalice and the chalice of demons at one and the same time. Perhaps my own unfortunate experience will serve to explain what I mean.

Many years ago, when I left home, parents, sister and relations, for God's sake, I also abandoned the comfortable style of life I was used to. I was off to Jerusalem to be a soldier of Christ. But I just couldn't do without the library that I had got together in Rome with so much effort. So, like a real booby, I used to fast *and* read Cicero. After interminable night vigils and countless tears for my past sins, I would reach for a nice volume of Plautus. But when I reverted to my devotional mode and took up one of the prophets to read, I couldn't bear the ghastly style. My sight was so bad that I found the light unbearable, yet it never occurred to me that it was not the sun but my vision that was faulty. Then I became sick with a fever. Preparations were made for my funeral and I imagined myself standing before the last court of judgement. It was so bright there that I dared not look up but fell to the ground. "What are you?" they asked, so of course I replied: "A Christian!" The one on the judgement seat retorted: "Rubbish! You're no Christian—you're a Ciceronian! Where your treasure is, there is your heart also". What could I say? I felt the blows I received—for he ordered me to be beaten—all the more because my conscience was troubling me. I repeated the words: "And who shall confess thee in hell?" Then I began to cry out and lament: "Have mercy on me, Lord, have mercy on me." My request re-echoed as the lashes came down on me. In the end, the onlookers threw themsleves down before the knees of the One presiding there and asked him to spare the young fellow, let me have a chance to repent of my errors and to punish me fully if I ever again read a work of pagan literature. Things were so bad that I would have promised even more than that. I started to take an oath and swore by His name: "O Lord, if ever I own or read secular works, I shall have denied you." As soon as I had said this I was allowed to return to the world above. They were all astonished when I opened my eyes and wept so copiously that even the incredulous believed. I hadn't been merely sleeping or experienced one of those pointless dreams that so often take us in. I had been before a very real tribunal and I had been scared stiff by the possibility of judgement. I trust that I shall never have to suffer such an interrogation again! My shoulders were black and blue from the drubbing I'd received and I could still feel the blows when I woke up. After all that, I read God's word more zealously than I had read human words in the past.

Jerome

How Mean are You?

St Bernard of Clairvaux   c. 1150

To Baldwin, bishop of Noyon

This delightful letter is a rare survival as such amusing and personal notes were not usually preserved in archives or anthologies.

To the Lord Baldwin, Bishop of Noyon, something better than he deserves, from Brother Bernard, styled Abbot of Clairvaux:

I am sending you the small boy who is bringing this letter to eat your bread, that I may find out how mean you are from the sort of welcome you give him. But you have no cause for tears or lamentations, he has a small stomach and will be content with little. I shall be grateful if he returns wiser rather than stouter. The tone of this letter will have to serve as my seal because it is not to hand, neither is your Godfrey.

Brother Bernard

Admonish Me

St Robert Bellarmine

June 16th 1599

To the Jesuit provincial

In 1597 Pope Clement VIII made Bellarmine a papal theologian and in 1598 a cardinal, "as he had no equal for learning." This relentless self-scrutiny reveals his profound humility.

Dear Father Provincial,

I constantly think of giving up the purple, and cannot see how. I rather think that my efforts would be useless and that people would say that it was only another of my poses. Furthermore, I do not know that God would like this renunciation, for it was by his will that I was forced to accept this dignity. To introduce novelties into my way of life by reducing the number of people in my suite, or by adopting simple dress would make people think that I wished to start reforms which the most austere and virtuous cardinals have neither advised nor adopted. St Antoninus, for instance, teaches in his treatise "De statu cardinalium" that a certain amount of splendour is necessary if the dignity of the Sacred College is to be treated with the respect due from the world in general. I try as hard as ever to keep my splendour and dignity as modest as possible. Among my colleagues who are neither extravagant nor showy but follow a middle way that is not without its own elegance and distinction, I am accounted the least elegant and distinguished. Indeed, within the limits of order and decency, I am just not shabby.

My reason for talking thus to you, Father, is that you as the guide and master of my soul may admonish me if I go wrong in any way, and that thus, with your advice, I may be converted to wiser ways. I shall now give some precise details. There are ten gentlemen in my suite who carry out various higher duties. Most of them have two servants apiece, but some of them have only one. In addition, I have fourteen servants for ordinary house and stable work, so that the sum total of the domestic servants is not beyond thirty. I told each of them privately when I took them on that, according to the rules of my house, swearing, impurity, or any other serious sin would mean instant dismissal. I bring them together every week and exhort them as earnestly as possible to lead good lives and to carry out their religious duties. I continue to say the Office at the canonical hours, as in the past. I have not stopped my former custom of fasting on Wednesdays and Fridays.

I try never to send a poor man away unhappy or empty-handed, but as I am poor myself I can give only small sums at a time. If I ever become rich I shall be generous with my alms, as Tobit advises. The Lord knows that it is not a desire to hoard that stops me from giving a lot to everyone who asks, for I never had the slightest love of money or possessions. As for austerity, I fear that hair-shirts, sleeping on the floor, a bread and water diet, and so on are not right for me, for I am almost sixty and my health is almost broken. I do not think that I could stand such hardships for long. Nevertheless, if a spiritual and prudent man were to recommend them, I think that unless I was quite deceived by self-love, I should be quite prepared to adopt them. At first I decided to have only one carriage, but I soon found that a second was needed for the convenience of my suite, without whom you may not attend the papal services and consistories. Of course I could have obtained a lift from my friends on the way to these events, but the return journey was the difficulty. My friends' coaches were not available then, so, if I had not possessed a second carriage of my own, the gentlemen-in-waiting would have been forced to return home on foot and that would not have been right. The furniture in my house is as simple and plain as possible and I did not have my arms embroidered on the tapestries or couches in the hall, though it is the general custom to have them put on. All the chairs except four are plain leather. The four are in velvet but are brought out only when cardinals, royal ambassadors, and other eminent people visit us. The rest of the furniture is very ordinary indeed, and no-one would call it valuable. I wear no silk at all and there is nothing grander than plain, cheap wool in my wardrobe.

I an writing to you in this vein so that you can relieve my doubts with your wise advice and tell me straightforwardly what I should do. You are my close friend and that is why I tell you all these things, but I should not like others to learn what I have told you. The Pope wanted me to accept the bishopric of my native area, Montepulciano, but only if I were to remain in Rome. I did not accept these terms as I know the dangers of being an absentee bishop. But if he would allow me to stay in the diocese I should not be so reluctant, because I think that the office of a bishop is more spiritual, more religious, more productive of good, and more secure, than that of the cardinalate alone, which is certainly sacred but has much of the secular about it. I do not forget the difficulties and dangers involved in the cure of souls, but when God summons us we cannot cry safety first. Obedience is certainly the safest state for, as St Francis says, in obedience there is profit and in prelacy peril. But we should rather choose the way of life that is most pleasing to God and at the same time least dangerous for our souls. I apologize for the length of this letter. Pray for me, Father. I shall anxiously await your good advice. I beg you with all my heart to draw me with you to heaven, somehow, even though I am reluctant.

Farewell,

Robert Bellarmine

A Great Hour-Glass

John Donne   September 1608

To Sir Henry Goodyer

This letter is one of Donne's most beautifully composed and profoundly spiritual, reflective and self-analytical pieces, in which, as befits a great poet and preacher, the use of imagery, sound and other stylistic devices is one with the development of the thought. Henry Goodyer was Donne's closest friend and was so impressed by Donne's letters that he took many thoughts and phrases from them for use in his own correspondence and other writings.

Sir,

Every Tuesday I make account that I turn a great hour-glass, and consider that a week's life is run out since I writ. But if I ask myself what I have done in the last watch, or would do in the next, I can say nothing; if I say that I have passed it without hurting any, so may the spider in my window. The primitive monks were excusable in their retirings and enclosures of themselves: for even of them every one cultivated his own garden and orchard, that is, his soul and body, by meditation, and manufactures; and they owed the world no more since they consumed none of her sweetness, nor begot others to burden her. But for me, if I were able to husband all my time so thriftily, as not only to wound my soul in any minute by actual sin, but not to rob and cousen her by giving any part to pleasure or business, but bestow it all upon her in meditation, yet even in that I should wound her more, and contract another guiltiness: As the eagle were very unnatural if because she is able to do it, she should perch a whole day upon a tree, staring in contemplation of the majesty and glory of the sun, and let her young eaglets starve in the nest. Two of the most precious things which God hath afforded us here, for the agony and exercise of our sense and spirit, which are a thirst and inhiation after [desiring] the next life, and a frequency of prayer and meditation in this, are often envenomed, and putrified, and stray into a corrupt disease; for as God doth thus occasion, and positively concur to evil, that when a man is purposed to do a great sin, God infuses some good thoughts which make him choose a less sin, or leave out some circumstance which aggravated that; so the devil doth not only suffer but provoke us to some things naturally good, upon condition that we shall omit some other more necessary and more obligatory. And this is his greatest subtlety; because herein we have the deceitful comfort of having done well, and can very hardly spy our error because it is but an insensible omission, and no accusing act. With the first of these I have often suspected myself to be overtaken; which is, with a desire of the next life: which though I know it is not merely out of a weariness of this, because I had the same desires when I went with the tide, and enjoyed fairer hopes than now: yet I doubt worldly encumbrances have increased it. I would not that death should take me asleep. I would not have him merely seize me, and only declare me to be dead, but win me, and overcome me. When I must shipwrack, I would do it in a sea, where mine impotency might have some excuse; not in a sullen weedy lake, where I could not have so much exercise for my swimming. Therefore I would fain do something; but I cannot tell what, is no wonder. For to choose, is to do; but to be no part of any body, is to be nothing. At most, the greatest persons, are but great wens, and excrescences; men of wit and delightful conversation, but as moles for ornament, except they be so incorporated into the body of the world, that they contribute something to the sustenation of the whole. This I made account that I begun early, when I understood the study of our laws: but was diverted by the worst voluptuousness, which is an hydroptic immoderate desire of humane learning and languages: beautiful ornaments of great fortunes; but mine needed an occupation, and a course which I thought I entered well into, when I submitted myself to such a service, as

I thought might employ these poor advantages, which I had. And there I stumbled too, yet would try again: for to this hour, I am nothing, or so little, that I am scarce subject and argument good enough for one of mine own letters: yet I fear, that doth not ever proceed from a good root, that I am so well content to be less, that is dead. You, Sir, are far enough from these descents, your virtue keeps you secure, and your natural disposition to mirth will preserve you; but lose none of these holds, a slip is often as dangerous as a bruise, and thou cannot fall to my lowness, yet in a much less distraction you many meet my sadness; for he is no safer which falls from an high tower into the leads, than he which falls from thence to the ground: make therefore to yourself some mark, and go towards it alegrement. Though I be in such a planetary and erratic fortune, that I can do nothing constantly, yet you may find some constancy in my constant advising you to it.

Your hearty true friend,

J. Donne

Opportune Kindness

St Teresa of Avila

January 17th 1570

To Don Lorenzo de Cépeda

St Teresa thanks her brother for helping their sister and describes her own attitude to possessions. The sister's husband was a difficult partner, always in financial straits and thus a source of great anxiety.

May the Holy Spirit be ever with you ...

I have already written to tell you how opportune was the kindness which you showed my sister. I have been amazed at the dire straits into which the Lord has led her, and she has endured them so well that he is now pleased to grant her some relief from them. For myself, I lack nothing; in fact, I have enough and to spare of everything; I shall give some of what you send me to my sister and spend the rest in good works, which I shall regard as having been done by you. Your last present arrived most opportunely, as I was troubled by scruples at the time; for with these foundations certain occasions keep arising when, careful though I am, I feel I should give less in the way of gifts to the learned men whom I always consult about spiritual matters. Of course I do it solely for the sake of the foundations, and they are the merest trifles, anyway; but still it was great relief to me to get your money, so as not to have to accept relief from anyone else. Though others would not have failed me, I much prefer to be completely independent of these gentry, so that I can express my opinions to them freely. There is so much worldliness these days that I simply hate having possessions, so I shall keep none of your present for myself, but give part of it to the Order, and then be free to dispose of the rest in the way I said; for I have all possible freedom, from both the General and the Provincial, to receive postulants, to move nuns from one house to another, and to help any one house from the funds of others.

People have such blind confidence in me—I don't know how they can do such things, but they seem to trust me so implicitly that they will give me as much as a thousand or two thousand ducats. So, although I used to detest money and business matters, it is the Lord's pleasure that I should engage in nothing else, and that is no light cross. May his Majesty grant me to serve him in this, for everything will pass away.

Your unworthy servant,

Teresa of Jesus, Carmelite

What Good have you Done?

Gerard Manley Hopkins SJ   January 19th 1879

To Robert Bridges

Robert Bridges the poet was one of the few people with whom Hopkins was able to discuss his own poetry. Occasionally he ventured beyond literature and related subjects to describe, say, his conversion, or even, when he thought it called for, to offer measured moral advice on such matters as Bridges' excessive harshness as a critic or, as here, on the need for charity.

Dearest Bridges,

. . .

When we met in London we never but once, and then only for a few minutes before parting, spoke on any important subject, but always on literature. This I regret very much. If it had ended in nothing or consisted in nothing but your letting me know your thoughts, that is some of them, it would have been a great advantage to me. And if now by pen and ink you choose to communicate anything I shall be very glad. I should also like to say one thing. You understand of course that I desire to see you a Catholic or, if not that, a Christian or, if not that, at least a believer in the true God (for you told me something of your views about the deity, which were not as they should be). Now you no doubt take for granted that your already being or your ever coming to be any of these things turns on the working of your own mind, influenced or uninfluenced by the minds and reasonings of others as the case may be, and on that only. You might on reflection expect me to suggest that it also might and ought to turn on something further, in fact on prayer, and that suggestion I believe I did once make. Still under the circumstances it is one which it is not altogether consistent to make or adopt. But I have another counsel open to no objection and yet I think it will be unexpected. I lay great stress on it. It is to give alms. It may be either in money or in other shapes, the objects for which, with your knowledge of several hospitals, can never be wanting. I daresay indeed you do give alms, still I should say give more: I should be bold to say give up to the point of sensible inconvenience. "Fieri non potest ut idem sentiant qui aquam et qui vinum bibant": the difference of mind and being between the man who finds comfort all round him unbroken unless by constraints which are none of his own seeking and the man who is pinched by his own charity is too great for forecasting, it must be felt. I do not say the difference between being pinched and being at one's ease, that one may easily conceive and most people know, willynilly, by experience, but the difference between paying heavily for a virtue and not paying at all. It changes the whole man, if anything can; not his mind only but the will and everything. For here something applies like the French bishop's question to his clergy whenever one of them came to tell him that he had intellectual difficulties and must withdraw from the exercise of his priestly functions—"What is her name?" In some such way a man may be far from belief in Christ or God or all he should believe, really and truly so; still the question to be asked would be (Not "who is she?", for that to him is neither here or there but) "what good have you done?" I am now talking pure Christianity, as you may remember, but also I am talking pure sense, as you must see. Now you may have done much good, but yet it may not be enough: I will say, it is not enough ....

Believe me your affectionate friend,

Gerard M. Hopkins SJ

Wavering

St Jerome   384

To Eustochium

When in Rome as secretary to Pope St Damasus, Jerome became friendly with and a spiritual director to a number of noble, yet scholarly and devout, Roman women. They included St Paula and her daughter Eustochium, who later succeeded her mother as head of a convent in Bethlehem. He said that he wrote to them every day. This is the autobiographical section of one of several letters to the daughter. It bears no trace of the sarcasm or irony which are often features of Jerome's correspondence. In this instance he is laying down rules for a life of virginity, and uses a typically strong and graphic illustration, drawn from his own life, of the hazards of the ascetic way.

My Lady Eustochium,

    ...

How often when I was established in the desert and in that great wilderness burnt by the sun's heat where monks dwell among natural savagery, I imagined myself back in the pleasures of Rome. I sat alone because I was so bitter. I wore rough sackcloth and looked rather ghastly. I neglected my skin which looked like an Ethiopian's. I shed tears each day, I groaned each day, and whenever sleep overtook me I bruised my awkward bones on the harsh ground. I shall not mention meat and drink, for even the sick drink only cold water, and cooked food is something of a luxury. Out of fear of hell I had sentenced myself to this prison with scorpions and wild beasts as my only friends. But I was often surrounded by dancing girls. My face was wan from fasting and my mind was burning from desire in an ice-cold body. My flesh was almost dead but passionate fires were alight within me.

I lay helpless at Jesus' feet. I bathed them in my tears and wiped them with my hair. When my flesh rebelled I punished it with weeks of fasting. I shall not blush at my ridiculous condition, indeed I am rather sorry that now I am not what I was then. I remember often weeping and groaning day and night and continuing to beat my breast until the Lord's rebuke brought me peace again. I even feared to enter my tiny cell, as though it knew what I was thinking. I was angry with myself and very nervous, and went alone into the desert. When I came upon a deep valley or craggy peak and cliff I made this place my prayer centre, and a place of punishment for the miserable flesh. As God will testify, after weeping and looking up to heaven, I seemed sometimes to be surrounded by crowds of angels and rejoiced while singing....

But if people with a worn body are tempted by thoughts alone, what about a girl who is delighted by luxuries? The apostle has said: "She is dead while alive." If you will believe me as someone who knows what he's talking about, I beg you as a bride of Christ to run a mile from wine. Devils use wine especially as a weapon in their struggle to win over young people. Greed, pride and ambition are all less effective than drink. We can put away the other vices. This enemy is inside us. We bear it with us wherever we go. Wine and youth doubly fan the flames of pleasure....

There are women who make a show of themselves in public by the way they walk and attract a crowd of young men with their sly winks. They are the targets of the prophet's words: "You had a harlot's face, you never blushed." ... They just need a touch of purple in their clothes and a loosely-bound head, with a little cloak fluttering on their shoulders, sleeves tight on their arms, and a clever movement of their knees when walking— and before you know it, that's all their virginity amounts to. Women like that can keep their followers. I'm glad to be unpopular with girls like that who can earn a higher reward for their ruination precisely because they have a reputation for virginity....

You are the first noble woman in the city of Rome who has chosen to be a nun. You will have to try all the harder not to lose present and future advantages....

    Jerome

Dangerous and Terrible

Gerard Manley Hopkins

June 13th 1868

To the Revd E. W. Urquhart

In what seems to be his last letter to a close friend at Oxford, a High Church curate who eventually became an Anglican priest and married, and with whom he shared a number of interests, probably including the same sexual inclination, Hopkins conveys the high seriousness of his own conversion to Catholicism.

Dear Urquhart,

   ...

I do not at all understand what you mean by my treating you shamefully in the way of correspondence ... I think argument is not only useless but tends to encourage the way of thinking of yr. position as if intellectual and not moral hindrance stood between you and the Catholic Church. If I tell you the truth it is that you are trying the forbearance of God and that the most terrible things our Lord uttered were spoken to some who had to all appearance more excuse than you. The way you write, peculiar so far as I know among your school to yourself, whether blindness or as I suppose irony, I can only call desperate. I know that living a moral life, with the ordinances of religion and yourself a minister of them, with work to do and the interest of a catholicwards movement to support you, it is most natural to say all things continue as they were and most hard to realize the silence and the severity of God, as Dr Newman very eloquently and persuasively has said in a passage of the Anglican Difficulties; but this plea or way of thinking—all things continuing as they were—is the very character of infidelity. The difference between a state of grace and a state of reprobation, that difference to which all other differences of humanity are as the splitting of straws, makes no change in the outer world; faces, streets, and sunlight look just the same: it is therefore the more dangerous and terrible. And if God says that without faith it is impossible to please him and will not excuse the best of heathens with the best of excuses for the want of it, what is to be said of people who knowing it live in avowed doubt whether they are in his church or not? Will it comfort you at death not to have despaired of the English Church if by not despairing of it you are out of the Catholic Church?—a contingency which by the fact of doubt you contemplate. Will God thank you for your allegiance and will he excuse you for it? He asks obedience before everything else. Make half an hour's meditation on death and suppose you have received what you call the last sacrament: it will then occur—perhaps this is not a sacrament and if not it is mockery to me and God; secondly, if it is, perhaps it is received in schism and I have wounded my soul with the "instrument of salvation": this perhaps which gives little trouble on an ordinary Sunday will be very terrible then... Until you prefer God to the world and yourself you have not made the first step....

Believe me, yr. affectionate friend—

Gerard M. Hopkins

Energy and Passion

Søren Kierkegaard   1843

From "Judge William" to the young man and author "A"

In the assumed identity of the letter-writer of his pseudonymously published "Either/ Or", Kierkegaard seeks to impress upon the reader the necessary intensity and energy of self-awareness—a major aspect of his conviction that "Subjectivity is the truth": that choosing, or knowing, oneself is supremely important if one is to reach a state of profitable dissatisfaction with one's actual self and become conscious of the true self one might be if one fulfilled one's possibilities.

My Friend,

When with all his energy a person has felt the intensity of duty he is then ethically mature, and in him duty will emerge of itself. The chief thing is, not whether one can count on one's fingers how many duties one has, but that a man has once felt the intensity of duty in such a way that the consciousness of it is for him the assurance of the eternal validity of his being. I, therefore, by no means extol a man for being a man of duty, any more than I would commend him for being a bookworm, and yet it is certain that the man before whom duty has never revealed itself in its whole significance is quite as poor a sort as is the scholar who thinks like the foolish inhabitants of the village of Mol that learning comes to one without further ado....

When I was five years of age I was sent to school. It is natural that such an event always makes an impression upon a child, but the question is, what impression. Childish curiosity is engrossed by the various confusing conceptions as to what significance this may properly have. That this was the case with me too is quite likely: however, the chief impression I got was an entirely different one. I made my appearance at school, was introduced to the teacher, and then was given as my lesson for the following day the first ten lines of Balle's "Lesson-Book," which I was to learn by heart. Every other impression was then obliterated from my soul, only my task stood out vividly before it. As a child I had a very good memory, so I had soon learned my lesson. My sister had heard me recite it several times and affirmed that I knew it. I went to bed, and before I fell asleep I catechized myself once more; I fell asleep with the firm purpose of reading the lesson over the following morning. I awoke at five o'clock, got dressed, got hold of my lesson-book, and read it again. At this moment everything stands as vividly before my eyes as if it had occurred yesterday. To me it was as if heaven and earth might collapse if I did not learn my lesson, and on the other hand as if, even if heaven and earth were to collapse, this would not exempt me from doing what was assigned to me, from learning my lesson. At this age I knew little about duties. I had not yet, as you see, learned to know them from Balle's "Lesson-Book," I had only one duty, that of learning my lesson, and yet I can trace my whole ethical view of life to this impression. I may smile at a little nipper of five years who takes hold of a thing so passionately, and yet I assure you I have no higher wish than that at every time of life I may take hold of my work with the same energy, with the same ethical earnestness as then. It is true that in later life one acquires a better conception of what one's work is, but still the chief thing is the energy.... What is really important in education is not that the child learns this and that, but that the mind is matured, that energy is aroused. You often talk about how glorious a thing it is to have a good head. Who will deny that this is important? And yet I am nearly inclined to believe that one can make oneself that if one will. Give a man energy, passion, and with that he is everything.

Yours sincerely,

Judge William

What Can I Say to You?

St Bernard of Clairvaux   12th century

To someone who broke his word

Even in his most kindly and charitable letters of paternal concern, Bernard does not hesitate to use a short, sharp shock image in order to provoke his correspondent into realizing his condition.

Dear Friend,

Although you care not for yourself, yet I do not cease to care for you since I am fond of you and grieve over you. Because I am fond of you I grieve over you; because I grieve over you, I think of you. But how sad and unhappy are my thoughts! I wonder what is preventing you from coming as you promised. I cannot believe that you would break your word, so solemnly given, except for some compelling reason, for I gather that you are a faithful and tolerably truthful young man. And I am not deceived in my opinion; it is indeed something grave and compelling that is keeping you back. The same thing that overcame David the mighty, the same thing that deceived Solomon the wise. What can I say to you? In the words of

the Prophet, I say: "A man falls but to rise, errs but to retrieve his path."
I have much that is important to say to you, too much for a letter. But this
much I do say: If there lives in you the faintest spark of your old love for
me; if you have any hope at all of eventually escaping from your wretched
captivity; if you do not wish that confidence in the prayers and friendship
of this community, which I am told you have even while living as you are,
to be utterly empty and false, come at once to Clairvaux ... that is if you
are free and sufficiently master of yourself to dare to leave, even for a short
time, the bloodstained monster which daily devours both your substance
and your soul. Otherwise know you that from now on you are cut off from
the fellowship of our brotherhood, and will never again be able, except in
vain, to flatter yourself on their friendship with good men, because, by
refusing to take their advice, you will prove yourself unworthy of their
fellowship. But if you do not loiter but come at once, you can be sure that
before you leave you will be, by God's mercy, freed of the deadly thraldom
that now grips you.

Yours ever,

Bernard

True Feelings and Practices

St Vincent de Paul

July 25th 1640

To Fr Peter Escart

*An excellent psychologist, Monsieur Vincent was well aware of Fr Escart's tendency
to self-righteousness and excessive anger masquerading as the defence of virtue. He
eventually killed a friend in a fit of rage.*

Dear Father Escart,

...

I find your zeal for the advancement of this Company is always
accompanied by a harshness of some kind, which can even become
bitterness. All you say about certain people and everything you call
cowardice and sensuality in them shows me this and especially the spirit
in which you say it. Good Lord! You must be very wary of that. In the
case of the virtues it is very easy to pass from fault to excess, from being just
to being rigorous and foolishly zealous. They say that good wine easily
becomes vinegar and that excellent health is a sign of approaching sickness.
We know of course that zeal is the soul of the virtues, but surely it must

be according to knowledge, which means, according to experimental knowledge. As young people as a rule do not have this experimental knowledge, their zeal becomes excessive, especially in the case of those who are naturally severe. You must be very wary indeed of that, and mistrust most of the movements and ploys of the mind when you are young and have a temperament like that. Martha complained about the holy idleness and holy self-indulgence of her dear sister Mary Magdalen, and thought the latter was behaving badly because she was not busy, as she was herself, attending on our Lord. You and I would perhaps have felt the same if we had been there. Yet, "O the depth of the riches of the wisdom and of the knowledge of God! How incomprehensible are his judgements!" (Rom. 11: 33). Behold our Lord saying that the idleness and self-indulgence of Magdalen were more pleasing to him than the indiscreet zeal of Martha! Perhaps you will say that there was some difference between listening like Magdalen and our listening, as we do, to our own minor weaknesses. But are we sure that it is not our Lord himself who has inspired the two persons you write about with the notion of travelling and also of enjoying those little comforts you mention?

I am quite sure of one thing; that is: "For those who love God all things work together unto good" (Rom. 8: 28), and I do not doubt that the very same persons really love God. How otherwise would they have left their parents, friends, puissance, and all the natural pleasures which they had in them, in order to go looking for the poor sheep that have been lost among the mountains, if they did not love God? And if the love of God is in their hearts, surely we must think that God inspires them to do everything that they do, and not do what they leave undone, and that everything they do and leave undone is for the best! In the name of God, let us practise these really true feelings and behaviour, and let us fear lest the evil spirit leads us from our excessive zeal to a lack of respect for our superiors and charity towards our equals. As a rule, that is what our less discreet zeal eventually becomes, and that is the advantage which the evil spirit gets out of it. Therefore I beseech you in the name of our Lord to work with me to lose such manifestations of zeal and, especially of those which harm respect, esteem, and charity. Because I think that the evil spirit has such designs on you and me, let us work hard to find how we should interpret our neighbour's behaviour favourably and bear with him in his weaknesses....

Yours,

Vincent de Paul

Birmingham People

John Henry Newman

July 25th 1864

To Monsignor Talbot

Here Newman appears as the master of the short, sharp, tart reply to an ineffably patronizing letter (amounting even to an unworthy rebuke) to one of the greatest, most respected but also most castigated and envied religious thinkers and writers of the age. Talbot had asked the author of the recently successful Apologia pro Vita sua to preach at his church in the Piazza del Popolo, and, apart from the disparaging remarks about English Protestants, had tried to apply pressure by saying: "When I told the Holy Father that I intended to invite you, he highly approved of my intention, and I think myself that you will derive great benefit from revisiting Rome, and again showing yourself to the Ecclesiastical Authorities there, who are anxious to see you ... I am afraid that you may plead age &c. as an excuse for not taking so long a journey, as some persons have told me you are likely to do, but I feel convinced that you are prepared to make any sacrifice when the greater glory of God, and the Salvation of Souls are concerned, and that you are prepared to forgo your own comfort, when the high interests of the Church are concerned, and you have an opportunity to serve the Holy See." As Newman told another correspondent, not only had the author of this "pompous" and "insolent" letter spread lies about him previously, saying for instance that he was a supporter of Garibaldi, but the invitation was "suggested by [Cardinal] Manning—the Pope had nothing to do with it. When Talbot left for England he said, among other things, 'I think of asking Dr Newman to give a set of lectures in my church', and the Pope, of course, said, 'a very good thought', as he would have said if Mgr Talbot had said, 'I wish to bring Your Holiness some English razors'."

Dear Monsignore Talbot,

I have received your letter, inviting me to preach next Lent in your Church at Rome to "an audience of Protestants more educated than could ever be the case in England."

However, Birmingham people have souls; and I have neither taste nor talent for the sort of work which you cut out for me. And I beg to decline your offer.

I am, yours truly,

John H. Newman

A Gentle Corrective

St Bernard of Clairvaux   12th century

To the Count of Angoulême

Bernard was a master of the short, witty but, one suspects, stinging, rebuke that would echo much more effectively than a long one in its recipient's mind and conscience.

My dear Count,

Do not be surprised at my thinking that the rent you are charging my brethren for the domain of Boisse is too high, for we have not been accustomed to pay anything like that. We have founded many abbeys, but none of them has been liable to such exactions. But because you wish it and because the Lord loves a ready rather than a grudging giver, I will keep the agreement which my brethren have made with you, until God shall inspire you with better dispositions, which I have no doubt he will do. For the rest love, cherish, protect, and support them, because you will be able to appear with greater confidence before the tribunal of Christ if you have the poor to love you and intercede for you.

Yours ever,

Bernard

Christian Love

John Wesley   March 1790

To Dr Pretyman Tomline, bishop of Lincoln

Sir George Pretyman Tomline, tutor and Secretary to the younger Pitt, was Bishop of Lincoln and Dean of St Paul's 1787-1820 and Bishop of Winchester 1820-7. He shared and voiced the typical Establishment view of Methodist enthusiasm as a form of dangerous and possibly treasonable disloyalty to the state church and even the State itself. This is a good example of Wesley's ability succinctly to combine an assertion of factual truth and moral reproof.

My Lord,

I am a dying man, having already one foot in the grave. Humanly speaking, I cannot long creep upon the earth, being now nearer ninety than eighty years of age. But I cannot die in peace before I have discharged this office of Christian love to your Lordship. I write without ceremony, as neither hoping nor fearing anything from your Lordship or from any man living. And I ask, in the name and in the presence of Him to whom both you and I are shortly to give an account, why do you trouble those that are quiet in the land? those that fear God and work righteousness? Does your Lordship know what the Methodists are? that many thousands of them are zealous members of the Church of England, and strongly attached not only to His Majesty but to his present Ministry? Why should your Lordship, setting religion out of the question, throw away such a body of respectable friends? Is it for their religious sentiments? Alas, my lord, do as you would be done to. You are a man of sense; you are a man of learning; nay, I verily believe (what is of infinitely more value), you are a man of piety. Then think, and let think. I pray God to bless you with the choicest of his blessings.

I am, my Lord, your obedient and humble servant,

John Wesley

No Evil for Evil

St Bernard of Clairvaux   1150

To a certain layman

Here the adviser of popes and monarchs administers a carefully modulated rebuke to an odious correspondent.

Dear ...,

I have never met you, but I have heard of you. You have the reputation of being a wise man and you enjoy a respected position in the world. But my dear son Peter, to whom you seem to be well known and related by blood, has asked me to write to you or, I should say, to write back to you. For you have written to him, and I could wish that your letter had been creditable to yourself and profitable for him. This is not the case, for you have had the audacity to try and dissuade a soldier of Christ from the service of his Lord. I tell you, there is one who will see and judge this. Are not your own sins enough for you that you must saddle yourself with the sins of another by doing your best to entice a repentant young man back to his follies and thus, in your hard and unrepentant heart, to lay up wrath for yourself on that day of wrath? As though the devil were not tempting Peter enough without the help of you who are supposed to be a Christian and his friend and leader. You have behaved towards him like another serpent, but he has not yielded to you like another Eve. He was shaken but not overthrown by what you wrote, for he is founded upon a firm rock.

I shall not return evil for evil. On the contrary I shall try to overcome evil with good by praying for you, by desiring better dispositions for you, and by trying to impart them with my letter. First of all, so that you may be in very truth as wise as people say you are, I send you to the Wise Man, saying: "Suffer him to do good who may, and you yourself, when you may, do good." You have the time to do good, but for how long will you have it? How much of life is there left to you, especially now that you are an old man? "For what is life but a vapour which appears for a little while, and afterwards vanishes away?" If you are truly wise then that curse will not come upon you: "Never did I see a fool secure in his possessions but I prophesied disaster, there and then, for his fair prospects." The truly wise man did well to call the falsely wise fools, for the wisdom of this world is foolishness with God. "Ah, if you would but take thought, learn your lesson, and pay heed to your final end." If only you were wise in the things of God, if only you had a true estimation of the things of this world and paid more heed to the depths beneath you, surely then you would dread what is beneath you, crave for the heights above you, and scorn what lies to your hand! My mind, or rather, my soul, suggests much that I might say to you. But until I know from your answer how you have taken what I have already said, I will refrain from adding anything more. I do not wish to become burdensome to one with whom I hope to be on friendly terms in future, and whom I would gladly help to salvation if he would permit me. Although she has done nothing to deserve it, I greet your dear wife in Christ.

Bernard

He Loves You

Corrie ten Boom   June 19th 1945

To the person who betrayed her to the Germans

Corrie ten Boom and her family were reported to the Germans as helpers of Jews, then under persecution unto death merely because of their race and faith. After the war she writes to her betrayer.

Dear Sir,

Today I heard that most probably you are the one who betrayed me. I went though ten months of concentration camp. My father died after nine days of imprisonment. My sister died in prison, too.

The harm you planned was turned into good for me by God. I came nearer to him. A severe punishment is awaiting you. I have prayed for you, that the Lord may accept you if you will repent. Think that the Lord Jesus on the cross also took your sins upon himself. If you accept this and want to be his child, you are saved for eternity.

I have forgiven you everything. God will also forgive you everything, if you ask him. He loves you and he himself sent his son to earth to reconcile your sins, which meant to suffer the punishment for you and me. You, on your part, have to give an answer to this. If he says: "Come unto me, give me your heart," then your answer must be: "Yes, Lord, I come, make me your child." If it is difficult for you to pray, then ask if God will give you his Spirit, who works the faith in your heart.

Never doubt the Lord Jesus' love. He is standing with his arms spread out to receive you.

I hope that the path which you will now take may work for your eternal salvation.

Corrie ten Boom

CHAPTER 4

Comfort and Encouragement

The Ocean Thrown Up

St John Chrysostom   June 404

To deaconess Olympias

In 404 the Empress Eudoxia banished the over-critical Chrysostom for the second time—to the Caucasus. He wrote several times to St Olympias, a close personal friend, who was persecuted for remaining loyal to him, and carried out his commissions until his death on the way to a further place of exile. This letter is one of the great recommendations of confidence in spite of overwhelming and unjustified oppression.

Dear Sister Olympias,

Please listen to what I have to say. I am going to try to make you a little less depressed and to get rid of the dark clouds in your mind. Why are you so worried, sad and agitated? Because the storm that has attacked the churches is harsh and menacing, and because it has wrapped everything in unrelieved darkness? Because it is approaching crisis-point? Because it brings dreadful shipwrecks every day, while the whole world collapses about us?

We see the ocean whirling up from its uttermost depths and sailors' bodies floating on it. We see others overcome by the force of the waves, broken decks, torn sails, shattered masts, oars ripped from the oarsmen's grasp, and the helmsmen idle on deck opposite the tillers, with their hands resting on their knees. It is all so hopeless that they can only scream, groan, cry and weep. Neither sky nor sea can be seen. Profound, unmitigated and desolate darkness covers everything. No one can see anyone else. The waves rise up and thunder all about. Everywhere monsters of the deep rear up and threaten travellers. But no mere words can express the unutterable.

No terminology I can think of can adequately convey the terrors of these times.

Though I am well aware of all these miseries, I never cease to hope. I always remember the universal Pilot. He does not rely on steersmanship to suffer the storm and come through it. He merely nods to calm the roaring oceans, and if he takes his time in doing so, well that is this Pilot's way. He does not stop dangers straightaway, as soon as they start to menace us, but banishes them only when they get close to their most ghastly point, and almost everyone has abandoned hope. Only then does he show us marvels and miracles. Only then does he reveal the power which he alone possesses, and teach the suffering how to be patient.

Do not be discouraged when this happens. You must fear only one thing that comes to try you, and that is sin. I have told you this many times. Everything else is of of no account at all: plots, quarrels, betrayals, lies, abuses, accusations, confiscations, exile, sharp swords, the dangers of the ocean or the threat of universal warfare. Nothing lasts. All these things pass away. They may affect our mortal body but cannot injure our wary soul.

When the apostle Paul wished to bring home to us the insignificance of earthly worries and pains, he put it in a nutshell: "The things that are seen are transient" (2 Cor. 4: 18). Why then should you fear transient things that will come and go in never-ending line? The present may be happy or sad, but does not last for ever.

Do not be worried by all these things. Stop clamouring to this person or that. Stop running after shadows, for all human efforts are no more than that. Instead, call out again and again to Jesus whom you adore, and ask him just to turn towards you. Then your sorrows will be banished in the twinkling of an eye.

Yours,

   J. Chrysostom

Dryness and Darkness

Friedrich von Hügel   April 21st 1920

To his niece, Gwendolen Greene

One of the Baron's best descriptions of his practice in his letters of personal and spiritual advice—well exemplified in the following—is his own account of a "very wonderful thing in Fénelon: It is the combination of a rarely seen light (not frivolous), a light

and elastic open temperament with an earnest will and gently concentrated determi-
nation ... By that combination—the earnestness without rigorism—he always strikes
me as belonging, in his measure, to that minority of Christian teachers who have
reached closest to that same combination in our Lord himself."

Dear Gwen-child,

I have four letters of yours—three of them long. But I think they give me chiefly one big subject-matter for consideration—the stress of dryness and darkness, and what to do then. I know—oh, well, well—what that means. And I do not doubt that with your special temperament, such times must be particularly trying. But—mark this well, Child—irreplaceably profitable. If you but gently persevere through them, you will come out at the other end of the gloom, sooner or later, into ever deeper, tenderer day.

Let me give you three images, all of which have helped me on along "many a flinty furlong." At eighteen I learnt from Father Raymond Hecking, that grandly interior-minded Dominican, that I certainly could, with God's grace, give myself to him, and strive to live my life long with him and for him. But that this would mean winning and practising much desolation—that I would be climbing a mountain where, off and on, I might be enveloped in mist for days on end, unable to see a foot before me. Had I noticed how mountaineers climb mountains? how they have a quiet, regular, short step—on the level it looks petty; but then this step they keep up, on and on, as they ascend, whilst the inexperienced townsman hurries along, and soon has to stop, dead beat with the climb. That such an expert mountaineer, when the thick mists come, halts and camps out under some slight cover brought with him, quietly smoking his pipe, and moving on only when the mist has cleared away.

Then in my thirties I utilized another image, learnt in my Jesuit retreats. How I was taking a long journey on board ship, with great storms pretty sure ahead for me; and how I must now select, and fix in my little cabin, some few but entirely appropriate things—a small trunk fixed up at one end, a chair that would keep its position, tumbler and glass that would do ditto: all this, simple, strong, and selected throughout in view of stormy weather. So would my spirituality have to be chosen and cultivated especially in view of "dirty weather".

And, lastly, in my forties, another image helped me—they all three are in pretty frequent use still! I am travelling on a camel across a huge desert. Windless days occur, and then all is well. But hurricanes of wind will come, unforeseen, tremendous. What to do then? It is very simple, but it takes much practice to do well at all. Dismount from the camel, fall prostrate face downwards in the sand, covering your head with your cloak. And lie thus, an hour, three hours, half a day: the sandstorm will go, and you will arise, and continue your journey as if nothing had happened. The old Uncle has had many, many such sandstorms. How immensely useful they are!

You see, whether it be great cloud-mists on the mountain-side, or huge, mountain-high waves on the ocean, or blinding sandstorms in the desert: there is each time one crucial point—to form no conclusions, to take no decisions, to change nothing during such crises, and especially at such times, not to force any particularly religious mood or idea in oneself. To turn gently to other things, to maintain a vague, general attitude of resignation—to be very meek, with oneself and with others: the crisis goes by, thus, with great fruit. What is a religion worth that costs you nothing? What is a sense of God worth which would be at your disposal, capable of being comfortably elicited when and where you please? It is far, far more God who must hold us, than we who must hold him. And we get trained in these darknesses into that sense of our impotence without which the very presence of God becomes a snare.

As to your feeling the facts of life and of religion complicated—that would be, I expect, in any oppressive way, openly during such desolations.... I wanted you, even in times of temptation, to feel the realities you were called to, perhaps straining at times—even apparently mere illusions— but not cramping, not petty. You can thus settle quietly into your little cabin with the huge billows buffeting you, the ship; their size has not been minimized: they are huge: well, God is in the storm as in the calm! But, of course I am deeply glad that sunshine and calm are back again. And certainly these, and those at their utmost, are intended for our eventual life!

U.

The Very Gates of Hell

St Thomas More   October 23rd 1504

To John Colet

The twenty-five-year-old More, who had finally decided not to become a contemplative in the Charterhouse, but to practise law and marry (as he did a month after this letter), is still dependent on the spiritual direction and advice of the humanist Colet. His attitude to the world remains coloured by his longing for a religious life. Even

twenty years later, when a married man, he would withdraw to a separate building
in the grounds of his Chelsea house for devout prayers and exercises. At the time of this
letter, Colet was absent from London (he was vicar of Stepney and a prebendary of
St Paul's Cathedral) and probably staying at Dennington, Suffolk, where he had a
country living.

My dear Colet,

As I was walking in the law-courts [at Westminster Hall] the other day, not myself being very busy, I met your servant. I was delighted to see him both because I have always been fond of him and especially because I thought he would not be here without you. But when I heard from him not only that you had not returned but that you would not do so for some time, my joyful expectation was changed to unutterable dejection. No annoyance that I could suffer is to be compared with the loss of your companionship, which means so much to me. I have come to rely on your prudent advice, to find my recreation in your pleasant company, to be stirred by your powerful sermons, to be edified by your life and example; in short, to be guided by even the slightest indications of your opinions. When I had the advantage of all these helps, I used to feel strengthened; now that I am deprived of them I seem to languish and grow feeble. By following your footsteps I had escaped from the very gates of hell, and now, driven by some secret but invisible force, I am falling back again into the gruesome darkness....

For city life helps no one to be good, but, rather, when a man is straining every nerve to climb the difficult path of virtue, it tempts him with every kind of allurement and drags him down to its own level with its manifold deceits. Wherever you turn, what do you see around you? Pretended friends and the sweet poison of smooth flatterers, fierce hatreds, quarrels, rivalries, and contentions. Look again and you will see butchers, confectioners, fishmongers, carriers, cooks and poultrymen, all occupied in serving sensuality, the world and the world's lord, the devil. Houses block out from us a large measure of the light, and our view is bounded not only by the round horizon but by the lofty roofs.

I really cannot blame you if you are not yet tired of the country where you live among simple people, unversed in the deceits of the towns. Wherever you cast your eyes, the smiling face of the earth greets you, the sweet fresh air invigorates you, the sight of the heavens charms you. You see nothing but the generous gifts of nature and the hallowed traces of innocence. But yet I do not wish you to be so enamoured of these delights as to be unwilling to return to us as soon as possible. But if you are repelled by the unpleasantness of town life, then let me suggest that you should come to your country parish of Stepney. It needs your fatherly care, and you will enjoy there all the advantages of your present abode and be able to come from time to time for a day or two into the city as if to an inn where so much useful work awaits you. For, in the country, where men are for the most part innocent, or certainly not enslaved by gross vices, the services of any physician can be helpful. But in the city, because of the great numbers that congregate there and because of their long-standing habits of vice, no physician can do much good unless he be of the highest skill.

Certainly there come from time to time into the pulpit of St Paul's preachers who promise us health, but although they speak very eloquently, their life is in such sharp contrast to their words that they do more harm than good. For they cannot bring men to believe that though they are themselves obviously in direst need of the physician's help, they are yet fit to be entrusted with the cure of other men's ailments. Thus when men see that their diseases are being prescribed for by physicians who are themselves covered with sores, they immediately become indignant and refuse to accept their remedies. But if, as patient observers of human nature assert, he is the best physician in whom the patient has the greatest confidence, it is beyond all doubt that you are the one who can do most for the cure of all in the city. Their readiness to allow you to treat their wounds, their trust, their obedience, has been proved to you by past experience, and is, in any case, clear now by the eagerness amd expectation with which all are looking forward to your coming.

Come then, my dear Colet, for Stepney's sake which mourns your long absence as deeply as a child his mother's, for the sake of your native city which should be no less dear to you than are your parents; finally, though I cannot hope that this will be a powerful motive for your return, come for my sake who am entirely devoted to you and anxiously await your coming.

Meanwhile I pass my time with Grocin, Linacre and our dead friend Lily. The first, as you know, is the sole director of my life during your absence; the second my master in study; and the third the beloved partner in all my concerns.

Farewell, and, as I know you do, ever love me.

Thomas More

Like a Bird on the Air

## St Robert Southwell												c. 1587

To other Catholics persecuted and in prison

While on the English mission, and living at Arundel House in the Strand, London, Southwell wrote a series of letters to his protector's husband, Philip Howard, who had already spent two of his eleven years in the Tower of London. These formed the basis of the letters in St Robert's major treatise "An Epistle of Comfort," intended to console and encourage English Catholics in penal times. They are notable for their lyrical style, lively metaphor, scriptural basis, and references to the Fathers.

Dear fellow-Catholics,

If we consider the poor, their life is led in such agony, pain and neediness that every one must loathe it. If we behold the rich and mighty, their felicity is folly and their joy is vanity. If we look on potentates who seem the very flower of mankind, we find oftentimes that they are poor in their riches, abject in their honours and discontented in their delights. Their bodies are sacks of dung; their souls, sinks of sin; miserable their birth, wicked their life and damnable their end.

Look, says St Augustine, into the graves, survey all the emperors, dukes, states and worthies of former ages, and see who was master, who man; who rich, or who poor. Discern, if you can, the captive from the king, the strong from the weak, the fair from the deformed. These words import that, if after life there is no more difference of persons than there is in the ashes of velvet and coarse canvas or of divers woods burnt up in one fire, it surely is folly to care for these bodies or to desire their long continuance. For in the end they must be resolved into earth and dust and cannot live here without a multitude of cumbers as we find in almost every other thing. And therefore after having perused all the miseries of our life, we may think it a great benefit of God that whereas there is but one way to come into this world, yet there are very many to go out.

What can there be in life, either durable or very delightsome, when life itself is so frail and fickle a thing? Our life is like the print of a cloud in the air, like a mist dissolved by the sun, like the passing of a shadow, like a flower that soon fades, like a dry leaf carried with every wind, like a vapour that soon vanishes out of sight. St Chrysostom calls it a heavy sleep, fed with false and imaginary dreams; another time he calls it a comedy, or rather, in our days, a tragedy of transitory shows and disguised persons. Sometimes he calls it a bird's nest made of straw and dung that the winter soon dissolved. St Gregory Nazianzen likens it to the child's game of building houses of sand on the shore where every wave washes them away; yes, as Pindar says, it is no more but the dream of a shadow. It passes away like one that rides in post; like a ship in the sea that leaves no print of the passage; like a bird in the air of whose way there remains no remembrance; like an arrow that flies to the mark, whose track the air suddenly closes up. Whatsoever we do, whether we sit, stand, sleep or wake, our ship, says St Basil, always sails towards our last home. Every day we die, and hourly lose some part of our life; even when we grow, we decrease. We have lost our infancy, our childhood, our youth and all, till this present day. What time soever passes, perishes. And this very day death secretly by minutes secretly purloins from us. This St Gregory well expresses, saying, our living is a passing through life, for our life, with her increase, diminishes, and by that always impairs, whereby it seems to profit. Future things, says Innocent, are always beginning, present things always ending, and things past are quite dead and done. For while we live we die, and when we leave living then we leave dying. Better therefore it is to die to life than to live to death, because our mortal life is nothing but a living death, and life continually flies from us and cannot be withheld and death hourly comes upon us and cannot be withstood. No armour resists, no threatening prevails, no entreaty profits against death's assault. If our life be spared despite all other other perils and chances, yet time and age in the end will consume it.

We see the flood that rises in the top of a mountain fall and roll down with a continual noise; it gushes out with a hollow and hoarse sound, then it runs roaring down other craggy and rough cliffs; it is continually crushed and broken with divers encounters till at the foot of the hill it enters into the sea. And so it fares with man's life, he comes into the world with pain, begins his course with pitiful cries and is continually molested with divers vexations; he never ceases running down till in the end he falls into the sea of death. Neither is our last hour the beginning of our death but the conclusion; for then is come what has been long in the coming, and fully finished what was still in the ending. Why therefore should we be willing to lose that which cannot be kept? Better it is, since death is debt and nature's necessary wreck, to follow St Chrysostom's counsel: Let us make voluntarily that which must needs be necessary, and let us offer to God for a present that which of due and debt we are bound to render.

What marvel if, when the wind blows, the leaf falls; if, when the day appears, the night ends? Our life, says the same saint, was a shadow and it passed; it was a smoke and it vanished; it was a bubble, and it was dissolved; it was a spider's web and it was shaken asunder. No wise man laments that he lived not a year sooner than he was born, so why should

he lament that within a year or less he shall live no longer? For he loses nothing that he then had, and he shall be to the world but as he then was.
Farewell,
Robert Southwell

Keep in the Seed

George Fox   1670

To Friends

Having already suffered much persecution for their beliefs and practice of religion, the Friends were severely threatened by the Conventicle Act, which came into force on May 10th 1670 and forbade meetings of more than four people, ostensibly to prevent seditious assemblies under the guise of religion. His wife having just been freed from prison after an appeal to the King, Fox left the country for the streets of London, where ministers and Friends intended to hold their meetings as usual: "... drums beat for every household to send forth a soldier into the trained bands to be in readiness, the Act being then come into force. As I had endeavoured to soften the magistrates, and to take off the sharpness of their edge in the execution of the Act, so it was upon me to write a few lines to Friends to strengthen and encourage them to stand fast in their testimony, and bear, with Christian patience and content, the suffering that was coming upon them." Fox himself was soon arrested but set at liberty after a discussion with the magistrate in which they exchanged scriptural citations.

My dear Friends,

Keep in the faith of God above all outward things, and in his power, that hath given you dominion over all. The same power of God is still with you to deliver you as formerly; for God and his power is the same; his seed is over all, and before all; and will be, when that which makes to suffer is gone. And so be of good faith in that which changeth not; for whatsoever any do against the truth, it will come upon themselves, and fall as a millstone on their heads. If the Lord suffer you to be tried, let all be given up; and look at the Lord and his power, which is over the whole world, and will remain when the world is gone. In the Lord's power and truth rejoice over that which makes to suffer, in the Seed, which was before it was; for the life, truth and power of God is over all. All keep in that; and if ye suffer in that, it is to the Lord.

Friends, the Lord hath blessed you in outward things; and now the Lord may try you, whether your minds be in the outward things, or with the

Lord that gave you them. Therefore keep in the Seed, by which all outward things were made, and which is over them all. What! Shall not I pray, and speak to God, with my face towards heavenly Jerusalem, according to my wonted time? Let not anyone's Delilah shave his head, lest he lose his strength; neither rest in its lap, lest the Philistines be upon you. For your rest is in Christ Jesus; therefore rest not in anything else.

George Fox

Take Care!

St Francis de Sales   1620

To a lady

St Francis was a masterly spiritual director, always able to find appropriate examples to make his advice consoling yet appropriate to the individual's state of mind.

Dear Madam,

I am not at all surprised to learn that you feel rather dull-witted and depressed. After all, you're pregnant! When your body is weighed down like that, you can't expect to be bright, cheery and ready for anything. Still, your soul can please God just as much as if you were the most cheerful person in all the world. In fact, you can please him all the more because it's that much more of a struggle. When we are depressed, the only way to rise above that state of mind and to turn it to a good end is to face up to it exactly as it is. If you are patient with yourself, and accept depression humbly, you can turn your leaden self into a new golden you—a you that is far more pure than you at your brightest beforehand. Make your higher self put up with your lower self. Offer the tiny creature inside you to the greater glory of God. But take care of your health. Don't put yourself out, or force yourself to pray. If kneeling makes you tired, then sit down. If you can't pray for half an hour, pray for a quarter. If not for a quarter, then for seven and a half minutes; and so on. Remember, we have an artist in the house here who paints pictures solely for God's sake. But when he is working he has to concentrate so hard that he cannot pray and paint at one and the same time. He feels worried about that, of course, yet he works as hard as ever for the sake of the honour done to God, and the effect his pictures have on other people. Think of your baby as the work of art that you are producing as a likeness of God.

Francis de Sales

Comforted Completely

Corrie ten Boom   May 8th 1944

To her family and others

Corrie ten Boom and her family helped to shelter Jews from persecution and eventual extermination during the German occupation of the Netherlands. Suffering months of solitary confinement in Scheveningen prison in the Netherlands, before transportation to a concentration camp, unsure whether she will survive or die like her father, she writes to describe her feelings and strengthen her family's faith.

Dear Nollie and all other loved ones,

On May 3rd I received your letter. First I was sad, but now I am comforted completely. Father can now sing:

> I cannot do without you,
> You Jesus, my Lord,
> Thanks, praise, adoration,
> Never will I be without you again.

How beautiful his voice will sound. I am so happy for him. When I think of those nine days I quickly switch to the present and concentrate on how happy he is now for he sees the answer to everything. On the wall of my cell is written in English, "Not lost, but gone before." He will leave a great emptiness in my life. For the love and help I gave him, the Lord will surely provide many others. But what I received from him can never be replaced. What a privilege though that we could for so long so intensely enjoy him. For a few days I was upset. Now that has passed. During the last few days there was such a tension within me. I did not dare to think things through and when you are so alone it is difficult to get away from your thoughts. Now that is gone and I am thinking much about the future. I make plans and am experiencing much peace. How good the Saviour is to me! He not only bears my burdens. He carries me, too...!

What a pleasure all the notes are. Every day I re-read the letter at least once. I so hope you will succeed in obtaining the business interview. There is so much to be discussed. How wonderful, Casper, that you made a profession of faith. I know that you did it with all your heart. May God bless this step. Don't be concerned any more about my being alone, Nollie. The Saviour is everything to me. Everything I lack he supplies....

Yes, Nollie, how difficult your path is, but the Saviour will give you a strong heart to go on at this time. I pray much for you. Please pray much for me. Bye, dear children and friends. God bless you all....

Pray for guidance for me when I have to appear before the judge. I am not afraid. The Saviour never leaves me alone and he will not here either.

Much love,

        Corrie

Smuggled out:

There is now no longer such a strong expectation in looking towards England—only when I look at the Saviour, does it become peaceful. Often I can give thanks that I may experience this but mostly there is a strong wish that it may be over. Now I really know what it means to cast my anxieties on the Lord when I think of Father. Is there still a future for the Beje here on earth or are we now going straight towards the return of Christ? Or are we going to die? How wonderful to know that the future is secure, to know that Heaven is awaiting us. Sometimes I have self-pity, especially at night, when my arm hurts very badly. This has to do with the pleurisy, but then I think of how much Jesus suffered for me and then I feel ashamed.

CHAPTER 5

Enthusiasm, Zeal and Scruples

The Language of Perfection

St Francis de Sales

April 26th 1617

To a lady

St Francis was a tender-hearted but witty correspondent. Here he finds an admirable metaphor with which to make his point about right attitudes.

My dear Daughter ...

Tell yourself, dear Barbe-Marie who loves me very much and whom I love even more, to talk as freely as you wish about God whenever you think it apposite, and happily ignore what those listening to you may think or feel about you. In short, I have already plainly declared your duty: never do or say anything to seek praise, never leave anything undone or unsaid out of fear of being praised. It is not hypocritical if your deeds fall short of your words. Well, well! Where should we be if that were the case? I would have to keep silence to avoid being hypocritical, since it would mean that if I spoke of perfection I would believe I was perfect. Of course not, dear child. I no more believe I am perfect because I speak of perfection than I would think I was Italian because I spoke Italian.... Nevertheless, I do think that I know something about the language of perfection, for I have learned it by talking to people who spoke it.

Tell yourself to powder your hair, Barbe-Marie, because you do it with the right intention. Going into detail over that kind of thing isn't worth the trouble. Do not worry about getting your mind caught in such cobwebs. The hair of my daughter's mind is much finer than the hair of her head, and that is why she finds it troublesome. She mustn't split hairs as she does, or waste time on objections which our Lord just isn't interested

93

in. So tell her to go ahead quite confidently, and to steer a middle course according to the fine virtues of simplicity and humility, instead of going to extremes by preferring subtle distinctions and arguments. You may boldly powder her hair. Remember: pheasants, those gorgeous birds, give their feathers a thorough dust-bath in order to avoid lice....

Glory and honour to God for ever,

Francis de Sales

No Grief Beyond Measure

St John Chrystostom   404

To deaconess Olympias

Chrysostom, sentenced to exile by the unjust Empress Eudoxia, writes to condemn excess and to encourage his friend and supporter, St Olympias, who was persecuted for her loyalty, carried out his commissions, survived his death and withdrew into near self-exile until her death in 408.

Dear Sister Olympia,

Excessive grief about faults for which we are responsible is neither safe nor necessary. It is usually injurious or even destructive. Then it is even worse and quite pointless to wear yourself out worrying about others' faults. Above all, it means supping with the devil and damages the soul.

Here is a well-tried example. A man from Corinth had taken the holy waters, was purified through baptism, had shared in the sacred rites of the holy table, and, in short, participated in all our mysteries. Many people say that he was a teacher. After this sacred initiation and all the great benefits to which he had been admitted, and in spite of his important position in the Church, he became a serious sinner. He lusted after his father's wife and did not stop there but carried the thought into action. This shocking act went beyond fornication and adultery, and passed to an even worse stage.

Blessed Paul heard of this and since he had no appropriate and sufficiently serious words for this particular sin, he indicated the vileness of the crime in another way. "It is actually reported," he says, "that there is sexual immorality among you, and immorality of a kind that even pagans condemn." Trying to stress the extreme nature of the crime, he does not say "of a kind that is not committed," but "that even pagans condemn."

So he hands him over to the devil, separates him from the whole Church, and will let no one share with him at the common table. It is not right, he says, even to eat with a person like that, and he immediately demands that the sinner should suffer the severest punishment: he makes use of the devil as the means of vengeance to punish the man's flesh.

Yet he who cuts the sinner off from the Church, and will not allow anyone to eat at the same table, who demands that everyone should mourn on his account, he who drives him away from all directions as if he were a leper, who has shut him out from every house, handed him over to Satan, and demanded so extreme a punishment for him, this very same Paul, when he finds the man contrite and repentant for the sins he has committed, and that his actions show that he is truly repentant and wishes to lead a new life, wholly changes his approach. He now orders the same people whom he had instructed as I have described, to act in the very opposite way. The man who had said: "Cut him off, turn him away, mourn over him, and let the devil have him," now says—what? "Now is the time to offer him forgiveness and comfort, for it is possible for a man in his position to be completely overwhelmed by remorse. I ask you to show him plainly now that you love him. We don't want Satan to win any victory here, and well we know his methods!"

Surely you can see that the tendency to be far too upset over something like that comes from Satan and is the work of his cunning? By pushing us to excess, he turns a healing medicine into a vile poison, and whenever he or she behaves excessively, a man or woman hands himself or herself to the devil. That is why Paul says: "We don't want Satan to win any victory here...." His words really mean: "This sheep was afflicted with a terrible disease. He was separated from the flock and cut off from the Church. But he has corrected his evil and has become the wholesome sheep he was beforehand. That is the power of repentance. Let us welcome him wholeheartedly. Let us receive him with open arms. Let us embrace him and hug him to our breasts. Let us make him one of our company. If we do not do so, we give the devil the advantage. When we are careless, Satan seizes the advantage and takes not what belongs to him but the soul who belonged to us. He drenches him in excessive mourning and makes him his own property for the future". And so St Paul goes on to say: "... and well we know his methods". We know very well how often, when plans to help someone go wrong, the devil uses them to trip up the unwary.

Indeed, Paul will not allow someone who has fallen into even so shocking a sin to mourn too much, but instead encourages him, urges him on, and does everything he can to take the burden of his depression from his shoulders. He points out that excess is the work of Satan, and to Satan's advantage; in fact excess is a proof of his wickedness and the work of his evil intentions. Surely, then, it the utmost folly and insanity where other people's sins and the final accounting are at issue to mourn and afflict the soul to the extent of enveloping oneself in a cloud of depression which ends in turmoil, confusion, and unbearable mental anguish.

J. Chrysostom

A Difficult Request

St Gregory the Great   593

To Augusta's lady-in-waiting

Pope St Gregory finds time to treat an impossible demand with polite but firm advice.

Dear Lady Gregoria,

At last the letter I have waited for so long has arrived. You scrupulously and precisely describe your many sins. But Almighty God is merciful. Knowing his profound love for you, I am sure that the voice of Truth is judging you with the same judgment which he gave in favour of a certain holy woman: "Her sins, many as they are, shall be forgiven her, because she has loved much" (Luke 7:47). What is the most trustworthy proof of her forgiveness? That she followed our Lord, sat at his feet, and listened to what he said (Luke 10:39)....

But when your Ladyship threatens to give me no peace until I assure you that I have had a revelation that your sins are forgiven you, you ask something difficult and pointless. It is difficult because I am unworthy of revelations and pointless because it is not intended that you should be unconcerned about your sins, unless on the very last day of your life, when you no longer have enough strength to mourn them. Until then your faults should always arouse apprehension, and every day in fear and trembling you should try to wash them away with your tears. Paul the apostle, as we know, was taken up to the third heaven and conducted into Paradise, where he heard secret words which no man may pronounce. Even then he was kept in suspense. "I am my body's sternest master," he said, "for fear that when I have preached to others I should myself be disqualified" (1 Cor. 9:27). He had been taken up even into heaven, yet he was still worried, and we must ask if any person on earth has any right to feel free from fear. Weigh my words carefully, most beloved daughter.

Security is very often the mother of negligence. You are not intended to feel safe in this world. That would only make you careless. "Blessed is the man that is always fearful" (Prov. 28:14), says the Bible; and again: "Serve the Lord in fear, and rejoice unto him in reverence" (Ps. 2:11). Your soul is necessarily uncertain during this fleeting life, if afterwards it is to enjoy the happiness of everlasting security. May Almighty God fill your soul with the grace of his Holy Spirit, and when the fears you have poured out in prayer are wiped away, may he bring you to eternal happiness.

Farewell,

Gregory

Wretched Scruples

François Fénelon   June 23rd 1702

To Countess Elizabeth de Grammont

Fénelon reproaches his long-term spiritual dependant for excessive scruples, and subtly advises her to follow the main lines of the "new spirituality" of self-renunciation, inimical to what Thomas Merton in this context called the "self-centred, self-complacent, tyrannically demanding superego," over-emphasis on which "produces the frightful mask of false, pharisaical devoutness, the imago wrought by self-will."

Dear Madam,

I really feel quite unable to express all my concern for your distress. You accuse yourself of unimportant things, which you, not God, have invented. God is not interested in trivialities. To be sure, he may draw attention to our faults, but kindly, and even his condemnations are consoling. He humbles us tenderly and allows us to discern our misdeeds though his eyes, and so that his peace can relieve the misery of guilt. "The Lord is not in the earthquake." I am sure that you were misled by your liking for conversation and that because you wanted to sound impressive you exercised your natural wit too freely. I do not take seriously what you are certainly exaggerating out of excessive imagination and clever scrupulousness. What, then, are we to make of all this? Are you going to renounce society entirely? Do you want to cut yourself off from friends who need you, and from those whom, in your search for God, you also need? Are you to reject all those medicines which your weak body needs to recover? Do you really intend to lead the life of a hermit, with all the consequences for your health and strength that this would imply? It is said that St

Bernard, when he had just preached a first-class sermon and was about to quit the pulpit in self-satisfaction, was suddenly suffused with guilt because he felt so pleased at doing well. But God enabled him to see that this worrying about vanity was an over-scrupulous conscience tempting him ever so subtly. Therefore, before deciding to continue with his sermon, he told himself: "I did not enter this pulpit because of vanity and, whatever the temptation it offers, it will not make me leave it." Even if you do fall into error at such times, you cannot turn the clock back. And mortal sin does not come into it. These are venial faults which our self-regard often lets us commit and which no one in this life can entirely escape. The things you want to evade are, rather, providential, useful and belong to your vocation. If you shunned them you would do yourself spiritual harm by incurring the guilt of another person's fall. You would harden your heart and the springs of grace would dry up. Moreover, you must surely see that, after these conversations, God punishes you by withdrawing himself and depriving you of the grace of prayer. Your scruples and nothing else cram your mind with all kinds of imagined wrongdoing, make you harden your heart, and virtually dry up the springs of grace within you. Don't heed your miserable scruples. Try to remain peaceful and get used to ignoring anything that takes your attention away from God. Learn to express only that amount of sorrow for your minor faults that God's quiet presence may suggest. Then you will see that your present inability to enjoy the sweetness of prayer is not heaven's punishment for wrongdoing but, on the contrary, the result of your own drying up of the channels of grace because you have returned to your own devices. Before God, I know no condition which is more dangerous or more contrary to perfection than what you are striving for when you try to be perfect. The correct way for souls in a state of grace to behave is characterized by simplicity, peacefulness, sober conduct and avoidance of extremes. But you are excessively scrupulous about trivialities which deserve no attention whatsoever. Nevertheless, you go so far as to do yourself physical harm, turn your inner life into a wilderness, and reject all spiritual and material help, for the sake of things so trivial that they would shame a seven-year-old. Believe what I say in God's name and try to rise above such matters as what you possibly have or possibly have not said in everyday conversation. If you could do just that, you would rejoice in the freedom of God's children. Then you would not be unable to pray but instead find that the very act of praying makes you stronger and takes you much closer to God. Whenever you are afraid that something you have said is not what God wants, just accuse yourself silently and then carry on with what you are doing. Anything more than that means exceeding the bounds of what is required and putting a cloud between yourself and God.

Fénelon

Sleeping on the Ground
John Keble

18—

To a penitent

Like many spiritual advisers before the latter half of the present century, Keble directed many of the souls in his charge largely by correspondence. This conflation of two letters to a lady, one more specifically concerned with the observance of Lent, and the other with meditation on diverse occasions, shows him giving sound and specific advice while dealing gently with two constant problems of spiritual direction and therapy: excessive penitential zeal and adulation of the adviser.

Dear child,

What you feel about Lent is, I imagine, what all, or almost all, feel, who set themselves to observe it in earnest; even though they are ever so much guided: *how* to do it, or how they have done it, must be to them as unsatisfactory a question as what to do can be to you. Those who have been, or yet in some sense are, under the dominion of some known and wasting sin, have so far a more definite course; where, by God's mercy, that is not the case, the perplexity you speak of, painful as it is, may well be borne with true thankfulness, that one's case is not far more miserable. That will be one way of improving it. Another, of course, is to make it an occasion fo prayer, e.g., if you were to turn the substance of your last letter to me into an address to Him, pouring out yourself to Him at large, stating to Him all the difficulties and cravings which He knows already, but loves to be told of, as Moses, Job, Jeremiah, David did. The 143rd Psalm, if I mistake not, is just in the key to which your heart will respond. And among uninspired writings there is a book on the list of the Christian Knowledge Society, "The Meditations of James Bonnell, Esq.," in which spiritual troubles are dealt with in a way, perhaps, to soothe and help you. If you cast yourself before Him as well as you can in this spirit, and tell Him all, and beg Him to think for you of all that you know not how to tell Him; He will as surely help and guide you as He has taught you to call Him Father. You will judge better than I whether it would not help you to do all this in writing. I would wish it to be done quite at large, and not to take up any very long time at once, so as either to excite or weary you more than can be helped. I should hope and expect that upon using this, or some such devotional help, you would be guided in the choice of times and forms of prayer, and exercises of self-denial, as may best suit your case. Meanwhile, I would propose one or two obvious things. 1. That you should annex something Lenten—a collect, a verse, or part of a hymn—to each of your stated offices of private devotion. 2. That you should at some time in the day practise meditation, for at least half-an-hour (and here again the pen might be useful), on some Lenten subject: e.g. on Monday on contrition: Tuesday, confession; Thursday, intercession; Friday, our Lord's Passion in some of its details; Saturday, resignation. The Sunday subject might be suggested by the Sunday services. Direct self-examination might, and prayer of course ought, to be always part of this exercise. Modes of self-examination are more difficult to suggest. Sleeping on the ground is rather an extreme measure, and I could not recommend it in your case, as far as I can judge. It would either hurt your health, or you would soon become used to it, and it would make small difference. Two cases appear to me, in which it is desirable—as penance or check to grievous sin, or as inuring people to necessary privation in missionary labours: but these are not here in point. Dress, I believe, I have mentioned before. I suppose that in this respect ladies are not altogether free agents. otherwise one might fancy there might be a good deal of room for self-denial, without ostention or singularity. You mention amusing books and talk; perhaps the quantity of these, incidental to your position, might be lessened by a little arrangement; and it seems to me that it would be probably be a real, and therefore an acceptable, sacrifice. Again, it is a good Lenten exercise to refrain from speaking, when it would tend to blame others, or get credit to oneself, unless it be a matter of duty; and this alone will furnish a good deal of matter for watching and self-examination. Then there is going oneself to pay or prolong unpleasant visits to people of various ranks; to do useful work, writing or study against the grain, and other disagreeable things, which experience will suggest: and some of these which I have mentioned may, perhaps, not inconveniently be appropriated to some one day of the week, or otherwise practised on something of a system.

. . .

My notion is, that in the "Devotional Helps," you have just what you asked of me for meditation. But I will set down what occurs to me, endeavouring to combine the subject of the season in each case with the matters which you specify as troubling you. The subject of next week is the light of God's truth (collect) shining in us before men (epistle), even in trouble (gospel). Think, then, with yourself, when you are dispirited about the matters temporal or spiritual which trouble you, on such places as (1) Isaiah. 1:10,11; (2) when you forget your prayers or the like, on Luke 23:45-6; (3) when you cannot get over dislike to anyone, on Matthew 26:47-50; (4) when it vexes you to be treated as bodily weak or ill, think of John 19:28-30; (5) when it is hard not to be with sick friends, etc., think of John 11:3-6; (6) when your soul refuses comfort, think of David (Ps. 77), and of Jacob (Gen. 48:15-6), and of our Lord (John 29:27-8); (7) When you feel as if you had been hasty towards—, think of her love as an image of God's, and how He loves and turns all to good (Isaiah. 66: 13). Try this for the present, and let me know how it works. I will not now assign you any further penance, but serve God, be cheerful, and do not lean too much on any of us. Beware of "Hero worship."

Your affectionate Friend in Him whom we serve,

J. K.

Meeting in Paradise
St Catherine dei Ricci

January 6th 1561

To a lay person

St Catherine was an ecstatic mystic who received the stigmata, but in this letter to Filippo Salviati, as elsewhere, she uses very practical things to illustrate her straight-forward message about making the right decisions.

Dear Salviati,

I hear that you are sick. I can believe you though I cannot think of a solution. Religious separated from the world and with no business or family ties necessarily lead a more harsh and rigorous life than others. But you are the head of a great house and have all the cares of a family to bear; you must be very careful about your life and health, not in order to enjoy the pleasures of this world, but to support your family as you should, and to give your children a good Christian education. Never forget that we shall have to give an account at the judgment of our indiscretions as well as of our self-indulgence. Now that you are both at Florence, I am sure no one will offer you soup and biscuits at supper, so I am sending you a basket of chestnuts, and order you to eat at least four each night. We must look to life not death as our goal, and seek to do good in order to honour and glorify God in ourselves. I do wish you would not do things that are really beyond you. You will do yourself irreparable harm. For example, you ought not to have left here. You were told this often enough, but all you said was: "I shall go whether it snows or hails." You cannot argue with someone who has made up his mind, and you were determined to go whatever the result, although I was sorry to hear of it, and if it had been possible I should have stopped a single drop falling on your dear head. But you wouldn't do what I advised.... It is now nine o'clock on Tuesday evening. I assume that your day is at an end and that you have gone to bed. I am sure that this weather is really bad for your health, so I beg you to take care of yourself in all simplicity, at least until mid-April. Do it out of love of our Lord, and to gain time to work for God: that should be our real aim.

The wine got here and I was given some of it at collation last night after reading your letter, for my throat had swollen considerably on hearing of your problems. But your news was so harsh that I ignored the wine's sweetness. Yet this morning it tasted sweet. Thank you. I remembered you last night and this morning and offered our Lord your body, soul, heart, memory, intellect and will. They are the six water-pots whose contents I asked him to change into wine. I prayed that as wine purifies and preserves, so your mind may be liberated from everything untoward, and your good will be preserved by good actions. Please do the same for me. I look forward to the day when we see one another not at St Peter's or at Florence or at the Prato but in Paradise when Jesus, his blessed Mother and the whole company of heaven come to fruition.

Yours,
                    Catherine

For Peace and Order's Sake
George Fox   1657

                                                          To Friends

Some of George Fox's new disciples were over-enthusiastic in responding to the inner voice and he hastened to instruct them: "... many mouths were opened in our meetings to declare the goodness of the Lord, and some that were young and tender in the truth would sometimes utter a few words in thanksgiving and praises to God. That no disorder might arise from this in our meetings, I was moved to write an epistle to Friends, by way of advice in that matter."

All my dear Friends in the noble Seed of God, who have known his power, life and presence among you, let it be your joy to hear or see the springs of life break forth in any: through which ye may have all unity in the same, feeling life and power. And above all things, take heed of judging any one openly in your meetings, except they be openly profane or rebellious, such as be out of the truth; that by the power, light and wisdom ye may stand over them, and by it answer the witness of God in the world, that such, whom ye bear your testimony against, are none of you: so that therein the truth may stand clear and single. But such as are tender, if they should be moved to bubble forth a few words, and speak in the Seed and Lamb's power, suffer and bear that; that is, the tender. And if they should go beyond their measure, bear it in the meeting for peace and order's sake, and that the spirits of the world be not moved against you. But when the meeting is done, then if any be moved to speak to them, between you and them, one or two of you that feel it in the life, do it in the love and wisdom that is pure and gentle from above: for love is that which doth edify, bears all things, suffers long, and doth fulfil the law. So in this ye have order and edification, ye have wisdom to preserve you all wise and in patience; which takes away the occasion of stumbling for the weak, and the occasion of the spirits of the world to get up: but in the royal Seed, the heavy stone, ye keep down all that is wrong; and by it answer that of God in all. For ye will hear, see, and feel the power of God preaching, as your faith is all in it (when ye do not hear words), to bind, to chain, to limit, to frustrate; that nothing shall rise nor come forth but what is in the power: for with that ye will hold back, and with that ye will let up, and open every spring, plant and spark; in which will be your joy and refreshment in the power of God....

And Friends, though ye may have been convinced, and have tasted of the power, and felt the light; yet afterwards ye may feel a winter storm, tempest, and hail, frost and cold, and temptation in the wilderness. Be patient and still in the power and in the light that doth convince you, to keep your minds to God; in that be quiet, that ye may come to the summer, that your flight be not in the winter. For if ye sit still in the patience, which overcomes in the power of God, there will be no flying.

George Fox

Prayer and Orange-Flower Water

St Teresa of Avila   March 28th 1578

To Mother María de San José

St Teresa writes from Avila to the Seville community with practical as well as spiritual counsels and a request for a little orange-flower water.

Jesus be with you, my daughter,

I am amused at what you say about the defects of Fray Bartolomé's slow-witted sisters. Even if their dowries were sufficient to pay for the house outright, the situation would be intolerable. On no account take postulants who are not sensible people, for it is against our Constitution to do so, and the harm done is incurable. Thirteen is very young—I am referring to the other one now—for at that age girls are so unsteady. However, you will be able to decide. Believe me, I only want what is best for you.

I do not approve of your nuns writing on subjects to do with prayer; there are many disadvantages in the practice which I should like to mention. You must realize that it is not only a waste of time; it interferes with the soul's freedom of action; and then, too, it may lead the nuns to imagine all kinds of things. If I remember, I will say this to our Father; if I do not, you should speak to him about it yourself. If their experiences are of any substance, they will never forget them; and if they are of a kind that can be forgotten, there is no point in their writing them down. It will be sufficient if they tell our Father what they remember of them when they see him. It seems to me that they are quite safe if they do that, and if there is one thing which can do them harm, it is attributing importance to things they see or hear. If they have scruples about anything, let them talk about it to your Reverence, for, if they believe what you say, I feel sure God will give you light to guide them. The reason I insist so much upon this is that I know what a bad thing it is for them to keep thinking of what they are going to write—the devil can so easily suggest things to them. If anything they say demands really serious consideration, your Reverence can write it down and they need not even know. If I had appeared to attach any importance to the things Sister San Jerónimo told me, she would never have stopped, so I said nothing, though actually I thought some of them genuine. Believe me, the best thing for the nuns to do is to praise the Lord who gives these things, and, as soon as they are over, just let them be: what matters is the profit they bring the soul.

I have been suffering a good deal from my heart lately, as well as from my bad arm. Send me a little orange-flower water, and send it in such a way that whatever it comes in does not get broken—it is only the fear of that that has kept me from asking you for it before. That bottle of angel-water [*flower-scented water for freshening and fumigating clothes and rooms*] was so nice that I had scruples about using it, so I gave it up for use in the church, as my tribute of honour to the festival of the glorious St Joseph.

Today is Friday of the Cross.

Send only a very little orange-flower water, till we see how it comes.

Your Reverence's

Teresa of Jesus

CHAPTER 6

Charity, Mercy and Compassion

By Example and Charity

Charles de Foucauld

July 17th 1901

To a Trappist

Shortly after his ordination in June 1901, Charles de Foucauld summarizes the missionary purpose that has brought him to North Africa.

Dear Friend,

If I trusted to myself I should think my ideas crazy, but I trust to God who said: "If you would serve, follow me," and again and again he said: "Follow me," and "Love your neighbour as yourself, and do to others as you would they should do to you." My idea of practising this brotherly charity is to consecrate my life to helping these brothers of Jesus who lack everything since they lack Jesus.

If I were one of those unhappy Moslems who know neither Jesus nor his Sacred Heart, nor Mary, our Mother, nor the Holy Eucharist, nor any of the things that make our happiness in this life and our hope in the next, and knew my sad state, how grateful I should be if someone would come and save me from it. So what I should wish for myself, that I ought to do for others. "Do to others as you would they should do to you." I must do this for the outcast and abandoned, must go to the lost sheep and offer them my banquet and my divine food, rather than to my brothers and my wealthy neighbours (rich in all the things those unfortunate people are ignorant of), to the blind and the beggars and the lame, who are a thousand times more to be pitied than those who suffer bodily ills. And I see no better way to help them than to bring them Jesus, as Mary brought him to the house of John at the Visitation. Jesus, the best of all good things, the Supreme Sanctifier, Jesus who will always be present with them in the Blessed Sacrament. Jesus offering himself every day at the altar for their conversion, and blessing them every day at Benediction, is the best of all things to bring them. Jesus, our All. And at the same time, though I am silent, I can make known to those ignorant brothers of mine the meaning of our holy religion, and of the Christian spirit, and the Sacred Heart of Jesus, not by preaching, but by example and charity to all....

Amen,
    Charles de Foucauld

The Poor and Destitute

St Bernard of Clairvaux   1146

To his Brothers

A terrible famine raged in 1146. The compassionate Bernard straightforwardly recommends direct action and, if that is not possible, similar advice to others.

My dear Brothers,

You know who it is that said: "Blessed are the merciful for they shall obtain mercy" and "Blessed is the man who takes thought for the poor and the destitute," and again, in the book of holy Job, "Thou shalt visit thy fair lands, and nought shall go amiss." My reason for quoting to you these few texts out of so many of the same nature in the Scriptures is that the poor and destitute are in greater need than usual at this time of famine. And so if you have any mercy at all in your heart, any capacity at all for compassion, now is your opportunity to show it. However wretched and disreputable they may appear, they are still your flesh and blood, and it is only right that they should be made to feel that you do not regard them otherwise than as this; that they should be made to feel this, if not by your gifts then at any rate by your kind thoughts and words. For instance, you should instruct your chaplain to excite and exhort the people, both privately and in public, to relieve their needs.

Yours,
    Bernard

The Way of Charity

George Herbert   Autumn 1630

To Sir Henry Herbert

Herbert had become rector of Bemerton. His widowed sister Margaret had died leaving three daughters who could not inherit their father's estate as it had to pass to male heirs. Her brother Edward had asked George to adopt one niece but he decided to take two or none and hoped that his brother Henry would take the third and youngest. Now, in spite of a very low income, he offers to take her too.

Dear Brother,

That you did not only entertain my proposals, but advance them, was lovingly done, and like a good brother. Yet truly it was none of my meaning, when I wrote, to put one of our nieces into your hand but barely what I wrote I meant, and no more; and am glad that although you offer more, yet you will do, as you wrote, that also. I was desirous to put a good mind into the way of charity, and that was all I intended. For concerning your offer of receiving one, I will tell you what I wrote to our eldest brother, when he urged one upon me, and but one, and that at my choice. I wrote to him that I would have both or neither; and that upon this ground, because they were to come into an unknown country, tender in knowledge, sense, and age, and knew none but one who could be no company to them. Therefore I considered that if one only came, the comfort intended would prove a discomfort. Since that I have seen the fruit of my observation, for they have lived so lovingly, lying, eating, walking, praying, working, still together, that I take a comfort therein; and would not have to part them yet, till I take some opportunity to let them know your love, for which both they shall, and I do, thank you. It is true there is a third sister, whom to receive were the greatest charity of all, for she is youngest, and least looked unto; having none to do it but her schoolmistress, and you know what these mercenary creatures are. Neither hath she any to repair unto at good times, as Christmas &c. which, you know, is the encouragement of learning all the year after, except my Cousin Bett take pity of her, which yet at that distance is some difficulty. If you could think of taking her, as once you did, surely it were a great good deed, and I would have her conveyed to you. But I judge you not: do that which God shall put into your heart, and the Lord bless all your purposes to his glory. Yet, truly, if you take her not, I am thinking to do it, even beyond my strength; especially at this time, being more beggarly now than I have been these many years, as having spent two hundred pounds in building; which to me that have nothing yet, is very much. But though I both consider this, and your observation, also, of the unthankfulness of kindred bred up (which generally is very true), yet I care not; I forget all things, so I may do them good who want it. So I do my part to them, let them think of me what they will or can. I have another judge, to whom I stand or fall. If I should regard such things, it were in another's power to defeat my charity, and evil should be stronger than good: but difficulties are so far from cooling Christians, that they whet them. Truly it grieves me to think of the child, how destitute she is, and that in this necessary time of education. For the time of breeding is the time of doing children good; and not as many who think they have done fairly, if they leave them a good portion after their decease. But take this rule, and it is an outlandish one, which I commend to you as being now a father, "the best-bred child hath the best portion." Well, the good God bless you more and more; and all yours; and make your family a houseful of God's servants.

So prays your ever-loving brother,

G. Herbert

Not Open to Objection

Gerard Manley Hopkins   January 29th 1879

To Robert Bridges

Hopkins was aware that Bridges had a strong dislike of dogmatic religion, and was dedicated to poetry as if to a religion. In one of the few attempts to "convert" Bridges recorded in the extant correspondence Hopkins does not engage in apologetics but concentrates on suggesting a means by which his friend may obtain grace: the giving of alms until it begins to hurt. Bridges rejected this intrusiveness, but he was more distressed by Hopkins' adverse criticism of his own work.

Dearest Bridges,

Morals and scansion not being in one keeping, we will treat them in separate letters and this one shall be given to the first named subject....

Can you suppose I should send Pater a discipline wrapped up in a sonnet "with my best love"? Would it not be mad? And it is much the same to burst upon you with an exhortation to mortification (under the name of "sensible inconvenience")—which mortification too would be in your case aimless. So that I should have the two marks of the foolish counsellor—to advise what is bad to follow and what will not be followed.

...I spoke then of alms—alms whether in money or in medical or other aid, such as you from the cases you come across at the hospital might know to be called for. And I said "sensible inconvenience"; that is, for instance, you might know of someone needing and deserving an alms to give which would require you in prudence to buy no books till next quarter day or to make some equivalent sacrifice of time. These are sensible inconveniences. And to submit to them you cannot, nevertheless, call the reverse of sensible....

I added something about it needing the experience to know what it feels like to have put oneself out for charity's sake (one or more might say for truth's sake, for honour's sake, for chastity's sake, for any virtue's sake). I meant: everybody knows, or if not can guess, how it feels to be short of money, but everybody may not know, and if not cannot well guess, how it feels to be short of money for charity's sake, etc as above.

All the above appears to me to be put plainly. It reads to me in the blustering bread-and-cheese style.... My thoughts were these—Bridges is all wrong, and it will do no good to reason with him nor even to ask him to pray. Yet there is one thing remains—if he can be got to give alms, of which the Scripture says (I was talking to myself, not you) that they resist sins and that they redeem sins and that they will not let the soul go out into darkness, to give which Daniel advised Nebuchadnezzar and Christ the Pharisees, the one a heathen, the other antichristians, and the whole scripture in short so much recommends; of which moreover I have heard so-and-so, whose judgment I would take against any man's on such a point, say that the promise is absolute and that there is for everyone a fixed sum at which he will ensure his salvation, though for those who have sinned greatly it may be a very high sum and very distressing to them to give—or keep giving: and not to have the faith is worse than to have sinned deeply, for it is like not being even in the running. Yet I will advise something and it must improve matters and will lead to good. So with hesitation and fear I wrote. And now I hope you see clearly, and when you reply will make your objections, if any, to the practice of almsgiving, not to the use of hairshirts. And I take leave to repeat and you cannot but see, that it is a noble thing and not a miserable something or other to give alms and help the needy and stint ourselves for the sake of the unhappy and deserving. Which I hope will take the bad taste away. And at any rate it is good of you only to misunderstand and be vexed and not bridle and drop correspondence....

Believe me, your affectionate friend

Gerard M. Hopkins SJ

Melancholy in Oxford

John Keble   18—

To a friend

Keble was a noted spiritual director. Here he advises a friend how to counter depression by active kindness to others.

My dear Friend,

I am bound to thank you over and over again for your last letter; it was and is a real comfort to me: for I am tolerably sure you are in the right way; only don't dwell too much upon whatever may have been wrong; to some minds it may be necessary, but not to those who are in danger of becoming indolent by too much thinking about themselves: and when you find yourself, as I daresay you sometimes do, overpowered as it were by melancholy, the best way is to go out and do something kind to somebody or other. Objects either rich or poor will generally present themselves in the hour of need to those who look for them in earnest, although Oxford is not perhaps the most convenient place to find them in. However there they surely are if you will take the trouble of looking for them, and perhaps that very trouble is in some sort an advantage in doing away a moody fit.

Writing, too, I have known in many cases, a very great relief, but I almost doubt the expediency of preserving journals, at least of looking much back upon them; if one could summon resolution to do so, I fancy the best way would be to write on till one was a little unburdened, and then put one's confession in the fire. But in all these things, of course no one can judge for his neighbour, And whatever you do, don't put your confessions to *me* in the fire; for it does my heart good to resolve them: it makes me hope that I am sometimes useful, which is a sensation I don't very often experience.

Yours ever,

John Keble

Just and Merciful

Elizabeth Fry   1842

To her eldest son, on his becoming a magistrate

Even in her more personal, family letters, Elizabeth Fry's social conscience was to the fore. Here she is the affectionate mother as a good teacher, imparting information and a moral as well as factual framework for individually chosen judgment and action, based on her own experience and knowledge, which she knows are rare in the governing and executive class, and valuable to one who has been raised not only to cherish the precepts of religion and law but to inform his or her moral awareness by searching out the facts of the case. At the same time, although her approach seems to betray what would now be an extraordinary, even outrageous, determination to control the behaviour of her adult son, a professional man, she never talks down to him, for the pedagogical conventions of the time encouraged correspondence much more instructional than this.

My dearest John,

Ever since I heard of the prospect of thy being a magistrate, I have had it on my mind to write to thee; but alas! such is the press of my engagements, that in my tender state I cannot do what I would. I now, however, take up my pen to tell thee a little of my mind. I think the office of magistrate a very weighty one, and often, I fear, too lightly entered, and its very important and serious duties too carelessly attended to; and this I attribute to a want of a due feeling of the real difficulty of performing any duty; particularly one where much true wisdom is required in doing justice between man and man, unless governed and directed by that wisdom that cometh from above, which is pure, then peaceable, gentle, easy to be entreated, full of mercy and good fruits, without partiality and without hypocrisy. I believe it is thy desire to be governed by this wisdom, and to do justice, and love mercy; but remember this requires a very watchful and subjected spirit, and those who have to sit in judgement on others must often sit in judgement on themselves: this fits the mind for sympathizing with the wanderers, and adopting every right measure for their reformation and improvement. I think it is of the utmost importance to enter the duties attached to a magistrate in a very prayerful spirit, seeking the help and direction of the Spirit of God, and that the understanding may be enlightened to comprehend his will. I am perfectly sensible that a justice of the peace must keep to the laws of his country in his decisions, and, further, that he should be well acquainted with these laws; but I also know much rests with him, as to leaning on the side of mercy, and not of severity; and I know from my experience with so many magistrates, how much they do in the prisons, etc., etc., to instigate or increase suffering; and also how much they may do for the improvement, and real advantage of criminals. Much is in their power; they may do much harm or much good; too many are influenced by selfishness, party spirit, or partiality, both in individual cases and where public good is concerned; but the simple, upright, faithful, just and merciful magistrates, are too rare, and they are much wanted. Mayst thou, my dearest John, be of this number; but remember it can only be by grace, and being thyself directed and governed by the Holy Spirit of God.

I advise thy reading Judge Hale's life—I know a judge and a justice are different things; but the same wise, truly impartial spirit, should govern both. I wish to remind thee, that in petty offences, much is left to the magistrate's own judgement, and the utmost care is needful that crime is not increased by punishment, and the offenders become hardened, instead of being brought to penitence. I fear for young people. Our prisons in Essex generally only harden; therefore try any other means with boys or girls: get them to Refuges, or try to have such measures adopted as may lead them to repentance and amendment of their ways. My very dear love to thy wife, and all thy children; and with deep and earnest desires that through the grace of God thou mayst perform all thy duties, domestic and public, to His glory, thy own peace, and the good of mankind.

I am,

Thy very affectionate mother,

Elizabeth Fry

I forgot to say that a late Act of Parliament gives very great liberty in not sending young offenders to prison, but much rests with the judge or magistrate, as to what is to be done with them; this Act was I think about two years ago. Many of the late Acts of Parliament respecting persons need much studying.

Overweening Self-Assurance

St Bernard of Clairvaux   12th century

To the monk Alard

This is a superb example of Bernard's "paternal" letters, in which he quotes scripture and the Rule of St Benedict but makes his point about right conduct towards an unsettled novice mainly by examining the recipient's own character.

My dear Son Alard,

Brother Adamarus complains that you are behaving very disagreeably towards him: that not only was he expelled from the house at your instigation but also that, owing to your obstruction, he cannot be received back. I might have believed that you were acting from a good zeal, but when I call to mind that obstinacy of yours with which, as you know, you so often in friendly confidence reproach yourself, I begin to fear that your zeal may not be very well informed. For, to quote the words of the Rule, it is exceedingly presumptuous for anyone to strike or excommunicate, let alone expel, any of the brethren, especially during the absence of the abbot and without his knowledge. It would be more in keeping with your humility to behave towards others as you would wish them to behave towards yourself. Indeed it ought to be more conducive towards your perfection to act like the Apostle when he says: "With the weak I have behaved myself like one who is weak, to win the weak"; and again: "If a man is found guilty of some fault, you, who are spiritually minded, ought to show a spirit of gentleness in correcting him." You tell me it was the prior who turned him out. I know this; but it was you who persuaded him and did everything you could to induce him to do so. And now, so I hear, when the prior himself, moved by pity, wishes to recall him, you persist in your obduracy and will not permit him to correct the action he ill-advisedly allowed himself to be forced into taking. Whence, I ask you, such overweening self-assurance on your part that when everyone else would have pity on the man and the abbot himself is willing, you alone stand out implacably? Have you ever read those words: "The merciless shall be judged mercilessly"? Or have you forgotten that "award shall be made to you as you have made award"? Or do you scorn the reward of mercy that is promised to the merciful?

But, you tell me, I do not know what good reasons there were for his expulsion. I'm not interested, and do not greatly care whether there were good reasons or not. What I complain about, what I protest against, what astonishes me, is that the man by his humble satisfaction, by his urgent prayers, by his patient waiting, by his promises of amendment, has not yet deserved to receive from you that "assurance of good will" the Apostle advises and, in the words of our Master, to be tried again in all patience. Certainly, if he were unjustly expelled, it would be just to receive him back so that he does not turn away form the just and merciful God. I ask you, dearest son, to grant at any rate in answer to my prayers, which he has sought for so long, what he has been unable to obtain from you by his own.

With paternal affection,

Brother Bernard

In London They Practise Nobility

St Frances Xavier Cabrini   November 8th 1898

To her nuns, on leaving Liverpool

Mother Cabrini, a tireless founder of convents, schools and orphanages for the poor and unfortunate, especially Italian immigrants to North America, where Pope Leo XIII sent her in 1889, had a gift for conveying her impressions of a place, an occasion or even—as here—a nation, in a fresh and original way.

Dear Sisters,

I now leave Europe for the American missions, for the seventh time. A mysterious inspiration of the spirit persuaded me to visit this country England, once an island of saints, which unfortunately lost its faith because of its king's pride and passion. My dear daughters, you must pray constantly for the conversion of England. It is heartbreaking that this country is without the true faith. England has every quality that could make it worthy to be in Christ's fold. Its only fault is that it has merely half the faith, for it is no longer joined to the head who forms a perfect union of the Church with Christ.

On October 27th I left Paris for America by way of England. Although there was no time for me to do any work in England, I somehow wanted at least to visit this country where I wished so very much to do some good. My companion and I went out to see London after breakfast. The first thing I had to do was buy a new trunk to replace the one I had left at Victoria.

This first experience of shopping told us something about the incredible prices in London. We had to enter a small station to get from where the Sisters' house was to the business part of the city. We bought our tickets and then, with a number of other people, we stood in something rather like a room, waiting for the journey to start. Suddenly we started to go down into the earth. Then we stopped. People began to run as if for their lives— without a word. In London everyone goes on his or her way, so it seems, without saying anything. So we followed them and got into the actual train. Like lightning we were transported to the city's centre. We had gone the whole way underground. Then we went up into the daylight.

When we asked people the way, they answered us kindly, and even offered to carry our bag and umbrella. We asked one man the way and he pointed in the direction we should take, but apologized for not being able to go with us, for he had urgent business to attend to. We went into a shop about six times the size of Bocconi's in Milan to buy something we wanted:

they were extremely kind and civil to us. They offered us chairs and showed us whatever we wished to see. In other countries they talk about nobility and courtesy, but in London they practise them. In one shop where we could not buy a trunk, the manager made one of his clerks go with us, and told him how to help us find what we required. I could quote hundreds of similar examples. That is how they treat Sisters in England. God, who looks on what is done to his servants as done to him, will bless this nation.

On August 2nd we left London for Manchester, where some friends were waiting for us. We reached Victoria at nine in the morning and gave orders about our luggage. The porters were going to weigh it to find out how much it would cost to take with us, but the clerk told them to take it as it was to the train. "The Sisters," he said, "can go as they are!" he gave me a chit so that I could claim the luggage at the other end. This kindness was overwhelming. I silently asked God to bless this country England, which I should like to call "the Land of Angels."

Yours ever,
Mother Cabrini

Murder and Sacrilege

St Bernard of Clairvaux   12th century

To Archbishop Henry of Mainz

Bernard was very much ahead of his and our own times in forthright condemnation of the persecution of the Jews and of what we now know as anti-Semitism. In 1146, during the Crusades, the fanatical monk Raoul incited not only the rabble but people of different ranks to attack the Jews as a preliminary to an even more earnest crusade against the Mohammedans. Bernard does not shilly-shally in his utter condemnation of Raoul and his crude unchristian enthusiasm. His attitude to anti-Semitism on this and other occasions was admired for centuries by German Jews, who found few such models among the higher ecclesiastics of the mid-twentieth century.

My Lord Archbishop,

I received your kind letter with due respect, but my answer must be brief because of the press of business. By revealing to me your troubles you have given me a sure sign and pledge of your affection and, what is more, a mark of your humility. Who am I, or what is my father's house, that I should have referred to me a case of contempt for an archbishop and of damage to his metropolitan see? "I am no better than a child that has no skill to find its way back and forth." Yet ignorant though I be, I am not unmindful of those words of the Most High: "It must needs be that scandals come, but nevertheless woe to that man through whom the scandal cometh." The fellow you mention in your letter has received no authority from men or through men, nor has he been sent by God. If he makes himself out to be a monk or hermit, and on that score claims liberty to preach and the duty of doing so, he can and should know that the duty of a monk is not to preach but to pray. He ought to be a man for whom towns are a prison and the wilderness a paradise, but instead of that he finds towns a paradise and the wilderness a prison....

I find three things most reprehensible in him: unauthorized preaching, contempt for ecclesiastical authority, and incitation to murder. A new power forsooth! Does he consider himself greater than our father Abraham who laid down his sword at the bidding of him by whose command he took it up? Does he consider himself greater than the Prince of the Apostles who asked the Lord: "Shall we strike with our swords"? He is a fellow full of the wisdom of Egypt which is, as we know, foolishness in the sight of God. He is a fellow who answers Peter's question differently to the Lord who said: "Put back your sword into its place; all those who take up the sword shall perish by the sword." Is it not a far better triumph for the Church to convince and convert the Jews than to put them all to the sword? Has that prayer which the Church offers for the Jews, from the rising up of the sun to the going down thereof, that the veil may be taken from their hearts so that they may be led from the darkness of error into the light of truth, been instituted in vain? If she did not hope that they would believe and be converted, it would seem useless and vain for her to pray for them. But with the eye of mercy she considers how the Lord regards with favour him who renders good for evil and love for hatred. Otherwise where does that saying come in, "Not for their destruction I pray," and "When the fullness of the Gentiles shall have come in, then all Israel will be saved," and "The Lord is rebuilding Jerusalem, calling the banished sons of Israel home"? Who is this man that he should make out the Prophet to be a liar and render void the treasures of Christ's love and pity? This doctrine is not his own but his father's. But I believe it is good enough for him, since he is like his father who was, we know, "from the first a murderer, a liar, and the father of lies." What horrid learning, what hellish wisdom is his! A learning and wisdom contrary to the prophets, hostile to the apostles, and subversive of piety and grace. It is a foul heresy, a sacrilegious prostitution "pregnant with malice, that has conceived only spite, and given birth only to shame"! I should like to say more, but I must forbear. To sum up briefly what I feel about this fellow: He is a man with a great opinion of himself and full of arrogance. He shows by his works and teaching that he would like to make a great name for himself among the great of the earth, but that he has not the wherewithal to achieve this.

Bernard, Abbot of Clairvaux

Excess of Mercy
Simone Weil

early 1942

To Gustave Thibon

It has been said of Simone Weil that she stretched "out with all her soul towards a pure and absolute goodness of which nothing here below provides her with a proof but which she feels to be more real than anything existing in and around her. She seeks to establish her faith in this perfect being upon a base which no stroke of fortune, no affliction, no surging wave either of mind or matter can shake. For that it is important before all things to eliminate from the inner life all forms of illusion and compensation ... which too often usurp the name of God and which are really no more than shelters for our weakness or our pride." She saw Jesus as the supreme mediator because he accepted and assumed everything that was utterly wretched and tragic in human life. "Everything without exception which is of value in me comes from somewhere other than myself, not as a gift but as a loan which must be ceaselessly renewed. Everything without exception which is in me is absolutely valueless; and, among the gifts which have come to me from elsewhere, everything which I appropriate becomes valueless immediately I do." The selflessness of the writer of these words is very evident in the following letter (and the offer it contains) to the friend who welcomed her into his home when she was banned from the University and had to flee Paris because of the anti-Semitic laws enacted in France during the German Occupation.

Dear Friend,

... I hope that Destiny will spare the house at Saint Marcel—the house inhabited by three beings who love each other. That is something very precious. Human existence is so fragile a thing and exposed to such dangers that I cannot love without trembling. I have never yet been able to resign myself to the fact that all human beings except myself are not completely preserved from every possibility of harm. That shows a serious falling short in the duty of submission to God's will.

You tell me that in my notebooks you have found, besides things which you yourself had thought, others you had not thought but for which you were waiting; so now they belong to you, and I hope that after having been transmuted within you they will one day come out in one of your works. For it is certainly far better for an idea to be associated with your fortunes than with mine. I have a feeling that my own fortunes will never be good in this world (it is not that I count on their being better elsewhere; I cannot think that will be so). I am not a person with whom it is advisable to link one's fate. Human beings have always more or less sensed this; but, I do not know for what mysterious reason, ideas seem to have less discernment. I wish nothing better for those which have come in my direction than that they should have a good establishment, and I should be very happy for them to find a lodging beneath your pen, whilst changing their form so as to reflect your likeness. That would somewhat diminish my sense of responsibility and the crushing weight of the thought that through my many defects I am incapable of serving the truth as I see it when in an inconceivable excess of mercy it seems to me that it deigns to allow me to behold it. I believe that you will take that as simply as I say it to you. In the operation of writing, the hand which holds the pen, and the body and soul which are attached to it, with all their social environment, are things of infinitesimal importance for those who love the truth. They are infinitely small in the order of nothingness. That at any rate is the measure of importance I attach in this operation not only to my own personality but to yours and to that of any other writer I respect. Only the personality of those whom I more or less despise matters to me in such a domain....

I do not know whether I have already said it to you, but as to my notebooks, you can read whatever passages you like from them to whomever you like, but you must leave none of them in the hands of anyone else.... If you hear nothing of me for three or four years, you can consider that you have complete ownership of them.

I am saying all this to you so that I can go away with a freer mind. I only regret not being able to confide to you all that I still bear undeveloped within me. Luckily, however, what is within me is either valueless or else it exists outside me in a perfect form, in a place of purity where no harm can come to it and whence it will always be able to come down again. That being so, nothing concerning me can have any kind of importance.

I also like to think that after the slight shock of separation you will not feel any sorrow about whatever may be in store for me, and that if you sometimes happen to think of me you will do so as one thinks of a book one read in childhood. I do not want ever to occupy a different place from that in the hearts of those I love, because then I can be sure of never causing them any unhappiness....

Simone

CHAPTER 7

Loyalty, Honour and Justice

Be Loyal

St Joan of Arc

July 7th 1429

To the citizens of Tournai

Joan presents herself to the people of Tournai as the Lord's avenging angel. They were loyal to the Dauphin, though in the midst of a region owing allegiance to the Burgundians. They accepted her invitation and sent their representatives to the coronation. Falstaff was not taken prisoner, as she suggests, but probably another knight with a similar name.

To the loyal French people of the town of Tournai
+ JESUS + MARY

Good loyal French people of the town of Tournai, the Maid informs you that in eight days she scoured the English from all those strong places that they held on the river Loire, by assault or otherwise; and there were many deaths and captives, and she thwarted them in battle. Be sure that the Duke of Suffolk, his brother la Pole, Sir John Talbot, Scales, and Sir John Falstaff and several knights and captains were taken prisoner, and the brother of the Duke of Suffolk and Gloucester died. Remain loyal and steadfast, French people, I beg you, and I ask and require you to be ready to come to the coronation of the good King Charles at Rheims where we shall be shortly, and come before us when you know that we are approaching. I commend you to God, may God look after you and give you his grace to pursue the cause of the Kingdom of France. Written at Gien on the twenty-fifth day of June.

A Matter of Honour

St Joan of Arc   November 7th 1429

To the citizens of Riom

The King ordered an attack on La Charité, which was a nest of mercenaries, but left his forces without money, supplies and munitions. The people of Riom promised to help but did not. Orleans sent men, money, clothes and artillery, but not enough. Joan attempted to raise the siege, though without sufficient money or supplies, and failed.

To my dear and good friends, the churchmen, citizens and inhabitants of the town of Riom.

Dear and good friends, you know well how the town of Saint-Pierre le Moustier was taken under assault, and, with God's help, I intend to free the other places that are against the King; but because a great amount of gunpowder, many arrows and other necessities of war were used before the said town, and the lords in that town and I are poorly provided to lay siege to La Charité, where we shall soon make our way, I beg you by your great love for the well-being and honour of the King, and also of all others thereafter, without delay to assist us in the said siege by sending powder, saltpetre, sulphur, arrows, strong crossbows and other necessities of war. For, consider, if we have the said powder and other necessities of war, the matter will soon be settled and no one will accuse you of negligence or refusing to help. Dear and good friends, may our Lord take care of you. Written at Moulins, the ninth day of November.

Joan

Keep a Careful Watch

St Joan of Arc   March 28th 1430

To the citizens of Rheims

The people of Rheims had written to Joan about their fears of a siege. She had promised them that she would make the English buckle their spurs in haste. The English wanted to take Rheims and crown their own king there. But now there had been an anti-English conspiracy in Paris, there were hopes of a rising there, and Joan had other good news for the town, which was to be of good cheer, for the King would help them if they were besieged. The French had indeed been inordinately successful, but if the Anglo-Burgundian forces took Rheims Paris would be in danger.

To my very dear and good friends the churchmen, mayor and deputies, burgesses and citizens and masters of the good town of Rheims.

Very dear and good friends, rest assured that I have received your letters, saying that the King has been told that he has many enemies within the city of Rheims. You must know that truly he has heard that many there formed an alliance and planned to commit treason against the town and allow the Burgundians to enter it. Since then, the King has been made aware that the opposite is true, for you have sent him an assurance to the contrary: therefore he is well pleased with you; and you may rest assured that he looks with favour on you; and if you are in need, he will help you, in respect of the siege; and he is well aware that you must suffer greatly under the harshness of these traitrous Burgundian enemies; if he frees you shortly, God willing, he will do so as soon as ever he may. I ask and require you, very dear friends, to keep the said good city safe for the King, and to keep a very careful watch. Very soon you will receive more ample news from me. For now I have no more to tell you except that all Brittany is French and the Duke should send the King three thousand warriors paid for two months. I commend you to God's care. Written at Sully on the twenty-eighth of March.

Sell the Chalice off the Altar!

St Bernard

c. 1150

To Odo, abbot of Beaulieu

Some of Bernard's letters, as in this instance, were curt announcements that a particular injustice was now well known and must be put right immediately.

To his brother and friend, Odo, Abbot of the Clerks Regular of Beaulieu, greetings from Brother Bernard, the unworthy steward of the monastery of Clairvaux!

It is neither good nor honourable for you to hold on to the savings of this poor man (if indeed you are doing so), which, so he says, he gave you to keep for him. He came to me with his complaints because he had heard of the special and intimate friendship between us. And I, presuming on the friendship, ask you, with all due respect, why you have not chosen to sell the chalice off the altar so as to keep the man quiet, if you have not got an ox or horse to sell, so that he might receive back what belongs to him. Have some respect for your good name, for the good name of your house, for this holy season of Lent which is upon us, and return without delay this man's savings which you are keeping without excuse, before the matter should become so widely known that it could not be settled without greater embarrassment.

Brother Bernard

The Order Best to Take

St Thomas More   September 3rd 1529

To his wife

In this letter from Woodstock to his second wife Alice, whom he married in 1511, a few months after the death of Jane More, St Thomas applies to his concern for his neighbours the same fine sense of justice for which he was noted in affairs of state.

Mistress Alice,

In my most hearty wise I recommend me to you. And whereat I am informed by my son Heron of the loss of our barns and our neighbours' also with all the corn that was therein, albeit (saving God's pleasure) it were great pity of so much good corn lost, yet sith it hath liked him to send us such a chance, we must and are bounden not only to be content but also to be glad of his visitation. He sent us all that we have lost and sith he hath by such a chance taken it away again his pleasure be fulfilled. Let us never grudge thereat but take in good worth and heartily thank him as well for adversity as for prosperity and peradventure we have more cause to thank him for our loss than for our winning, for his wisdom better seeth what is good for us than we do ourselves. Therefore I pray you be of good cheer and take all the household with you to church and there thank God both for that he hath given us and for that he hath taken from us and for that he hath left us, which if it please him he can increase when he will and if it please him to leave us yet less, at his pleasure be it.

I pray you to make some good ensearch what my poor neighbours have lost and bid them take no thought therefore, for and I should not leave myself a spoon, there shall no poor neighbour of mine bear no loss by any chance happened in my house. I pray you be with my children and your household merry in God and devise somewhat with your friends what way were the best to take for provision to be made for corn for our household and for seed this year coming, if ye think it good that we keep the ground still in our hands, and whether ye think it good that we so shall do or not, yet I think it were not best suddenly thus to leave it all up and to put away our folk off our farm, till we have somewhat advised us thereon; howbeit if we have more now than ye shall need and which can get them other masters, ye may then discharge us of them, but I would not that any man were suddenly sent away he wot nere whither. I shall, I think, because of this chance get leave this next week to come home and see you, and then shall we further devise together upon all things what order shall be best to take.

Your husband,

Thomas

A Case of Justice

John Henry Newman
May 21st 1840
To his sister Jemima

The voluminous correspondence of Cardinal Newman contains many letters to the sisters to whom he was especially devoted. This one to Jemima (Mrs John Mozley), sent when he was still an Anglican, is typical of those which show his concern not only for high matters of ecclesiastical and political concern but for questions of practical moral interest in everyday life.

My dear Jemima,

Thanks for your tablets which I have already found very useful. You have not told me the name of Mr Mozley's banker, so I assume it is Williams', & have ordered Rivington to pay into his account £100 now and £100 in about 2 months' time—when it is paid, I will ask about the interest of money.—It seems to me you are quite right in what you do for Aunt [i.e. giving her money]—and I have talked to Aunt about it—and she assents. She would quite assent if left alone—and I think the best way will be to drop the subject till her return. I think she would like this. It is quite preposterous that a married woman should have nothing to spend but on herself (I am taking the lowest ground, as if John were out of the question—though you are a Mozley, you are a Christian). Can any husband, who is good for anything, like his wife to have only so much as she spends on herself? and if you are bound as a Christian to spend on others as well as yourself, who has claims before Aunt? must we not be just before we are generous? is it not a case of justice? Why even as a Governess, to take the very lowest ground, she has earned from our justice what she may claim from our gratitude. And when a certain sum of money has come to you virtually, I cannot see any impropriety. I am writing abruptly, having little room. It comes to this—are you to give nothing to God of what he has given you? I think you are right.

Ever yours affectionately,

John H. Newman

Do not be Inconsistent

St Bernard of Clairvaux

12th century

To the Bishop of Limoges

The apparent spontaneity of this warning soon reveals the artistry of Bernard's moral rebukes. One of his favourite devices is to correct the recipient by referring to a third person.

My Lord Bishop,

I am not writing to you in my own interests or to seek any advantage for myself. I am writing to you for your own sake. The days of men are short. As long as you are Bishop of Limoges try to be a credit to your position by letting us see your good works. I am glad to hear that the Pope has entrusted the cause of the bishop-elect of Limoges to you, with the power to conclude it canonically without appeal. You have it in your power to prove to the Church of God that the Pontiff has been justified in this action of his. But you will only succeed in doing this if you fear God, observe the canons, and love justice. In the church of Rodez there is a question of a shepherd and a bishop of souls, a successor of Christ, a man to raise up seed to his dead brother. Shall it be the man of foul life, burdened conscience, and scandalous reputation? Shall it be the man who has descended from abbey to abbey, or rather from abyss to abyss, so as to be at once a consecrator and violator of virgins? What of that saying of the Apostle: "A bishop must needs be beyond reproach"? Do not be inconsistent with yourself, let your actions correspond with your words, so that those words of the psalm cannot be applied to you: "Their tongues shall be turned against them." It rests with you. Keep a watch on your soul and have no share in the sins of others. Through you this man will either stand or fall; if the latter you will be blessed by the Lord.

Yours in Christ,

Bernard

Unlawful and Accursed Behaviour

St Bernard of Clairvaux

12th century

To Louis, King of France

Bernard wrote more than once to Louis the Younger of France to rebuke him for invading the territory of Count Theobald and for committing a vast number of inexcusable atrocities, such as the burning of a village together with its inhabitants, during the incursion. This letter, together with Fénelon's letter to another Louis (next but one in this section), belongs among the major ecclesiastical indictments of wayward and unrestrained monarchs.

Sir,

God knows how fond of you I have been ever since I first knew you, and how I have always wanted your honour. You too know with what anxiety and trouble I, with other faithful servants of yours, have striven during the last year to obtain peace for you. But I begin to fear that we have laboured in vain, for it is evident that you are too ready to kick aside frivolously and hastily the good and sound advice you receive; and, under I know not what devilish advice, to hasten back while their scars are still fresh to your former evil ways, which with good reason you were only lately deploring. From whom but the devil could this advice come under which you are acting, advice which causes burnings upon burnings, and slaughter upon slaughter, and the voice of the poor and the groans of captives and the blood of the slain to echo once more in the ears of the Father of orphans and the Judge of widows? Clearly the ancient enemy of our race is delighted with this hecatomb of slaughtered men, because "he was a murderer from the beginning." Do not try to "cover sin with smooth names" by citing Count Theobald as a futile pretext for your wrongdoing, for he says that he is ready and indeed very willing to abide by the terms which were arranged between you both when peace was made, and that he is prepared to make immediate satisfaction in everything if those who love your name, that is to say the mediators between you both, should find him to have offended your honour in any way which he does not think he had.

But you will not receive any peaceful overtures or keep your own truce or accept sound advice. On the contrary, by some mysterious judgement of God, you insist on turning everything round so perversely that you deem disgrace to be honour and honour to be disgrace and fear what is safe and scorn what you should fear. According to the rebuke that Joab gave the holy and glorious kind David, you have "nothing but love for your enemies and nothing but hatred for your friends." Those who are urging you to repeat your former wrongdoing against an innocent person are seeking in this not your honour but their own convenience, or rather not so much their convenience as the will of the devil; they are trying to use the power of the king to secure the mad purposes which they are not sure of being able to achieve by themselves, and are clearly the enemies of your crown and the disturbers of your realm.

But whatever you may be pleased to do with your own kingdom, crown, and soul, we, the sons of the Church, cannot overlook the injuries, contempt and ignominy to which you have subjected your mother and we perceive that this, besides what we grieve that she has already had to suffer from you, is partly being inflicted on her again, and partly threatened. Certainly we shall make a stand and, if necessary, fight even to the death for our mother with the weapons that are permitted to us, that is with prayers and lamentations to God, not with shields and swords. And, for my part, besides the daily prayers which, God is my witness, I offer in supplication for peace, for your kingdom, and for salvation, I have also endeavoured to further your cause with the Holy See by letters and messengers, almost, I must admit, against my conscience and, I cannot deny, even to the extent of arousing against myself the just anger of the Supreme Pontiff. But now I tell you that, provoked by the constant excesses you commit almost daily, I am beginning to regret having stupidly favoured your youth more than I should have done, and I am determined that in future to the best of my limited capacity, I shall expose the whole truth about you.

I shall not withhold the fact that you are again trying to make common cause with excommunicated persons, that I hear you are associating with robbers and thieves in the slaughter of men, the burning of homesteads, the destruction of churches, and the scattering of the poor, according to those words of the Prophet, "Swift art thou to welcome the thief who crosses thy path, to throw in thy lot with adulterers"; as if you are not able to do evil enough by yourself! I shall not conceal the fact that you have not even now corrected that unlawful and accursed oath you took against the church of Bourges, on account of which so many evils have arisen; that you do not allow a pastor to care for the sheep of Christ at Chalons; and moreover that you billet your brother and his soldiers, archers, and crossbowmen in the houses of the bishops against all right and justice, thereby rashly exposing the property of the Church to be squandered in disgraceful uses of this kind. I tell you, you will not remain long unpunished if you continue in this way. Therefore, my lord king, I admonish you in a friendly way and strongly advise you to give up your evil practices immediately, so that, like the King of Nineveh, you may be able to placate by humility and penance the wrath of God, if perhaps he is even now preparing to strike you. I have spoken harshly because I fear an even harsher fate for you. But bear in mind those words of the Wise Man: "Better the love that scourges, than hate's false kiss."

Bernard

A Question of Justice

St Joan of Arc   March 22nd 1429

To the king of England and the English

St Joan dictated this letter before her acceptance by the French commission of examination. On April 30th her two heralds delivered it to the English who put one of them in irons, intending, against all the laws of war, to burn him. They had put up a stake but were awaiting a ruling from Paris University. He was rescued when the city was taken. It is important to note that Joan offered peace if the English would do her justice and mercy to the ordinary men-at-arms if they would obey her rightful demands. At her trial she denied dictating a few unimportant words, but they are in the three key versions that have come down from historians of the French side.

To the Duke of Bedford, the self-styled regent of the Kingdom of France, or to his lieutenants before the town of Orleans.

+ Jesus Mary +

King of England, and you Duke of Bedford, who call yourself Regent of the Kingdom of France; you, William de la Pole, Duke of Suffolk; Sir John Talbot; and you, Sir Thomas Scales, who call yourselves lieutenants of the said Duke of Bedford, accept the justice of the King of Heaven, yield to the Maid sent here by God, the King of Heaven, the keys of all the fine towns of France that you have seized and violated. She has come hither by the power of God on behalf of the royal line. She is quite prepared to make peace if you agree with her what what is right, that you are usurpers in France, and pay for what you have taken. You archers, good soldiers and others who stand before the fine town of Orleans, depart in the sight of God to your own countries. And if you do not do so, await the deeds of the Maid who will shortly be with you to your great pain. King of England, if you do not do what you should, I am a commander, and in some place where I shall lie in wait for your people in France, I shall make them flee, whether they wish or no; and if they will not obey, I shall cause them all to die, and if they will obey, I shall not be harsh with them. I have come here by the will of God, the King of Heaven, body to body to throw you out of France, and against all those who would commit treason, mischief, or injury to the Kingdom of France. And do not think that you have any right from God, the King of Heaven, Son of Holy Mary, to hold the Kingdom of France. It is thus that King Charles, the true heir, will hold it, for God, the King of Heaven, wishes it to be so, and the Maid revealed this to Charles, who will enter Paris with his own. If you refuse to believe the message sent from God by the Maid, in some place where we shall come upon you we shall come to blows, and we shall make such a hubbub as never was heard for a thousand years in France, if you do not see reason. And believe surely that the King of Heaven will find more strength in the Maid than you can bring to bear in all your sorties against her and her good soldiery; and then it shall be clear who has more right: those who depend on the King or those who rely on you. Duke of Bedford, the Maid asks and requires you not to seek defeat. If you give way, you will share in the triumph of the finest thing that the French ever did for Christendom. Reply to the city of Orleans, if you wish to make peace; and if you do not do so, you will soon know to your cost what you should have done. Written on Tuesday of Holy Week.

On behalf of the Maid

Humble Yourself!

François Fénelon   1694-5

To King Louis XIV of France

Here one of the great moralists of the seventeenth century reproves and condemns the totalitarian abuse of government under the pretence of divine right. The situation he describes is not rare in our own century, and brave Christians, individuals and groups, still put their lives at risk in opposing greedy dictators and unjust regimes that unmercifully persecute and murder their own and other peoples. Though the original manuscript still exists, and is in Fénelon's own hand, this powerful document could be the first draft of the letter, which the writer perhaps toned down later. Even popes were slow to sound such blasts on the trumpet of truth when mighty princes were at fault.

Sire,

   The man who assumes the liberty of addressing you thus is not concerned with any worldly interest. He writes without resentment, ambition, or any desire to be known as one who has a share in high affairs of state. You do not really know him, but he is devoted to your person and, thereby, to God. You are indeed mighty but he desires nothing that you can bestow on him, and he is willing to bear any suffering in order to tell you truths concerning your salvation. Perhaps his message is blunt, but that should not dismay you, even though you seldom hear anything like it. People who are used to flattery are apt to explain the unvarnished truth when they hear it as the mere promptings of envy, annoyance or excessive enthusiasm. But failure to tell the whole truth means betraying trust. God himself will testify to the zeal, respect and loyalty of the writer. You may rest assured of his devotion to everything that may serve your true interests.

You, Sire, were born with a heart aware of the meaning of justice and honesty. The people charged with raising you taught you that as a ruler you ought to be jealous, suspicious and disdainful, mistrust virtue and fear undoubted merit; that you ought to favour only the servile and that your own selfish interests should always reign supreme. For about thirty years now, your leading ministers have ignored the ancient laws that governed this State, only to increase your authority which, because they exerted it, became their own. They no longer look to the State or to the laws of the realm but only to the King and to the King's own pleasure. They have unjustifiably increased your revenues and charges. They have elevated you yourself to a pinnacle of glory far above, so they say, the cumulative radiance of all your predecessors. This means in fact that they have made France destitute in order to support prodigality and ineradicable luxury at court. They wanted to raise you up among the ruins of the State without realizing that no elevation of this kind is possible when it depends on the wreckage of everything that promotes true greatness. Sometimes, to be sure, you have proved jealous of your ministers' authority (and excessively so, even, in foreign affairs), but, in general, each minister in his day has ruled as the unchallenged master of his own department. You thought you were ruling, but all you have done yourself is to set the bounds for those who actually rule. They have not been slow to show the public their power, that we know only too well. They have proved harsh, arrogant, unjust, violent and dishonest. Their only precept, either at home or abroad, has been first to threaten, then to crush and finally to destroy anyone who stands up to them. They have talked to you about things only to slander anyone whose real merits might put them in the shade. You have got used to hearing praise so extreme as to be tantamount to idolatry which, for honour's sake, you ought to have rejected angrily. They have not only made your name hateful but have turned us into a nation intolerable to all our neighbours. We have lost all our allies, for we wanted them not as confederates but as slaves. We have borne destructive wars for more than twenty years. In 1672, for instance, they forced your Majesty to declare war on the Netherlands in order to punish the Dutch for protesting too unrespectfully against our reneging on the trade agreements ratified by Cardinal Richelieu. I refer to this particular war only as an example, because all the others sprang from it. It was started for the sake of glory and revenge, which are both unjustifiable motives for warfare. Consequently, all the extended frontiers arising from these wars have been acquired unjustly. Of course, since possession of the occupied lands was confirmed by subsequent peace treaties, it might be claimed that there was was some modicum of justification for it. But success is no justification for an unjust war. Moreover, the conquered did not sign these treaties willingly, but under the threat of force and of worse losses if they refused. They signed them in the same spirit as one surrenders one's purse when one must either give it up or die. To examine before God the nature of all your conquests we have to return to the origins of the war with the Netherlands.

It is pointless to claim that all these conquests were necessary for your country's welfare. We have no right to look on others' possessions as necessary for ourselves. It is necessary, however, to behave in accordance with the demands of justice pure and simple. We should not pretend it is right always to hold certain fortresses because we need them to defend our borders. You should ensure this security through due alliances, by the moderate conduct of foreign affairs, or by establishing strong-points behind our own borders. Nevertheless, in spite of our duty to ensure our own safety, that can never justify taking territory belonging to our neighbours. Any wise and honest person will confirm the obvious truth of what I say.

All the foregoing, Sire, shows how far throughout your life you have departed from the main road of truth and justice, and therefore that of the Gospel too. All the calamities that Europe has suffered during the last twenty years, the bloodshed, the acts of violence, the ravaged provinces, and the towns and villages put to fire, have been the deadly results of the war of 1672 started to ensure your own glory and to discipline a few pamphlet-writers and medal-casters in the Netherlands. Ask honest people straightforwardly whether you can keep everything you own as a result of treaties that you have forced on your enemies through so inadequately justifiable a war.... You have not even observed the terms of your arrogantly imposed treaties. You have even made huge conquests without formally declaring war.... Such methods of conducting foreign affairs have united and aroused all Europe against you. Even those who have not dared openly to come out against you long for your decline and humiliation as the only hope of liberty and peace for all Christian nations. You had it in your power to be the father of your people and chief arbiter among your neighbours, but you are now their common enemy and known as a harsh ruler of your own people....

Now your people, whom you ought to love as if they were your own children, and who have loved you unreservedly hitherto, are dying of hunger. Agriculture is almost non-existent, the population in town and country is dropping, all trades are approaching extinction and producing fewer and fewer workers, and commerce does not exist. You have destroyed almost half the inner strength of your country in order to make and keep useless conquests beyond its borders. Instead of taking more and more cash from your own people, you should give it to them to buy food. The law is held in no respect, and is exhausted anyway. The nobility, who hold their possessions by decree, are entirely dependent on the State, and you live amidst a crowd of greedy, demanding parasites. But you yourself, Sire, have caused all these misfortunes. The kingdom is in ruins because you retain what there is in your own hands and everyone is dependent on your bounty. Yet this is that same great kingdom that is supposed to be so prosperous under a monarch always declared to be his people's joy—which he would indeed be if he had not been infected by flattery and malign advice.

Even the common people, to be sure, who loved and trusted you to such a degree, are beginning to lose the love, trust and even the respect they felt for you. They do not rejoice at your victories and conquests, but find them sources of resentment and despair. Sedition is apparent everywhere. The people believe that you are indifferent to their misery, and that all you are concerned with is your own power and glory. If the King, so they say, really looked as a father on his people, surely he would be more interested in their miserable state than in his own glory? He would find glory instead by ensuring that they had peace, and in enabling them to rest after so many evils instead of maintaining on the frontiers so many places that could spark off wars? How do you answer these questions, Sire? Popular riots, unknown for so many years, are now increasingly common. Even in Paris, right on your doorstep, the magistrates must secretly bribe the arrogant and discontented in order to obtain some peace. Those who ought to be punished are paid instead. You are put in the shameful state of either letting sedition go unpunished, and thereby increasing it, or of massacring the people you have brought to despair by taxing them for the sake of war, and thus stealing the bread they strive to earn by the sweat of their labour.

Others are without bread, yet you are without money, and still refuse to admit that you have been reduced to such a condition. You have always enjoyed good fortune and cannot believe that it will ever come to an end. You are afraid of opening your eyes but also that someone will do it for you. You are afraid that you will be forced to surrender some of your glory. This glory has hardened your heart but is more dear to you than justice, than your own peace of mind, and than the lives of your people who die every day from diseases caused by starvation. You cherish it more than your eternal salvation, which you cannot have as well as the idol you have made of your glory.

This is your condition: you live with your eyes bandaged. You heap up self-praise for transient successes that settle nothing. You do not see things as a whole when the situation is becoming irreversible....

Everyone can see what is happening but no one dare tell you. Perhaps you will understand when it is too late. Real courage means not deceiving yourself, and deciding firmly on a course of action when necessity demands.... But eventually God will remove the bandage from your eyes and reveal everything you refuse to see now. For some time his arm has been ready to strike you down. He is reluctant to do so because he is merciful to a Prince who has always been a victim of flattery, and because your enemies are his too. But he knows how to distinguish between just and unjust causes, and how he must reduce your pride in order to convert you. You can be a real follower of Christ only if you take the way of humiliation. You do not love God and your fear of him is base. You fear hell, not God. Your religion is sheer superstition and pointless trivialities.... You love only your own glory and your own convenience. You think only of yourself, as if you were God and everything had been created to be sacrificed to please you. But God has created you only for the good of your people. Unfortunately, you are blind to these truths. How can you see them when you do not know God, do not love him, do not pray to him from your heart, and make no attempt to know him better?

Your archbishop is corrupt, scandalous, irreformable, deceitful, spiteful, wily, inimical to all virtue, and saddens all people of good will. You suffer him merely because he seeks only to please you with flattery. For more than twenty years he has sold his integrity and remained your confidant. You betray good people to him and allow him to tyrannize the Church, yet he is better treated than any virtuous ecclesiastic.

Your confessor is vicious, afraid of true virtue, and fond only of profanity and wrongdoers. He loves his own authority, which you have increased immeasurably. No previous royal confessor has been allowed to create bishops and to make decisions regarding any matter of conscience. You are the only person in France unaware that he is ignorant, that his intellect is restricted and dull, yet that his vile behaviour still leaves room for guile. Even the Jesuits despise him and are angered by his obedience to his family's ludicrous ambitions.... His policy is to keep you in the dark. He follows good principles only when he fears that you will be scandalized. Here the blind are leading the blind; as Jesus said, they will all fall into the chasm.... Your counsellors possess neither the authority nor the will to do good. France is in desperation. Why do they not tell you the honest truth? Are they waiting for the debacle? Are they merely afraid to displease you? If that is so, they do not love you, for you must be prepared to offend those whom you love, instead of deceiving them or betraying them by saying nothing. What use are your advisers if they do not plainly declare that you must give back the countries you have stolen, that you have to place the life of your people before vainglory, that you must make restitution to the Church for the harm you have done to it, and that you must think of becoming a true Christian before death suddenly stops you short?...They should resign if they find you too obdurate and insistent on surrounding yourself with flatterers. But of course you will ask what, in that case, they should tell you. They should say that you must humble yourself under God's mighty hand unless he is to humiliate you; that you should ask your enemies for peace, and thus expiate the longing for glory that you have made your idol; that you should shun the advice of political flatterers; and that to save your country you should restore to your enemies the conquered territories which, anyway, justice does not allow you to keep. Surely, in the midst of the misfortunes God has brought upon you, you should be pleased to end the successes that have blinded you and now demand that you should make restitution. A reversion of this kind is necessary for your salvation, but you would never have decided on such a course of action in one recent instance if you had stayed powerful and triumphant. The man who writes these truths, Sire, scarcely wishes you misfortune but instead would give his life to see you in the state that God wishes you to be in. He will never cease praying for you.

Fénelon

Why Are People Starving?

John Wesley   Dover, December 9th, 1772

To the editor of "Lloyd's Evening Post"

In the Britain of 1772 a long-drawn-out foreign war was followed by bad harvests. The prices of necessities rose alarmingly and a vast number of ordinary people were in great distress. Unlike most of those in authority, Wesley travelled constantly about the country preaching to the masses. He was powerfully affected by the condition of the poor and destitute, and spent much time in prayer devoted to their sufferings. He also used his powerful gift for practical exposition and moral remonstration to awaken the consciences of influential persons with a detailed account of the state of the nation and the reasons for it. The following is extracted from a long letter which he also sent to the "Leeds Mercury" on December 29th, and in January 1773 revised and enlarged for publication as a pamphlet.

Sir,

Many excellent things have been lately published concerning the present scarcity of provisions. And many causes have been assigned for it; but is not something wanting in most of these publications? One writer assigns one cause, another one or two more, and strongly insists upon them. But who has assigned all the causes that manifestly concur to produce this melancholy effect? at the same time pointing out how each particular cause affects the price of each particular sort of provision?

I would willingly offer to candid and benevolent men a few hints on this important subject, proposing a few questions, and adding to each what seems to be the plain and direct answer.

I ask first, Why are thousands of people starving, perishing for want, in every part of England? The fact I know: I have seen it with my eyes in every corner of the land. I have known those who could only afford to eat a little coarse food every other day. I have known one picking up stinking sprats from a dunghill and carrying them home for herself and her children. I have known another gathering the bones which the dogs had left in the streets and making broth of them to prolong a wretched life. Such is the case at this day of multitudes of people in a land flowing with all the necessaries, the conveniences, the superfluities of life!

Now, why is this? Why have all these nothing to eat? Because they have nothing to do. They have no meat because they have no work.

But why have they no work? Why are so many thousand people in London, in Bristol, in Norwich, in every county from one end of England to the other, utterly destitute of employment?

Because the persons who used to employ them cannot afford to do it any longer. Many who employed fifty men now scarcely employ ten. Those who employed twenty now employ one or none at all. They cannot, as they have no vent for their goods, food now bearing so high a price that the generality of people are hardly able to buy anything else.

But to descend from generals to particulars. Why is breadcorn so dear? Because such immense quantities of it are continually consumed by distilling. Indeed, an eminent distiller near London hearing this, warmly replied, "Nay, my partner and I generally distil but a thousand quarters of corn a week." Perhaps so. Suppose five-and-twenty distillers in and near the towns consume each only the same quantity. Here are five-and-twenty thousand quarters a week—that is, above twelve hundred and fifty thousand quarters a year—consumed in and about London! Add the distillers throughout England, and have we not reason to believe that half of the wheat produced in the kingdom is every year consumed, not by so harmless a way as throwing it into the sea, but by converting it into deadly poison—poison that naturally destroys, not only the strength and life, but also the morals of our countrymen!

"Well, but this brings in a large revenue to the King." Is this an equivalent for the lives of his subjects? Would His Majesty sell an hundred thousand of his subjects yearly to Algiers for four hundred thousand pounds? Surely no. Will he, then, sell them for that sum to be butchered by their own countrymen? "But otherwise the swine for the Navy cannot be fed." Not unless they are fed with human flesh? not unless they are fattened with human blood? O tell it not in Constantinople that the English raise the royal revenue by selling the blood and flesh of their countrymen!

But why are oats so dear? Because there are four times the horses (to speak within compass), for coaches and chaises in particular, than were some years ago. Unless, therefore, four times the oats grew now as grew then, they cannot be at the same price. If only twice as much is produced (which perhaps is near the truth), the price will naturally be double to what it was....

Your humble servant,

John Wesley

Compassion and Tenderness

Elizabeth Fry   July, 1820

To Admiral Sir Thomas Byam Martin

Elizabeth Fry courageously investigated the conditions of the poor and needy, especially criminals who were hanged or transported in vile circumstances to the colonies, above all Australia, as virtual slave labourers and eventual breeding stock, having been convicted often for petty misdemeanours arising from their awful impoverishment. She knew the criminalizing effects of imprisonment, and that in conditions of neglect on board ship the innocent were soon efficiently instructed by more practised companions. In visits and numberless letters she resolutely informed and pestered influential but sometimes wicked, indifferent, stupid or vague people, developing a highly-nuanced approach in correspondence that showed those whom she petitioned her undoubted knowledge of the facts of material injustice and her determination to redress them. At a time when letters pleading for others were usually models of ghastly sycophancy, she was intent to repeat the truth, and to remind powerful people of their capabilities and duty. Many refused to listen, but miracles were worked. Byam Martin, Comptroller of the Navy 1813-32, came to appreciate Mrs Fry's efforts, and the first advances in the improvement of female convict ships were made under his direction.

Respected Friend,

...

There is one great encouragement to persevere in the care of prisoners, and in forming proper arrangements for them, that in the best regulated gaols the returns are small indeed in comparison to what they are in others; and even in Newgate, as far as we have been able to calculate from the information received from the former Governor of the Prison, a very small proportion return to the women's side, in comparison to the number before we had the care of them. I believe kindness does more in turning them from the error of their ways than harsh treatment; and that many a poor creature claims a compassion and a tenderness that is little known, but to those who visit prisons, as there are many of whom it may be said, that they were driven into guilt, and only want the way to be made open, to return with joy into the paths of virtue.

With respect to convict ships, government appears to us most liberal in its supplies for the poor convicts, more so indeed, than would be right for those under punishment, did not the great length of the voyage, and the frequently delicate state of the health of women and children render it almost necessary; and we are of opinion, that having such arrangements made amongst the women as tends to their good order and reformation would render the voyage less agreeable, and of course less tempting to the profligate, though no doubt more safe to the well-disposed, as it would be instrumental in protecting their remaining innocence and virtue; I believe no female convict ship sails without some of this description in her. Surely, for the welfare of such, both here and hereafter, and the hope that even the worst may be preserved from further evil; as well as the important consideration, that for the sake of the colony, the women's morals should be protected on the voyage, it is worth the effort to make even a convict-ship a place for industry, instruction, and reform. I do not doubt thy kindness of heart on this subject; but we so often find in every good work, that enemies arise, some of them perhaps for want of understanding the subject, that I have feared lest any should discourage either thyself, or any other gentlemen who are interested in the cause of prisoners, from adopting such arrangements as are most likely to promote their good, with that of society at large and the security and safety of the community.

I remain, &c.,

E. Fry

Establishing Order

Elizabeth Fry   1823

To the Right Honourable R. Wilmot Horton, M.P.

Elizabeth Fry was well aware that a humanitarian project had to be followed through. Her interests extended throughout Europe and even across the globe. In the case of the women prisoners despatched to Australia (Van Diemen's Land = Tasmania), she knew that more than one influential person had to be converted to her viewpoint by skilful persuasion and practical information if the arrangements made for the female convicts during the voyage were not to be wasted on their arrival in the colonies. The immediate occasion of this letter was a naval surgeon's attempt to discourage the Navy Board from improving good order in convict ships because such "comfort did not exist on troop ships." Sir Robert John Wilmot Horton (knighted in 1831) was Under-secretary for War and Colonies, 1821-8, and Lord Bathurst Secretary for War and the Colonies. Mrs Fry was able to press Horton's interest in reform (he was to support Catholic emancipation in 1829) to her good ends.

Respected Friend,

In compliance with thy obliging proposal, I take the liberty of stating in writing our views relative to the female convicts in Van Diemen's Land;

in order that they may be submitted to the consideration of Lord Bathurst; as we cannot but feel anxious that the care we extend to this degraded class of the community not only in the different prisons, but also on the voyage, should be rendered permanently beneficial, through the cooperation of government in the colonies. In the first place, we deem it expedient that a building be erected at Hobart Town for the reception of female convicts. The building, if raised by the male convicts, and composed of such materials as the country affords, would, it is supposed, be completed greatly within the present estimate. That a respectable and judicious Matron be there stationed, to superintend the whole establishment under the direction of the Governor, or some magistrate appointed by him for that service. That part of the building be appropriated to use of an adult and girls' school, and that school-mistresses be selected by the Matron from among the reformed prisoners, provided they be sufficiently qualified for the office. That immediately on the arrival of a ship, after it has been visited, either by the Governor, or by some other person appointed by him, for the purpose of inspecting its general condition; the convicts be quietly (and as privately as possible) conducted from the ship to the said building, where the deportment of every prisoner shall be scrutinized with exactness. If the Secretary of State for the Home Department were to direct, that the Surgeon-superintendent should be furnished by the magistrates with a written account of the general conduct and character of every individual, even previously to their commitment, together with the nature and extent of their offence; we think it would greatly aid the Governor in his decision with regard to the proper disposal of the prisoners in the colony. That those who merit a favourable report be selected, and allowed to be taken into service, by the respectable inhabitants, under such restraints and regulations as may be considered needful. The others to remain confined; receiving at the same time suitable instruction, and employment, until they evince sufficient amendment in habits and dispositions, to warrant the grant of similar indulgence; and we conceive that much benefit might result, if some of the regulations mentioned in the new Act of Parliament, relative to prisons, were enforced in this colony, and in New South Wales. We would also propose that a sufficient supply of strong and decent clothing (not parti-coloured) be provided for them during the voyage, to be put on when they enter the ship, in exchange for their own; of which an inventory shall be immediately taken by a female officer, and given with the clothes to the Surgeon (in the presence of their respective owners), who shall carefully keep them in reserve, and deliver them to the Matron of the prison, to which they are destined, who shall receive the same in the presence of the prisoners, and shall at the same time see if they tally correctly with the inventories. And upon their discharge from prison, but not before, she shall restore them to their proper owners. We consider that it would be a great advantage in the voyage, and more especially while lying in the river, that the women should wear a simple uniform dress, and we think it indispensable for establishing order, and for enforcing the needful regulations on board the ship, that a Matron be stationed constantly there, whilst they remain in the river—to attend to their clothing, &c., and to search their female visitors, in order that no spirituous liquors, or anything else that is improper, be introduced. Could a person in that capacity accompany them during the voyage, it would no doubt be highly useful. We are pleased to understand that the Factory in Paramatta has more than cleared its expenses during the last year; as the interest we feel in the welfare of the colonies induces us, not only to desire the religious and moral improvement of the population at large, but in all our plans we wish to keep in view such a system, as shall eventually prove the most economical to government, as well as the most beneficial to the Colonial States.

In consequence of thy friendly encouragement, I have ventured thus freely to offer with submission our sentiments; we are fully aware that much has been accomplished, that many of our requests have been granted with obliging readiness, and we shall feel our sense of gratitude much increased, if Lord Bathurst will condescend to peruse these remarks, and to act in compliance, as far as his judgment can approve, and his authority enforce.

Believe me, to remain
With respect and regard,
Thy obliged friend,
                    Elizabeth Fry

Wrongfully Accused
John Gerard, SJ
January 23rd 1606

To the Duke of Lennox, Lord of the Privy Council

From the original in the Public Record Office: one of three letters to Lords of the Privy Council when the hue and cry was on after the Gunpowder Plot against King and Parliament, and the missionary priest Gerard had been falsely accused of complicity. The authorities skilfully used the Plot to increase hatred and suspicion and justify the

persecution of Catholics, almost as in our own century the Nazis used the burning of
the Reichstag to justify intolerable measures against their political opponents. Even
later, some twenty-five years after the Plot, when he had long ago escaped from
England, Gerard was still forced to scotch rumours (some circulated by priests, and
many of them citing extraordinarily circumstantial details) reminiscent of those
deposed in false testimonies at the time, such as that which claimed that he, Gerard,
still boasted that "by working under ground in the mine of Mr Catesby and other
conspirators, by excavating and carrying out the soil with his own hands, he has often
found his shirt wet through and dripping with sweat as copiously as if it had been
dragged through a river."

Right Honourable,

Seeing all laws, both divine and human, do license the innocent to plead
for himself, and the same laws do strictly require and highly commend an
open ear in any of authority to give audience and equal trial to a plaintiff
in such a case, my hope is that your Grace will excuse this my boldness in
offering up by your hands my humble petition for trial of my innocence
touching the late most impious treason, whereof I am wrongfully accused,
by some lost companions, I assure me, who, to save themselves from
deserved punishment, will not stick to accuse any innocent of any crime
wherein their bare word may pass for proof. There is none so innocent but
may be wrongfully accused, since innocency itself in our Lord and Master
was accused and condemned as an enemy to the State and no friend to
Caesar. This servant must not look to be more free from wrongs than his
Master was. But happy is that man by whom the truth is tried in judgment
and innocency cleared.

I durst not presume, being branded with the odious name of traitor, to
offer my petition to my Sovereign (to whom, as God is witness, I wish long
life and all happiness as to my own soul). But if by your Grace's means (of
whose piety and worthy disposition I have heard so much good) the
humble suit of a distressed suppliant (prostrate at his Majesty's feet) may
be offered up, I hope it shall be found not unfit for your Grace to offer,
and most fit and reasonable for so wise and righteous a Prince to grant.

My humble petition is only this. That, whereas I have protested before
God and the world, I was not privy to that horrible Plot of destroying the
King's Majesty and his posterity, &c, by powder (wherewith I am now so
publicly taxed in the proclamation), that full trial may be made, whether
I be guilty therein or not. And if so it be proved, that then all shame and
pain may light upon me; but if the truth appear on the contrary side, that
then I may be cleared from this so grievous an infamation and punishment
not deserved. Two kinds of proofs may be made in this cause, which I

humbly beseech your Grace, for God's cause, may be performed. One is, that all the principal conspirators (with whom I am said to have practised the foresaid Plot of Powder against the Parliament House) may be asked at their death, as they will answer at the dreadful tribunal unto which they are going, whether ever they did impart the matter to me, or I practise the same with them in the least degree, or whether they can but say of their knowledge that I did know of it. And I know it will then appear that no one of them will accuse me, if it be not apparent they do it in hope of life, but do give signs that they die in the fear of God and hope of their salvation.

And as by this trial it will appear (in this time most fit for saying truth) that there is not sufficient reason against me, so I humbly desire also trial may be made examining a witness, who can, if he will, fully clear me, and I hope he will not deny me that right, especially being the place of right and justice himself. Sir Everard Digby can testify for me, how ignorant I was of any such matter but two days before that unnatural parricide should have been practised. I have, for full trial thereof, enclosed a letter unto him, which I humbly beseech may be delivered before your Grace and the other two lords, whose favour and equity I have likewise humbly entreated by these letters unto them. All which I am bold to direct unto your Grace's hands, presuming upon your gracious furtherance, not having other means, in this my distressed case, to have them severally delivered. God of his goodness will reward, I hope, in full measure, this your Grace's favour and pity showed to an innocent wrongly accused, who would rather suffer any death than not to be found ever faithful to God and his Sovereign.

John Gerard

Standing my Conscience

St Thomas More   15—

To his daughter

More's letter from the Tower whence he was eventually taken to be beheaded is not only a moving personal letter to a dearly loved child but one the great statements of justification for conduct. It is a straightward and moving explanation of his obedience to the rule of conscience. It reiterates the standards of judgment that he would certainly have discussed with all his children.

Daughter Margaret,

We two have talked of this thing ofter than twice or thrice, and that same tale in effect that you tell me now therein, and the same fear too, have you twice told me before, and I have twice answered you too, that in this matter if it were possible for me to do the thing that might content the King's Grace, and God not therewith offended, there hath no man taken this oath already more gladly than I would do; as he that reckoneth himself more deeply bounden unto the King's Highness for his most singular bounty, many ways showed and declared, than any of them all beside. But since standing my conscience, I can no wise do it, and that for the instruction of my conscience in the matter, I have not slightly looked, but by many years studied and advisedly considered, and never could yet see nor hear that thing, nor I think I never shall, that could induce mine own mind to think otherwise than I do. I have no manner remedy, but God hath given me to the straight, that either I must deadly displease him, or abide any worldly harm that he shall for mine other sins, under name of this thing, suffer to fall upon me. Whereof, as I before this have told you too, I have ere I came here [the Tower] not left unbethought nor unconsidered, the very worst and the uttermost that can by possibility fall. And albeit that I know mine own frailty full well and the natural faintness of mine own heart, yet if I had not trusted that God should give me strength rather to endure all things, than offend him by swearing ungodly against mine own conscience, you may be very sure I would not have come here. And since in this matter but only unto God, it maketh me little matter, though men call it as it pleaseth them, and say it is no conscience but a foolish scruple.

Your father

Right Testimony

Dietrich Bonhoeffer

January 25th 1936

To Brother S.,

Three years after the National Socialists took power in Germany, when the evil intentions and unbridled force of the regime were clear and a relatively small body of Christians in the Confessing Church had refused to align themselves with the near-complicity or silence of the mainline churches, Bonhoeffer re-stated the primacy of truth.

Dear Brother,

... The truth still remains the greatest service of love which men can show each other in the community of Christ....

When the right way or the wrong way for the church, truth or untruth, was at stake, a time when at every moment there was a danger that the church might be led fearfully astray, if at a time like that there should for once have been some slight "psychical" explosions, well, I cannot get all that worked up about it. There is something more important that really matters. That is that the truth of the Word of God alone should prevail. Lapses in the tone of speeches and in disciplined conduct can be made good. I know of each of my brothers here that they are ready to ask pardon when they recognize such a lapse, and for me in this case that is the main thing. It is much much harder to make amends however if the church leaves the way of faithfulness and truth in its testimony to Christ. A discipline which no longer leaves room for a passionate protest against the falsification of the truth no longer stems from a wholeness of obedience toward Jesus Christ, but becomes an arbitrary Christian ideal, a self-selected work.

In all speaking and acting in the church I am concerned with the primacy, with the sole honour and truth of the Word of God. There is no greater service of love than to put men in the light of the truth of this Word, even where it brings sorrow. The Word of God separates the spirits. There is no vindictiveness here, but only the humble and truly dismayed recognition of the way which God himself will go with his Word in his church. The bounds of this Word are also our bounds. We cannot unite where God divides. We can only bear witness to the truth, remain humble, and pray for each other.... I find that with you the Holy Spirit is not just the reality bound up with the true, clear word of Scripture, which inextricably binds us in life and in knowledge, but a formative principle of a Christian ideal of life. The Holy Spirit remains somehow neutral. Behind your remarks there lurks a concept of what is "Christian" which has been won not from the truth of Scripture but from our verdict as a result of a human examination.... The Confessing Church would surrender the promise given to it if any other factor were introduced alongside obedience to the truth achieved through the Holy Spirit, in order to give the church new life....

With brotherly greetings,

D. Bonhoeffer

CHAPTER 8

Love, Marriage and Family

A Blessing to Each Other

George Macdonald   October 23rd 1848

To Miss Louisa Powell, his future wife

This is the first of a series of betrothal letters from Macdonald to Louisa, once her prosperous but somewhat severe father had given the near-penniless student permission to visit and eventually marry his daughter. Already we can sense the man who, in G. K. Chesterton's words, "made for himself a sort of spiritual environment, a space and transparency of mystical light, which was quite exceptional in his national and denominational environment."

Dear Louisa,

... I meant to write a much longer letter to my Louisa and many, beautiful and wise things (to me) I wanted to say, but now the impulse has left me. May our Father in Heaven be with you and bless you, and make you better of your present suffering.

Is love a beautiful thing, dearest? You and I love: but who created love? Let us ask him to purify our love to make it stronger and more real and more self-denying. I want to love you for ever—so that, though there is not marrying or giving in marriage in heaven, we may see each other there as the best beloved. Oh Louisa, is it not true that our life here is a growing unto life, and our death a being born—our true birth? If there is anything beautiful in this our dreamy life, shall it not shine forth in glory in the bright waking consciousness of heaven? And in our life together, my dear dear Louisa, if it please God that we should pass any part of our life together here, shall it not still shine when the cloud is over my head? I may see the light shining from your face, and when darkness is around you, you may see the light on mine, and from this we shall take courage. But we can only expect to have this light within us and on our faces—we can only expect to be a blessing to each other—by doing that which is right....

George

The Responsibilities of Life

St Thérèse of Lisieux   July 16th 1894

To a cousin

Three years before her death, the saint writes a typically delightful letter to congratulate a friend on her marriage. It remains a model for those who on such occasions try to say profound things in an entirely simple yet fresh and memorable way.

My dear Cousin Céline,

How really happy your letter has made me! I can only wonder at the way in which our Lady has graciously fulfilled your every wish. Even before you were married she made sure that your future husband's ideals would match your own exactly. How happy you must be to feel yourself so perfectly understood, and especially to know that your union will last for ever, and that, when this life is at an end, your love for your dead husband will persist.

We have both said good-bye to carefree childhood days. Now we have to face the responsibilities of life. We all take a different road but each one leads to the same goal. You and I must have a single aim: to grow in holiness while following the way that God in his goodness has laid down for us.

I feel that I can talk quite openly to you, my dear childhood friend. You understand the language of faith much better than the conversation of the world, and the Lord whom you received in your first holy communion has remained the Master of your heart. It is in the Lord that you love the fine soul who will be one with your own from now on, and the Lord makes your love so affectionate and strong.

Our faith is glorious indeed. Instead of restricting our hearts, as the world supposes, it uplifts them and extends their capacity to love, and, indeed, to love with an almost infinite love, for it will continue without break beyond this mortal life. Life has been given to us only so that we may purchase our home in heaven, where we shall meet once again the dear ones we loved on earth.

Dear Céline, I have asked our Lady of Mount Carmel to grant the favour you received at Lourdes. I am very glad that you are wearing the sacred scapular. It is a sure sign of predestination and also joins you more closely to your little sisters at Carmel. You beg me, Cousin, to pray for your dear husband. Do you think that I would let you down? No. Even in my poor prayers I could not pray for one without the other. I ask our Lord to be as kind to you as he once was to the bride and groom at Cana. May he always change the water into wine! By that, I mean: may he prolong his gift of happiness and, as far as possible, sweeten the bitter trials you will encounter on your way. But "trials"? To think of using such a word in my letter precisely when I realize that life for you is all sunshine! Forgive me, Cousin dear, and peacefully enjoy the happiness that God gives, and do not worry anxiously about the next day. I am sure that he has other favours and many consolations in store for you.

Dear little Cousin, please give my respects and greetings to Monsieur Poitier. I think of him too as my cousin. Now I must take my leave, dear Céline, but we shall always be closely united in affection, and I shall always find it a pleasure to sign myself:

Your little sister in our Lord,

Thérèse of the Child Jesus

Marriage Counselling

St Jane Frances de Chantal

April 13th 1620

To her daughter

St Jane had to administer eighty-six convents, but also had to ensure the prosperous future of the surviving children—a son and three daughters—of her marriage to the Baron de Chantal, who had died in a hunting accident. This letter shows the degree of control over the choice of a partner then exercised by a responsible even if just and tender-hearted parent.

My dear Françon,

May God be blessed for having guided you so wisely and fortunately as you prepare for your marriage. May his divine goodnesss guarantee you perfect peace. My darling girl, as things progress I am all the happier. Monsieur de Toulonjon is, I am convinced, the kindest of men. He has returned as pleased as possible and there is every reason for us to feel the same way. Dear Françon, your trust has delighted me greatly, but for my part God knows how I have prayed and wished to see you settled happily. He knows how much more profoundly I have felt your problem than my own. Your contentment is always my main concern; never doubt that. Rest assured that my love for you carried me away on this occasion, because I saw that it was the best for you. We certainly owe all this to the goodness of our Lord, who has cared for you and for me and has heard our prayers. The enclosed letter will tell you how much his lordship of Bourges also wants this marriage to take place.

Stay firm and if anxieties about this or that cross your mind, shut them out and do not let them in again on any account. Follow reason in everything as well as my own everyday advice. Believe me, my dear child, it is very good for you; if you carry on heeding it, you will find how wise it is. Do not forget your promise to write out at length all you think and feel, and to let me know if God has joined your heart to that of Monsieur de Toulonjon. Above all, I hope and wish that to be so, and I trust that God will have blessed your first meeting accordingly. As for me, darling, I can only repeat what I have already told you most sincerely: I wholeheart-edly approve of him. The affection I have for him is warmer than I can express. Indeed, none of our friends and relatives who know him could be more satisfied with him than you and I.

Monsieur de Toulonjon is very anxious about your rings. He wants to send me a large selection of all the precious stones in Paris, so that I can buy whatever I choose for you. Actually I should prefer you to take none of them. Frankly, my dear, ladies of quality no longer wear jewellery at Court. That is left to the wives of the townsfolk. But you must make your own decision when you come here. However, I do not know how I can persuade Monsieur de Toulonjon to share my opinion, for he has begged me, just for a start, to send you pearls and earrings and a vanity bag full of diamonds, which is all that ladies now carry with their gowns. But we really must not let him have his own way in such extravagance. He so much wants to please you that he will go to any lengths to give you whatever you want. If ever a wife ought to be quite happy, it is you. But you must realize how discreet you have to be in trying to restrain him. It would be best to be rather economical and to spend your money on useful things rather than on fripperies and show. I really do not want my Françon to go in for that sort of thing. Anyway, my own reputation is at stake, for you are my daughter and therefore you should be discreet and careful and arrange your life appropriately and profitably.

Finally, you should wear a wedding-dress. I do not want any ostentation in your marriage. I mean that absolutely. Monsieur de Toulonjon told me that you did not wish to be married during May. Doesn't your conscience worry you in this regard? It is rank superstition. On the other hand, however much he wants it, I do not think May will be possible.

The more I see of him the more I like him. The more, too, I realize that we should thank God for your happy engagement. Send him a very polite and warm letter. Be quite frank and open with him and show that you return his love. In future there is no need to stand on ceremony with him. His servant is downstairs waiting for my letter. My sole desire, dearest Françon, is that you should love your future husband with your whole heart. Good-bye, my dearest. Be quite frank when you write to me.

Your Mother

A Sudden Marriage

John Donne   February 1601-2

To Sir George More

A letter of apology that Donne wrote to his father-in-law at the time of his runaway marriage to Anne More, which had caused not only his imprisonment but that of two friends, Christopher and Samuel Brooke, who had helped him in the venture.

Sir,

The inward accusations in my conscience, that I have offended you beyond any inability of redeeming it by me, and the feeling of my Lord's heavy displeasure following it, forceth me to write, though I know my faults make my letters very ungracious to you. Almighty God, whom I call to witness that all my grief is that I have in this manner offended you and him, direct you to believe that which out of an humble and afflicted heart I now write to you. And since we have no means to move God, when he will not hear our prayers, to hear them, but by praying, I humbly beseech you to allow by his gracious example, my penitence so good entertainment, as it may have a belief and a pity. Of nothing in this one fault that I hear said to me, can I disculpe myself, but of the contemptuous and despiteful purpose towards you, which I hear is surmised against me. But for my dutiful regard to my late lady, for my religion, and my life, I refer myself to them that may have observed them. I humbly beseech you to take off these weights, and to put my fault into the balance alone, as it was done without the addition of these ill reports, and though then it will be too heavy for me, yet then it will less grieve you to pardon it. How little and how short the comfort and pleasure of destroying is, I know your wisdom and religion informs you. And though perchance you intend not utter destruction, yet the way through which I fall towards it is so headlong, that being thus pushed, I shall soon be at bottom, for it pleaseth God, from whom I acknowledge the punishment to be just, to accompany my other ills with so much sickness as I have no refuge but that of mercy, which I beg of him, my Lord, and you, which I hope you will not repent to have afforded me, since all my endeavours, and the whole course of my life shall be bent, to make myself worthy of your favour and her love, whose peace of conscience and quiet I know must be much wounded and violenced if your displeasure sever us. I can present nothing to your thoughts which you knew not before, but my submission, my repentance, and my hearty desire to do anything satisfactory to your just displeasure. Of which I beseech you to make a charitable use and construction.

    Yours in all faithful duty and obedience,

J. Donne

Guidance for a Married Woman

St Francis de Sales   May 3rd 1604

To a married woman

St Francis, a noted spiritual director, suggests ways of reaching due equilibrium in everyday life.

Dear Madam...,

    Since you are married, the right way for you is to live in close union with God and your neighbour and anything pertaining to them....

    There are many ways and means that help us to enjoy correct relations with our neighbour, but I shall mention only a few here. We have to see our neighbour in God who wants us to love him and show him consideration. This is what St Paul says (Eph. 6) when he tells servants to obey God in their masters and their masters in God. We have to practise this love by showing our neighbour external marks of kindness. Although it may seem very difficult at first we must not give up, for our good intentions and the habit resulting from continual repetition will finally subdue the objections of our lower nature. We must give up all our prayer and meditation time to the problem, since we have to pray first for the love of

God and then always ask for love of our neighbour, especially of any whom we find humanly objectionable.

I would advise you to make the effort to visit the hospitals occasionally. Comfort the sick, show compassion for their afflictions, show clearly that their sufferings affect you, and pray for them as well as helping them in a practical way. But, whatever you do, take care never to annoy your husband in any way, your household, or your parents with too much churchgoing, being too reclusive, or neglecting your family duties. Don't fall into the common fault of being too critical of others' behaviour, or despise conversations which do not come up to your own high standards, for in all such things we must be governed by charity, so that we willingly accept our neighbour's wishes in anything that is not against the law of God.

You must not only be suitably devotional and lead a spiritual life, but make it acceptable to everyone around you. They will certainly respect it if you make it helpful and pleasant. The sick will respect your devotion if it brings them loving comfort; your family, when they realize it makes you more attentive to their welfare, more approachable in a crisis, more tender when reproving them, and so on; your husband, when he sees you making progress in your spiritual life and as a result smiling on him more and showing your love towards him by your gentle conduct; your parents and friends, if they notice your increased generosity, loyalty and generous concession to their wishes as long as they are not contrary to God's will. In short, as far as possible, make your piety attractive.

I have written a short work on perfection in the Christian life. I enclose a copy. Take it as it is meant together with this letter. They are both the work of a heart wholly devoted to your spiritual welfare. The ardent desire of that same heart is to see the work of God perfected in your soul.

Please remember me in your prayers and communions. In return I assure you that you will always be remembered in mine.

Yours in the Lord,

Francis de Sales

Sooner or Later

St Bernard of Clairvaux

12th century

To Mar and his wife

This is a model of brevity on weighty matters and a recommendation of what was probably a desirable change of heart.

My dear Mar,

I am writing to you and to your wife that you may love each other, but not so as to prefer your mutual love to the love of Christ.

It is very certain that sooner or later you will lose whatever possessions you have, unless you send them on ahead to heaven by the hands of the poor. Come, dearest friends, lay up treasure in heaven where moth cannot corrupt and where thieves will not break in and steal, and where the leader himself cannot take anything from you. You have not to look far for those who will bear thither your treasure, for they who will faithfully do so are at your door, not one but many. God has multiplied their miseries at this time so as to give you an opportunity of laying up treasure in a place of endless joy and inviolable security. Do you, for your part, recommend the same course to T—, to my brother and your good nephew, to W—, who has married your granddaughter, and to any others who you know would listen; and I hope that especially those who are in the house of God may have the blessing of a visit from you quite soon.

Yours ever,
  Bernard

Please God Best

St Philip Howard

1595

To his wife

Philip Howard was imprisoned in the Tower for ten years for trying to leave England after an accusation of recusancy. After hearing an eloquent address by St Edmund Campion, he was reconciled to the Church, and to his wife, whom he had treated with cruelty and indifference. This moving letter has to combine a very personal apology, a final resolute statement of faith that can serve as an example to others, and factual information about a decision to kill him that he had got wind of (he is said to have been poisoned by his gaolers).

My dear,

Mine own good wife, I must now in this world take my last farewell of you, and as I know no person living whom I have so much offended as yourself, so do I account this opportunity of asking your forgiveness, as a singular benefit of Almighty God, and I most humbly and heartily beseech you even for his sake, and of your charity, to forgive me in all whereinsoever I have offended you, and the assurance thereof is a great contentment to my soul at this present, and will be a greater I doubt not when it is ready to depart out of my body. And I call God to witness it is no small grief unto me that I cannot make you recompense in this world for the wrongs I have done you; for if it had pleased God to have granted me longer life, I doubt not but you should have found me as good a husband to my poor ability by his grace, as you have found me bad heretofore. He that knows all things, knows that which is past is a nail in my conscience, and burden the greatest I feel there: my will is to make satisfaction, if my ability were able: but though I should live never so long, I could never do it further than by a good desire to do it, which while I have any spark of breath shall never be wanting.

I beseech you for the love of God to comfort yourself whatever shall happen, and to be best pleased with that, which shall please God best and be his will to send. For mine own part I find by more arguments than those I understand from you, that there is some intent (as they think who work it) to do me no good, but indeed to do me the most good of all: but I am, I thank God, and doubt not but I shall be by his grace, ready to endure the worst which flesh and blood can do against me.

    Your
    Philip

The Divorce Problem

St Jerome

c. 394

To Amandus

St Jerome's letter to a fellow-priest (presumably St Amandus of Bordeaux) has often been cited as a lucid and now classic presentation of a rigorous view of the indissolubility of Christian marriage that, as stated, would seem to exclude many more recent instances of divorce and even declarations of nullity in several branches of the Christian Church.

Dear Amandus,

In your letter you sent me a short paper which asked whether a woman whose husband was an adulterer and a sodomist, and who had left him and had been made to marry another man, could be admitted to communion with the Church while the husband from whom she was separated was still alive. Did she have to do penance for her fault?

As I read your question, I recalled those words of the psalm, "To make excuses in sins" (Ps. 140/1). We are only human and therefore lax about our own faults. We like to think that what we do of our own will is forced on us by nature. It is as if a young man were to say: "My body is too strong for me. Nature's fires are making my passions red-hot. The way I am made just demands a sexual outlet." Or as if a murderer were to excuse himself by claiming: "I was in need. I was really hungry. I hadn't anything to wear. All right, I did kill someone, but it was to save myself from freezing and starving to death." So don't pass my advice but the Apostle's to this sister who asks me what she is to do about her predicament: "You know very well, my brothers (for I am speaking to those well acquainted with the subject), that the Law can only exercise authority over a man so long as he is alive. A married woman, for example, is bound by law to her husband as long as he is alive. But if he dies, then his legal claim over her disappears. This means that, if she should give herself to another man while her husband is alive, she incurs the stigma of adultery. But if, after her husband's death, she does exactly the same thing, no one could call her an adulteress, for the legal hold over her has been dissolved by her husband's death" (Rom. 7). Elsewhere he says: "A woman is bound to her husband while he is alive, but if he dies she is free to marry whom she likes—but let her be guided by the Lord" (1 Cor. 7:39). So the Apostle dismisses all special pleading with his plain statement that a wife who remarries during her husband's lifetime commits adultery. Don't tell me about a violent man, a mother's cajoling, a father's heavy hand, or all the relatives, the deceit and insolence of servants, and losses of household goods. As long as her husband is alive, even though he is an adulterer, a homosexual, a man who has committed every crime in the book and who was divorced by his wife because of his sins, he still counts as her husband and she may not marry another man. The Apostle doesn't say this on his own authority. It is Christ speaking through him. Paul only echoes the words of Christ who tells us in the Gospel: "I say to you that whoever divorces his wife except on the ground of unfaithfulness is making her an adulteress. And whoever marries the woman who has been divorced also commits adultery" (Matt. 5:32). Notice that Christ says: "And whoever marries the woman who has been divorced also commits adultery." Whether she has separated from her husband or he has separated from her, whoever marries her is an adulterer. This explains why the apostles, as soon as they realize how burdensome matrimony is, say: "If that is a man's position with his wife, it is not worth getting married!" Our Lord replies: "Let the man who can accept what I have said accept it" (Matt. 19:10, 12), and he immediately cites the example of the three eunuchs in order to show what a blessed state virginity is, not being shackled by any ties of the flesh.

I have not been able to understand exactly what the sister means when she talks about being forced to take a husband. How was she forced? Did the man get a crowd of people together and force her against her will? If she was unfairly assaulted in this way, why didn't she repudiate her attacker afterwards? If she reads the books of Moses she will discover that if a girl engaged to be married is violently attacked inside the city and she doesn't cry out, she has to suffer the punishment of an adulteress. If she is attacked in the fields, she is absolutely without guilt and only the man who brutalized her will be found guilty. If this sister whom you quote, who says she has been forced into a second marriage, wants to receive the Body of Christ and not to be branded as an adulteress, she must do penance. At the very least from the moment when she starts a new way of life, all further marital relations with her second husband have to stop. It would be more appropriate to call him an adulterer than a husband. If she finds this difficult and cannot leave a man she has fallen in love with, if physical pleasure comes before our Lord, she must remember what the Apostle says: "You cannot drink both the cup of the Lord and the cup of devils. You cannot be a guest at the Lord's table and at the table of devils" (1 Cor. 10:21). He also says: "How can light and darkness share life together? How can there be harmony between Christ and the devil?" (2 Cor. 6:14, 15).

Therefore I beg you to comfort her and persuade her to follow the way of salvation. Any rotten flesh has to be cut away and cauterized. Not the treatment but the wound is to blame if a surgeon is merciful yet severe in sparing by not sparing, and practising cruelty for kindness sake.

Yours,
Jerome

Bitter and Sweet

St Vincent de Paul   1636

To St Louisa de Marillac

St Louisa was a extremely intelligent and happily married woman widowed in 1625. She then became St Vincent de Paul's indispensable helper in founding the Daughters of Charity (now the Sisters of Charity of St Vincent de Paul). He wrote letters on family as well as religious matters, and often the two were combined, as is clear from the following.

Dear Mademoiselle de Marillac,

May our Lord's grace be always with you.

I have never known such a woman for taking some things tragically. You tell me that your son's choice is God wreaking his justice on you. It is quite wrong to think like that and worse still to say such things. I have often begged you in the past not to talk like that. In the name of God, Mademoiselle, correct this fault and remember once and for all that bitter thoughts come from the Evil One and sweet and tender thoughts from our Lord.

You must remember, too, that children's faults are not always due to their parents, especially if they have made sure that they were duly instructed and had good examples to follow, as, thank God, has been the case with you. Anyway, our Lord, in his marvellous providence, lets children break the hearts of pious parents. Abraham's was broken by Ishmael, Isaac's by Esau. Jacob's by most of his children, David's by Absalom, Solomon's by Roboam, and the Son of God's by Judas.

I must remind you that your son told Fr de la Salle that he was entering this state of life only because you wanted him to do so, that he would rather die than do that, and that he would take minor orders to please you. Is that really a vocation? I am sure that he would rather die himself than want your own death. However that may be, whether nature or the devil is at fault here, his will is not free in its choice of so important a matter, and you ought not to want it. Some time ago, a good youth of this city entered the subdiaconate in the same frame of mind and he has been unable to go on to the other orders. Do you want to let your son in for the same danger? Let God guide him. God is his Father, more than you are his mother, and He loves him more than you do. Leave God to arrange matters, He can call him later if He wants, or give him something else to do that will save his soul. I remember a priest who was here who was ordained in a similarly anxious state of mind. God knows where he is now.

I ask you to pray remembering the case of Zebedee's wife and her children to whom our Lord said, when she wanted to settle her sons: "You do not know what you ask."

Yours sincerely,

Vincent de Paul

Join with God

John Donne   c. 1616

To his mother

Many of Donne's letters are profoundly serious, for their main purpose is often to convey certain important ideas and subtle distinctions in a setting of personal commentary and friendship that illustrates or elucidates the points made. Here he writes to Elizabeth his mother, who had remained a Catholic though Donne had entered the Church of England and was now a recently ordained priest. The letter is not only a moving attempt to comfort her on learning of his sister's death, but a serious if lovingly respectful review of the course of his mother's life from her first prosperous marriage to his father, through the death of all other children of that union, to the loss of her present husband's (Rainsford's) prosperity.

My most dear mother,

When I consider so much of your life as can fall within my memory and observation, I find it to have been a sea under a continual tempest, where one wave hath ever overtaken another. Our most wise and blessed Saviour chooseth what way it pleaseth him to conduct those which he loves to his haven and eternal rest. The way which he hath chosen for you is strait, stormy, obscure, and full of sad apparitions of death and wants and sundry discomforts; and it hath pleased him that one discomfort should still succeed and touch another, that he might leave you no leisure, by any pleasure or abundance, to stay or step out of that way, or almost to take breath in that way by which he hath determined to bring you home, which is his glorious Kingdom. One of the most certain marks and assurances that all these are his works, and to that good end, is your inward feeling and apprehension of them, and patience in them. As long as the Spirit of God distills and dews his cheerfulness upon your heart; as long as he instructs your understanding, to interpret his mercies and his judgements aright; so long your comfort must needs be as much greater than others', as our afflictions are greater than theirs.

The happiness which God afforded to your first young time, which was the love and care of my most dear and provident father, whose soul, I hope, hath long since enjoyed the sight of our blessed Saviour, and had compassion of all our miseries in this world, God removed from you quickly. And hath since taken from you all the comfort that that marriage produced. All those children (for whose maintenance his industry provided, and for whose education you were so carefully and so chargeably diligent) he hath now taken from you. All that worth which he left, God hath suffered to be gone from us all. So that God hath seemed to repent that he allowed any part of your life any earthly happiness, that he might keep your soul in continual exercise and longing and assurance of coming immediately to him.

I hope therefore, my most dear mother, that your experience of the calamities of this life, your continual acquaintance with the visitations of the Holy Ghost, which gives better inward comforts than the world can outward discomforts, your wisdom to distinguish the value of this world from the next, and your religious fear of offending your merciful God by repining of anything which he doth, will preserve you from any inordinate or dangerous sorrow for this loss of my most beloved sister.

For my part, which am only left now to do the office of a child; though the poorness of my fortune, and the greatness of my charge, hath not suffered me to express my duty towards you as became me; yet, I protest to you before Almighty God and his angels and saints in heaven, that I do, and ever shall, esteem myself to be as strongly bound to look to you and provide for your relief, as for my own poor wife and children. For, whatsoever I shall be able to do, I acknowledge to be a debt to you, from whom I had that education which must make my fortune. This I speak not, as though I feared my father Rainsford's care of you, or his means to provide for you; for he hath been with me, and, as I perceive in him a loving and industrious care to give you contentment, so I see in his business a happy and considerable forwardness.

In the meantime, good mother, take heed that no sorrow nor dejection in your heart interrupt or disappoint God's purpose in you; his purpose is to remove out of your heart all such love of this world's happiness as might put him out of possession of it. He will have you entirely. And, as God is comfort enough, so he is inheritance enough.

Join with God, and make his visitations and afflictions, as he intended them, mercies and comforts. And, for God's sake, pardon those negligences which I have heretofore used towards you; and assist me with your blessing to me and all mine; and with your prayers to our blessed Saviour, that thereby both my mind and fortune may be apt to do all my duties, especially those that belong to you.

God, whose omnipotent strength can change the nature of anything, by his raising-Spirit of comfort, make your poverty riches, your afflictions pleasure, and all the gall and wormwood of your life, honey and manna to your taste, which he hath wrought, whensoever you are willing to have it so. Which, because I cannot doubt in you, I will forbear more lines at this time, and most humbly deliver myself over to your devotions and good opinion of me, which I desire no longer to live than I may have.

Your son,

J. Donne

Weigh Yourself

St Robert Southwell   October 22nd 1589

To his father

The gentle, kindly Robert Southwell was chaplain to Anne Howard, whose husband was imprisoned for recusancy at the time of writing this letter (clearly the work of an accomplished poet), which undertakes with grace and dignity the extremely hazardous task of administering a priestly yet filial reproof and warning to a difficult parent.

My dear Father,

I am not of so unnatural a kind, of so wild an education, or so unchristian a spirit, as not to remember the root out of which I branched, or to forget my secondary maker and author of my being. It is not the carelessness of a cold affection, nor the want of a due and reverent respect that has made me such a stranger to my native home, and so backward in defraying the debt of a thankless mind, but only the iniquity of these days, that makes my presence perilous, and the discharge of my duties an occasion of danger. Nature by grace is not abolished, nor destroyed, but perfected. And if its affections be so forcible, that even in hell, where rancour and despite and all feelings of goodness are overwhelmed by malice, they moved the rich glutton by experience of his own misery, to have compassion of his kindred, how much more in the Church of God, where grace quickens, charity inflames, and nature's good inclinations are abetted by supernatural gifts, ought the like piety prevail. If the most frozen and fierce mind cannot but thaw and melt with pity even when it knows a person to suffer his or her deserved torments, how much less can the heart of a child consider those that bred him or her into this world, to be in the fall to far more bitter extremities, and not bleed with grief at their uncomfortable case? Where can the child owe so great service as to him to whom he is indebted for his very life and being? With young Tobit I have travelled far, and brought home a freight of spiritual substance to enrich you, and medicinable receipts against your ghostly maladies. I have in this general famine of all true and Christian food, with Joseph, prepared abundance of the bread of angels for the repast of your soul. And now my desire is that my drugs may cure you, and my provision feed you, by whom I have been cured and fed myself. Despise not, good sire, the youth of your son, neither deem your God measures his endowments by number of years. Hoary senses are often couched under youthful locks, and some are riper in the spring than others in the autumn of their age....

Now to come to the principal drift of my discourse. Most humbly and earnestly I am to beseech you that, both in respect of the honour of God, your duty to his Church, the comfort of your children and the redress of your own soul, you would seriously consider the terms you stand in, and weigh yourself in a Christian balance, taking for your counterpoise the judgments of God. Take heed in time that the word "Tekel," written of old against Balthazar, and interpreted by young Daniel, be not verified in you. Remember the exposition: "You have been weighed in the balance and found wanting."

Remember that you are in the balance, that the date of your pilgrimage is well nigh expired, and that it now behoves you to look forward to your country. Your strength languishes, your senses become impaired, and your body droops, and on every side the ruinous cottage of your faith and feeble flesh threatens a fall. Having so many harbingers of death to pre-admonish you of your end, how can you but prepare for so dreadful a stranger? The young may die quickly, but the old cannot live long. The prerogative of infancy is innocence; of childhood reverence; of manhood maturity, and of age wisdom; and seeing that the chief property of wisdom is to be mindful of things past, careful of things present, and provident of things to come, use now the privilege of nature's talent to the benefit of your soul. To serve the world you are now unable and, though you were able, you have little wish to do so, seeing that it never gave you but an unhappy welcome, a hurtful entertainment, and now abandons you with an unfortunate farewell. You have long sowed in field of flint, which could bring you nothing but a crop of cares and afflictions of spirit, rewarding your labours with remorse, and for your pains repaying you with eternal damages. It is now more than a seasonable time to alter your course of so unthriving a husbandry, and to enter into the fields of God's Church; in which, sowing the seed of repentant sorrow and watering it with the tears of humble contrition, you may reap a more beneficial harvest and gather the fruit of everlasting consolation. Remember, I pray you, that your spring is spent and your summer overpast; you are now arrived at the fall of the leaf, yea, the winter colours have already stained your hoary head....

Howsoever ... the soft gales of your morning pleasures lulled you in slumbers; howsoever the violent heat of noon might awake affections, yet now in the cool and calm of the evening retire to a Christian rest, and close up the day of your life with a clear sunset; that leaving all darkness behind you, and carrying in your conscience the light of grace, you may escape the horror of eternal night, and pass from the day of mortality to the Sabbath of everlasting rest.

Humbly desiring that my sincere affection may find excuse of my boldness, I here conclude.

Your son
Robert

God's Will

St Vincent de Paul   c. 1646

To a priest of the Mission

Monsieur Vincent's wide-ranging concern for the impoverished, destitute and marginalized, and his gentle yet practical concern for the members of the Order he founded, were backed by a penetrating knowledge of all sorts and conditions of people that owed much to the experiences of his "worldly" years, as is shown in this subtly balanced letter in which he offers reassurance but also very practical advice on human psychology.

Dear and Reverend Father,

I know how anxious you have been made by your father's letter asking you to help him....

Your possible motive for withdrawal is to be found in your father's need. But you have to know the circumstances, according to the casuists, that force children to leave a community. For myself, I think that it is only when parents suffer from natural causes and not from their circumstances of life, as, for example, when they are very old or when, because of some other natural problem, they cannot earn their living. Now that is not true of your father, who is only forty or forty-five at most, and is indeed working. Otherwise he would not have married again, as he did recently, and a young eighteen-year-old, one of the most beautiful girls in the city. He says so himself, so that I can give her an introduction to the Princess de Longueville whose son she wants to nurse. I think that he is not too well off. But who is not suffering under the present conditions of public misery? Moreover it is not his actual difficult circumstances that force him to recall you, for they are not really so terrible. It is merely what he is afraid of, through his lack of even a little trust in God, although he has wanted for nothing till now, and has every reason to hope that God's goodness will not desert him in the future.

Perhaps you will persuade yourself that it is by your means that God does indeed want to help him in his need, and that it is for that reason that God's providence is now presenting you with a cure of souls worth six hundred livres through the intervention of this same good man. But you will realize that this is not the case, if you merely consider two things: first, that God, having summoned you to a state of life which honours that of his Son on earth, and which is of such great use to your neighbour, cannot want just now to remove you from this state in order to send you back to care for a family which is living in the world, which is only seeking its own comfort, which will always worry you by asking for what you may or may not have, and which will weigh you down with troubles and worries, if you cannot help it to its own satisfaction and yours; and in the second place it is incredible that your father has been promised a cure to the value of six hundred livres a year for you, because those of the Bruges diocese are the poorest in the kingdom. But even if that were the case, how much would be left after taking away your maintenance?

I do not tell you this because I am afraid that you will succumb to temptation, for I know how faithful you are to God, but so that you may write once and for all to your father and tell him why you should follow the will of God, rather than his will. Believe me, his natural disposition is such as to give you very little rest when you are close to him, any more that it does now when you are so far from him. The trouble he has been giving your poor sister, who is with Mademoiselle Le Gras, is extraordinary. He wants her to leave the service of God and of his poor, as if he were to receive some great assistance from her. You know that he is naturally restless, and indeed so much so that whatever he has he finds displeasing, and whatever he does not have awakens violent desires. Finally, I think that the best you could do for him is to pray to God for him, keeping for yourself that one necessary thing, which will one day prove your reward, and which will even, on your account, bring down the blessings of God on your relations. I pray for this with all my heart.

Yours,
Vincent de Paul

Remember That He is Your Son

St Alphonsus Liguori   October 1737

To his father

Don Giuseppe de Liguori had fiercely opposed Alphonsus' decision to abandon a successful legal career for the Church. Five years before this letter the future bishop and great moral theologian had established an Order to instruct poor peasants in the faith, which was scarcely to his father's taste. He now had the task of defending his brother.

Dear Don Giuseppe,

For pity's sake be more loving to your son. He visited me this morning at Naples and burst into tears before me. He could not prevent himself from doing so because he was so very unhappy. Good heavens! Surely you do not want to make him do something quite desperate, or cause him to jump down a well, or take some equally crazy course! I must implore you not to give him such black looks at table and to help him in some way, for the poor boy is now married, cut off from Naples, and with no encouragement of any kind. Take care not to push him into anything foolish. Now that he is so sick you should show him clearly how kind you can be. Remember that he is your son and not some kind of mongrel, and surely as such far dearer to you than property or money. You may rest assured that if you are loving in your own family God will help you outside it. What are you going to do about all this? What is done is done. It has been foreseen from all eternity. Who is at fault? I pray for you to God at Mass every morning and hope that our Lady will help you. Bless me.

Your son,
Alphonsus

CHAPTER 9

Religious Life and Church Behaviour

As if I had been Crushed to Powder

St Thérèse of Lisieux   November 20th 1887

To her sister Pauline

The saint's dearest wish was to enter the Carmel of Lisieux at an early age. Her wish was granted and she spent nine years there before her death.

Dear Pauline,

God is forcing me through a great number of trials before he opens the door of Carmel. I shall tell you what happened when I went to see the Pope. If you could have looked into my heart, you would have found me very confident. I think I have done what God wanted me to do. Now there is nothing left but prayer.

The Bishop was not there. Father Révérony took his place. To get any idea of the audience you would have had to be there.

The Pope was up there on a grand chair. Father Révérony stood right by him, looking at the pilgrims as they filed past the Pope after kissing his foot, and saying things about some of them. You will imagine how madly my heart beat when I saw my turn coming, but I wasn't going to leave without talking to the Pope. I did speak to him, but I didn't say all I wanted to, because Father Révérony wouldn't give me time. He interrupted me. "Most Holy Father", he said, "this is a child who wants to enter Carmel at fifteen years of age, but her Superiors have the matter in hand at the moment...." I wanted to go into detail about it, but I didn't get a chance. All the Holy Father said to me was: "If it is God's will, you will enter Carmel." Then I had to go on, into the next room. Pauline, I can't tell you how I felt. I felt as if I had been crushed to powder. I felt quite abandoned, and also I am so far away, so far away.

As I write to you I could cry my heart out. It's fit to burst. But don't mind. God can't try me more than I can bear. He has given me the courage I need to stand this last trial. It's an enormous one, but I am the Child Jesus' little ball. If he wants to smash his toy, he can do so. Yes, I want all and everything he wants.

I haven't said everything I want. I can't write these things. I have to tell them to you myself. Anyway you won't read this letter until three days from now. Pauline, I've got no one but God.

Pray for your little girl,

Thérèsita

Your Dust, Your Brooms, Your Chaff

St Edmund Campion   February 26th 1575

To the novices at Bruenn

After he had taken his vows and had returned to the Jesuit college at Prague, the future martyr wrote a letter to his fellow-novices at Bruenn, in Austria, where he was teaching the catechism in the neighbouring villages.

My dearest Brethren,

How much I love you in the bowels of Jesus Christ, my dearest brethren, you may conclude from this, that in spite of daily occupations, which scarce leave me time to breathe, I have managed to steal time from the midst of my functions and cares to write to you. How could I do otherwise, directly I heard of a sure messenger to Bruenn? How could I help firing up with the remembrance of that house, where there are so many burning souls, fire in their mind, fire in their body, fire in their words—the fire which God came to send upon the earth, that it might always burn there? O dear walls, that once shut me in your company! Pleasant recreation-room, where we talked so holily! Glorious kitchen, where the best friends—John and Charles, the two Stephens, Sallitzi, Finnit and George, Tobias and Gaspar—fight for the saucepans in holy humility and charity unfeigned! How often do I picture to myself one returning with his load from the farm, another from the market; one sweating stalwartly and merrily under a sack of rubbish, another under some other toil! Believe me, my dearest brethren, that your dust, your brooms, your chaff, your loads, are beheld by angels with joy, and that through them they obtain more for you from God than if they saw in your hands sceptres, jewels, and purses of gold.

Would not that I knew not what I say; but yet, as I do know it, I will say it; in the wealth, honours, pleasures, pomps of the world, there is nothing but thorns and dirt. The poverty of Christ has less pinching parsimony, less meanness, than the emperor's palace. But if we speak of the spiritual food, who can doubt that one hour of this familiar intercourse with God and with good spirits, is better than all the years of kings and princes? I have been about a year in religion, in the world thirty-five; what a happy change, if I could say I had been a year in the world, in religion thirty-five! If I had never known any father but the fathers of the Society; no brothers but you and my other brothers; no business of obedience; no knowledge but Christ crucified! Would that at least I had been as happy as you, who have entered the vineyard of Christ in the morning of your lives! I almost envy Cantensis and Charles, who have been brought in so young that they can spend their childhood with the child Jesus, and can grow up with Him, and increase to the perfect strength of the fulness of Christ. Rejoice therefore, my brethren, at the good you enjoy, and at the greatness of the honour God has done you....

I thank you all most heartily for the extraordinary charity which I experienced when with you, and when away from you, by your letters and remembrances, and at my departure as I was setting off; especially I thank Melchior—and who else is it that I named before?—my dearest brother, my friendly rival, my compeer in the society, but how high above me in merits! His letters gave me and will give me the greatest pleasure; so did the things he spoke about in his two epistles. I will join with the Father Rector in drawing up a plan, and after the affair is set in order, I will write out the whole for him, before the feast of the Annunciation, I hope. Stephen the Hungarian said that he would write, but he has never written a word. With my whole heart I congratulate George and Charles, who have lately made their vows. These are strong chains, my brethren, and most strongly do they bind you to our Lord. Who shall tear you from his hands?

I thank my dearest brother Cantensis, whose letter gave me the greatest pleasure, and I thank my God who has given him so good a mind at his age. I received from him the pictures, the Agnus Dei, and the relics of our holy father Ignatius—a great treasure, for which I return great thanks. I salute you all in Christ Jesus from the bottom of my soul.

I commend myself to the prayers of you all. Farewell.

E.C.

Missionary Successes

St John Eudes
July 23rd 1659

To Jean-Jacques Blouet de Camilly

St John Eudes was an indefatigable "home missioner." Apart from overseeing similar efforts elsewhere, in June-July 1659 he conducted a forty-five days mission at Vasteville, and in the autumn another of the same length at Villedieu. During these missions he wrote a number of letters to Blouet de Camilly, a recent entrant to the Order, now studying at Paris. This one describes the work of, response to and difficulties encountered during an immense effort to instruct and "conscientize" masses of socially disadvantaged and ill-educated people .

My dearest Brother,

I cannot describe the blessings of the Lord on this mission: they are so great. I have not preached in the church for some time now, though it is very big. On Sundays we are graced with more than 15,000 persons. There are twelve confessors but fifty would not be sufficient.... We hear only the weeping and groaning of poor penitents. The fruits brought forth by the confessors are wonderful indeed. The sad thing is that we can confess only a quarter of those who desire it. We are overwhelmed. Some wait over a week for confession and cannot obtain their wish. They fall on their knees before the priests, crying and begging them to hear their confessions. We have been here in Vasteville and Villedieu for six weeks now. The missions are a great good and are necessary indeed. To put anything in their way is a great evil. If only those who have prevented us from carrying out so many missions in this diocese knew what harm they do. Father forgive them....

We should pray the Lord to send workers for the harvest. What are so many doctors and teachers doing in Paris while souls are perishing in their thousands for want of those who could stretch out a hand to save them from damnation and everlasting misery?... I should be off to Paris to shout in the Sorbonne and in the other colleges: Fire, fire, fire! The fires of hell threaten the entire world! Leave Paris doctors, bachelors, reverend Fathers, all you priests, and help to extinguish the fires of hell!

Your brother,

John Eudes

Arriving in Rome

Charles de Foucauld   November 8th 1896

To Fr Jérome

In September 1896, Charles de Foucauld, then a Trappist who had entered Our Lady of the Snows monastery in France in 1890, was sent to Rome to study theology. There he began an extensive correspondence with Fr Jérome, a novice whom he had met at a Trappist monastery in Algiers.

May Jesus always be with you, dearest Father....

I am taking advantage of Sunday to write to you, dearest Father, but I certainly have not waited for the day of rest to pray for you.

Leaving Algiers was painful for all of us yet offered an opportunity to offer a sacrifice to God, which was a good thing, and one that unites us more closely to our blessed Saviour is the greatest good and the only real good that exists—when we love, what is sweeter than to give something to the loved one, especially to give him something we hold dear, to suffer for love of him, to give him our very heart's blood. And then not only have we offered something to our Lord Jesus—our tears—but it is so wonderful that he lets us offer him these on behalf of each other, so that through our sacrifice we not only give him a sign of love but do good to those whom we love.

I intend to describe our arrival in Rome, and here I am still at the departure from Algiers. You see, it was so painful for me. But God be praised and all pain be praised!

We arrived in Rome at 1.30 on Friday afternoon. We didn't leave the train at San Paolo station near St Peter's because it wasn't really practicable, and how we praised God for that! Had we got out there we would have had to take cab after cab, and it would have been really terrible for me to enter the city like that when St Peter and St Paul entered it so poorly, so wretchedly, and St Paul in chains. As it was, we walked from the station to the Procura and on our way stopped at two churches where we knelt in adoration before the blessed Sacrament and asked that we might live here—in this city where we had just set foot—in conformity with his will, and we prayed him to bless all his children and especially those whom he has given us particularly to love: as you will guess, you were not forgotten in these two first visits to God. First we went to St Mary Major where our Lord's crib is preserved (and also, I think, St Jerome's remains) and then to the church of St Alphonsus, where there is a picture of our Lady of perpetual succour, a title that suits the blessed Virgin so well! We need her perpetual succour so much, we who are weak and stumbling! For a long time now, and particularly for the last three years, I have been under her special protection. This is how it happened. Three years ago, I had many difficulties regarding my inner life: fears, anxieties, periods of darkness. I wanted to serve God, I was afraid of offending him, I couldn't see things straight, I suffered. So I placed myself with all my heart under the protection of our Lady of perpetual succour. I implored her to guide my footsteps as she had guided those of the infant Jesus and to lead me in all things in such a way as not to offend God, but rather to be a subject of consolation for our Lord Jesus; in such a way as to console as much as I could the heart of Jesus that sees and loves us. So it was very sweet for me to stand beneath the picture of our so dear and good Mother on my very first day, in my very first hour. Need I say that I commended you to her from all that is best in my heart, and I said for you as much as for myself: "Our Lady of perpetual succour, grant me your all-powerful help and the grace always to ask for it".

The day after our arrival, Saturday, we left the Procura early and went to St Peter's. It took one and a quarter hours. On our way we passed the Colosseum, where so many martyrs have given their blood with joy and love for our Lord Jesus. How Jesus has been loved within those walls! What burning love has risen from there to heaven! How sweet it is to think that our Lord has been so loved! What are we beside those people? Yet we have hearts like them, our Lord loves us as much as them, and we can and must love him as much! How we must try to love this divine spouse of our souls! If our hearts are capable of loving passionately, and they are, let us drown in this love!

The Colosseum isn't far from where we are. I can see it from my window. It's there that St Ignatius was ground to pieces with joy for our Lord! There this happened to thousands and thousands of martyrs. How those stones speak! What a song of love still rises from there to heaven! When we went to St Peter's we saw the windows of the Holy Father's apartments.

In St Peter's, after we had adored the blessed Sacrament and prayed at St Peter's tomb (I prayed that you would follow our Lord to your last breath as Peter did and console him to your utmost during your whole life), Fr Henri said holy mass a few paces from St Peter's remains at an altar overlaying the bodies of the blessed apostles Simon and Jude: I served his mass and received God. Next day, Sunday, we continued our pilgrimage by going to the place of St Paul's martyrdom: it is marked by a pillar in a chapel a hundred yards from the monastery of the Three Fountains.

Fr Henri is well, rather exhausted by the journey and the complete change, but on the whole he's doing well and hasn't stopped. I hope you are well too, especially your soul, for what does the body matter? I cannot love you differently from how I love myself, nor desire for you anything other than what I desire for myself: to grow in virtue, to grow in the love of God, to do his will, to fulfil his desire, to love him passionately in thought, word and deed, to breathe nothing but his love and to console him as much as possible at every moment of our lives. I ask this for you with my whole heart, dearest Father, for I love you with my whole heart in the heart of our Lord Jesus.

Br Marie Albéric (Charles de Foucauld)

Today the Wind is Falling

St Edmund Campion   June 20th 1580

To his superior in the Jesuits, Everardus Mercurianus, the general

Having been sent on the English mission, the future martyr waited anxiously at St Omer, across the Channel, for news of Fr Persons, who was visiting a number of Catholic gentlemen in the counties round London. While waiting, he described his feelings in a letter to his Superior. As soon as he had finished this letter, he heard from Persons, waited four days in Calais for a good wind, and crossed over to England: "He landed on the sands, and retired behind a great rock, to fall on his knees and commend his cause and his whole coming to God, whether it might be for life or for death."

Dear Father in God,

Father Robert, with Brother George his companion, had sailed from Calais after midnight, on the day before I began writing this; the wind was very good, so we hope that he reached Dover some time yesterday morning, the sixteenth of June. He was dressed up like a soldier—such a peacock, such a swaggerer, that a man needs must have very sharp eyes to catch a glimpse of any holiness and modesty shrouded beneath such a garb, such a look, such a strut. Yet our minds cannot but misgive us when we hear all men, I will not say whispering, but crying, the news of our coming. It is a venture which only the wisdom of God can bring to good, and to his wisdom we lovingly resign ourselves.

According to orders, I have stayed behind for a time, to try, if possible, to fish some news about Father Robert's success out of the carriers, or out of certain merchants who are to come to these parts, before I sail across. If I hear anything, I will advise upon it; but in any case I will go over and take part in the fight, though I die for it. It often happens that the first rank of a conquering army is knocked over. Indeed, if our Society is to go on with this adventure, the ignorance and wickedness against which this war is declared will have to be overthrown. On the twentieth of June I mean to go to Calais: in the meantime I live in the College at St Omer, where I am dressing up myself and my companion Ralph. You may imagine the expense, especially as none of our old things can be henceforth used. As we want to disguise our persons, and to cheat the madness of this world, we are obliged to buy several little things, which seems to us altogether absurd. Our journey, these clothes, and four horses, which we must buy as soon as we reach England, may possibly square with our money; but only with the help of the Providence which multiplied the loaves in the wilderness. This, indeed, is our least difficulty, so let us have done with it. I will not yet close this letter, that I may add whatever news reaches me during these three days. For though our lot will be cast one way or other before you read this, yet I thought I ought, while I am here, to trace every particular of this great business, and the last doings, in which the rest, as yet unwritten, will hang.

There is a certain English gentleman, very knowing in matters of state, who comes often to me; he tells me that the coming of the Bishop of St Asaph is canvassed in letters and conversation. Great expectations are raised by it; for most men think that such a man, at his age, would never undertake such a task, except there was some rising on foot. I told him in the simplest manner the true cause of his coming. Still he did not cease wondering; for the episcopal name and function is in high honour in England.

Today the wind is falling, so I will make haste to the sea. I have been thoroughly well treated in St Omer College, and helped with all things needful. Indeed, in our whole journey we received incredible comfort in all the residences of our fathers. We also enjoyed the hospitality of two most illustrious cardinals, Paleotto and Borromeo, and of the Archpriest Collenis. We purposefully avoided Paris and Douai. I think we are safe, unless we are betrayed in these seaside places. I have stayed a day longer than I meant, and as I hear nothing good or bad of Father Robert, I persuade myself that he has got through safely. I pray to God every day to protect your reverence, and your assistants, and the whole Society.

Farewell,

E. Campion

Problems with Nuns

St Teresa of Avila   July 2nd 1577

To Mother Ana de San Alberto, prioress of Caravaca

St Teresa writes from Toledo to advise the Prioress on governing her house. The sister referred to was one of three girls from the generous Doña Catalina de Otalora's house, and in fact Doña Catalina's niece; she had been too depressed to take the habit when the convent was founded, but her health improved, and she did so eventually, on July 1st 1578.

Jesus be with your Reverence, my daughter....

I am not the least worried at your having to help the souls under your care to attain greater perfection, but do realize that you cannot regulate all souls by the same yard-stick. You must treat the sister to whom our Father gave the habit as though she were ill; do not trouble in the least about how perfect she is. It will be sufficient if she does what she can as well as she can, as they say, and does not offend God....

There is always a great deal to put up with, especially when one is beginning; for, until a foundation is established, we take such nuns as we can get, provided they have some money, and so can help the rest. It would be particularly fitting that you should receive this person, as it was she who began the foundation. Do what you can with her, my daughter. If she has a good soul, reflect that it is one of God's mansions....

If you are satisfied with those novices—I mean the old lady's daughters—it only remains for you to profess them: they may occasionally have bad turns, but there is no woman who does not....

It would be ridiculous to have fish brought, unless your Reverence can send for it yourself, and it would be very expensive for us to have it brought here.

With regard to the serge habits which our Father mentions, if you have not enough money to buy enough frieze habits for the sisters all at once, you should get rid of those you have, little by little, until you have none left. Sell them, and get as much for them as you can.

You should be on the best of terms with Doña Catalina de Otalora in every way. Try to please her as much as you can, for you know what you owe her and ingratitude does not look well. If she writes to any of the nuns, give them the letters, and see that they are answered.

May our Lord make you very holy....

Your Reverence's unworthy servant,

Teresa of Jesus

I Got the Coconuts

St Teresa of Avila   July 11th 1577

To Mother María de San José, Seville

St Teresa writes from Toledo with sympathy and advice about problems with postulants.

Jesus be with you, my daughter....

Take the postulant by all means: the dowry you say she can bring is not a bad one. I wish that widow had already entered. I wrote the other day telling you to take the little black girl without hesitation, and her sister too: it will do you no harm to do so. You have not told me if you got that letter also. I was sorry to hear of Garcialvarez's illness: don't forget to tell me how he is, and if the improvement in your Reverence's health continues. I got the coconuts: they are a grand sight. I shall send them to Doña Luisa. The one you sent for me is a fine specimen: our Father will be cutting it tomorrow....

God repay your Reverence for all the gifts you are sending me—you must be imagining you are a queen—and for sending the porterage money too. For pity's sake, think of yourself a little, and look after yourself, for if you do that you are doing me a kindness too. The sisters were delighted to see the coconuts, and so was I. Blessed be He who created them: they are certainly something worth seeing. I am so glad you have the heart to do these things, in spite of all your troubles: the Lord certainly knows the right people to send troubles to!

I have just been talking to our Father about that postulant of the Archbishop's: I am most displeased to see how they are importuning you and what little interest the Archbishop shows in the case. Our Father says he thinks she is a beata [*a woman living in a religious community without being a member of it, or living under a rule in her own house*] suffering from depression; experience should have warned us about people of that kind and if we take her and then have to get rid of her it will be worse than ever. See if you can have a few talks with her and find out what sort of person she is. If you see she is unsuitable for us, I think it would not be a bad idea if Father Nicolao were to have a talk with the Archbishop, and tell him how unfortunate we have been with these beatas, or perhaps you could keep the matter in suspense....

I am your Reverence's

Teresa of Jesus

The Discomfort of a Canoe

St John de Brébeuf   1636

To the French Jesuits

St John, the future martyr of North America, warns fellow-missionaries of the hardships that certainly face them among the native Americans/Canadians among whom he laboured for thirty-four years.

My dear Brothers,

You need not fear that you will find hearts full of love when you reach the Hurons. We shall welcome you with open arms, as if you were angels from paradise. Yet, though we want to do everything possible for you, we are in a situation that prevents us doing much. Even if you are quite worn out and in difficulties, all we can offer you is a poor mat or at best a skin coverlet for a bed. Moreover, the season you come in will make sure that fleas keep you awake almost all night. This minor martyrdom (not to mention mosquitoes, sandflies and similar creatures) usually lasts no less than three or four summer months.

How do you think you will pass the winter? I do not exaggerate when I say that you will spend five to six winter months in almost continual discomfort: bitter cold, smoke and the tedious behaviour of the natives. Our log cabin is a very basic affair, but it is so well put together that we have to send someone outside to find out what the weather is like. Often the smoke is so heavy, stifling and continuous, that unless you are quite used to it, for five or six days at a time you can hardly read a couple of lines of your breviary. All day long natives surround our hearth and are hardly ever absent at mealtimes. The food is not too bad. We usually find that a little corn, some smoked fish or some fruit is enough for our needs. You can find great numbers of strawberries, raspberries and blackberries, according to the season. The grapes are abundant and not so bad. Sometimes the squashes last four or five months. There are so many of them that you can have them for next to nothing.

But so far I have looked only on the bright side of things. There are Christians in almost every village, and therefore we have to go from one to the other in all seasons. We have to stay anywhere if necessary for two to three entire weeks, with all the troubles that implies. And our lives are constantly in danger. The cabin is quite flimsy and could be burned down at any moment, and the natives are inimical enough to make us constantly afraid. Some villain could set you alight or waylay you in some lonely place and split your skull. What is more, you are responsible for barren or fruitful ground on pain of your life. You are responsible for drought. If you cannot make rain, then they even threaten to kill you. Do you think, then, that we have any reason to relax?

Here there is no attraction at all in being virtuous. We live among tribes that have no idea what you are talking about when you speak about God, and whose mouths often spout the most frightful blasphemies. Sometimes you have to do without saying Mass. When you can say it, then your chapel is a tiny corner of your cabin which smoke, snow or rain will stop you from decorating—even if you can think of something to use for the purpose.

You will realize that with the natives all round you there is not much possibility of being on your own. They hardly ever leave you alone. They do not really know what speaking softly means. One difficulty I cannot go into in detail—the risk of following their impurity if God is not so firmly with you that you can resist that poison.

And then you will say: "Is that all? Do you think that all you have to say will put out the fire of my ardour? Everything you say is nothing compared with what I am ready to suffer for God's sake. If I knew anywhere in the world where there was more suffering, I would go there." Yes, dear Brothers, you must come here. You whom God has filled with this desire and light are the kind of workmen we need out here. Do not be afraid of the problems. You will find none, for the only comfort you seek is to be crucified together with the Son of God. You have learned to talk with God and with angels and saints in heaven. You will find silence sweet. You would find the food dull if the gall our Lord suffered did not make it more tasty and appetizing than the most flavoursome food in the world. Anyone who thinks of his loving Saviour taunted by cruel enemies and ascending Calvary under the weight of the Cross will find it sheer joy to shoot these rapids and climb these rocks. The discomfort of a canoe is no problem for anyone who remembers our Lord crucified. It is a consolation (I have to use words like that to satisfy you) to run the risk of being deserted by Indians while travelling, worn out by illness, or dying from hunger in the woods, and to be able to say to God: "Lord I am suffering like this since I came here to do your will." Thinking only of the God-Man who died on the cross, once again you will echo his cry to the Father: "My God, my God, why have you left me?"

Brother John

Getting Used to Strange Ways

Bd Philippine Duchesne   1822

To nuns of the Sacred Heart at home in France

In 1818 Mother Duchesne took charge of a party of five Sacred Heart nuns and conducted them to New Orleans. This was the start of immense labours which gave the Society a firm basis in North America. This letter home shows her characteristic interest in the varieties of human nature, life and environment wherever she went.

My dear Sisters,

I often want to be with you and to take advantage of your holy pursuits. Although I should prefer just to listen to you, I am sure you would say that I must talk instead, having crossed the ocean and experienced things that I should relate to you.

We are most pleased by the Osage tribe sending a deputation to Bishop du Bourg. The chief came to St Louis to ask the Bishop to visit his people. My Lord is going there next month with some traders from Missouri who say they will help him in every way possible to gain respect for his holy office. The Bishop gave the chief a crucifix which he received respectfully. Afterwards, when he went into a store in St Louis, the shopkeeper wanted to find out if the Indian valued the cross, and tried to get him to exchange it for a superb saddle, then alcohol, and finally a considerable sum in cash. The chief refused every time and said that he would never part with anything he had accepted from "the one who talks with the Author of Life."

Bishop Flaget has lost three missionaries who went back to Europe. One was the founder of the Daughters of Penitence and a saint. We have four children from Prairie de Chien, a month's travelling from here. The councils held between the Indians and the government representatives usually take place there. They cover the meeting-place with beaver skins. The most skilful Indian is the one who talks. He always begins with the words: "The Author of Life has made everything and the earth for all people to enjoy." But he ends up with a request for liquor, gunpowder and bread.

Everywhere among the Indians, even the very savage Sioux, there is affection for the "Blackrobes." One priest who has lived among them and often visits us here, says they would give him everything he needs if he were willing, but he is not anxious to be indebted to them in case they ask him for fire-water—that is, brandy. One Indian was converted in a remarkable way. He was dying and mentioned a previous sickness when he had imagined he was approaching death. He said aloud: "That was when I saw the Author of Life who told me: 'Go back, your hour has not come!' But this time I know that I shall be with the Author of Life!" A Christian Iroquois called Francis, who was present, said: "The Author of Life probably sent you back to have water poured over your head." The dying Sioux replied: "I am sure that that was exactly why I was told to return to life." Francis asked: "Shall I get a Blackrobe to pour water on you?" The Sioux said: "Go quickly. It is urgent." The priest came at once and was satisfied with the dying man's answers. He baptized him and a few minutes later he was dead. The priest gave him a solemn burial and also baptized the dead Sioux's son, who was very sick. The priest, one Father Acquaroni, is a Lazarist from Rome, and one of our most zealous friends here.

I am sending you a writing case and some slippers made by the Indians. You will see from them what the native handicrafts are like. They call visitors by animal names. For instance, the priest at St Geneviève is "Son of White Fish." One day an Iroquois from Canada who had been away from home at a place called Florissant returned and died at a time of year when travelling is out of the question. So his father hollowed out a tree trunk with one of his weapons, placed his son's body inside, and tied it to a tree. In the spring the other Indians told the father that the boy was crying out: "We must go to Florissant!" His father took the body of his son all those eighteen hundred miles and paid the priest of Florissant two hundred francs to bury it in consecrated ground.

They tell me that this country has an earth with the same qualities as soap. The natives use it as soap, in fact, washing and rubbing themselves with it and exchanging it for gunpowder, necklaces and blankets. All house-holders make their own soap from ashes which have been standing in water for some days before slow filtering. The product is mixed with oil and boiled for several days. The soap they have in the end is red and very effective. The most common grain here is Indian corn and bread is made from it. We often eat it and many Americans prefer it to bread made from wheat, which also grows here plentifully. You can get beans, pumpkins, melons and water melons. Potatoes are very popular, and come in white, red, yellow and bluish or even purple varieties. There are also sweet potatoes which taste like strawberries; they grow wild, as does a small fruit which looks rather like a lemon and tastes like one too. It is called "citron" in English. They eat the Indian corn or "maize" on the cob while it is still tender.

Your sister

Philippine

An Alaskan Mission

St Frances Xavier Cabrini   May 31st 1904

To some schoolchildren

St Frances was an extraordinary woman, who by the time of her death had founded sixty-seven houses of her Institute of the Missionary Sisters of the Sacred Heart. She established many schools and orphanages in America, where the welfare of poor immigrants was one of her main concerns. This letter shows that she had one of the essential gifts of a good teacher: an ability to arouse children's interest with striking details that convey the sense of a place or occasion.

My dear young Friends,

During my stay in Seattle I was asked to open a mission in Alaska. The natives of Alaska are supposed to have come from Lapland. I should think that it would be very interesting if the Sisters who are going there visited the ice-huts. Their system of building is very simple. They need no architects or masons. With a few planks of wood which the sea-waves, guided by the hand of God, throw in quantities on the coast of a country where there is perpetual snow and ice, these Eskimos build their roofs and walls, which are supported against the side of the mountain. Then they pour water over the huts, and this freezes at once. This operation is repeated until the walls reach a thickness that renders them inaccessible, even to icy winds. The Eskimos pass their lives in these huts, which are more like dens than houses, and they enter them by crawling through a low narrow opening.

In the summer, the sun is still shining at ten p.m., and in winter at three p.m. it is dark night. Now and then, by a mirage similar to that observed in the African desert, one sees suspended in the air an entire city, which is supposed to be the far-away city of St Petersburg. The Eskimos' manner of taking food is very strange. If you are invited by some great personage, such as the head of a tribe, you must not imagine that you are going to eat a piece of salmon or roast codfish (in which these coasts abound). In front of the head of the family you see two plates, one with the dressed meats, and the other empty. Now his work begins, and this must be very hard, for he chews all the food which is given to the guests. When this has been done, it is placed on plates and handed round accordingly. This ceremony over, all the guests eat of this well-prepared dish. The white people, however, have begun to build houses and villages there, so if any of you wish to join the Sisters who are going there, you need not live in ice-huts.

The journey from Seattle to Denver is very interesting. You pass through cities all so different from one another. In Utah I saw the lakes and mountains of salt of a transparent milk colour. But it is more interesting still to see the Indian Reserves. Though the Indians retain a few of their old habits, they are now more civilized, owing to the progress of religion, especially through the apostolate of the Jesuit Fathers. There is much to be done yet, for there are still many superstitions among them. When an Indian dies, all the friends are called to weep over the corpse, whether they want to or not. They even have to chant their grief in a more or less monotonous strain, like this: "You were very good, oh, oh, oh! You had a lovely house, ah, ah, ah!" You may imagine what the rest of the chant is like, and it continues through the dead of night. When the morning dawns, the Chief arrives, and they beg him to tell them if the dead man has gone to heaven or to hell. They hold the strange belief that while the corpse is on earth it needs nothing, but if it goes to hell it has to be provided with bread and water, as these items are not to be found in hell. If the corpse is destined for heaven, it needs nothing, so it does not return to take bread and water. Naturally, the dead man does not return for his bread and water; consequently, the tribe concludes that he has gone to heaven and makes merry over him, partaking of a great banquet.

Yours,

Frances Xavier Cabrini

Difficulties

Charles de Foucauld   November 18th 1907

To a friend

Charles de Foucauld succinctly conveys his feelings about a major dilemma of the missionary life. Together with a Brother Michael, he had left for the inhospitable Hoggar in December 1906; Brother Michael had departed in March 1907.

Dear Friend,

Does my presence do any good here? If it does not, the presence of the Blessed Sacrament most certainly does. Jesus cannot be in any place without radiating. Besides, contact with the natives familiarizes and instructs them, and gradually their prejudices and antipathies disappear. It is very slow work with very little result. Pray that I may do more good, and that better labourers than I may come to cultivate this corner of the Father's field.

In the Sahara, which is eight or ten times as big as France, and which, though it is not thickly populated, is inhabited all over, there are only ten or fifteen priests, at El-Golea and Wargla. There are difficulties of every sort on all sides. It is hard not to be saddened at the evil that reigns, and the small amount of good, the enemies of God so active, his friends so hesitating, and oneself so feeble in spite of all one's graces. Nevertheless, one must not be cast down, but look, above all that happens, to our Beloved.

    Charles de Foucauld

The Wrong Choice

St Bernard of Clairvaux   1145

To all the members of the Roman Curia

In 1145, on the death of Lucius II, Bernard Paganelli, a former monk of Clairvaux and then the Cistercian Abbot of St Anastasius near Rome (now the abbey of Tre Fontane), was elected Pope. The event allows Bernard to exercise his gift of irony to considerable effect.

Dear Lords and Reverend Fathers, Cardinals and Bishops,
    Members of the Roman Curia, your son greets you.
    May the Lord have mercy on you!
    What on earth do you think you've done? You've dragged a dead man out of the grave and stuck him back among the living, that's all that you've achieved! He had run away from crowds and worries, and you've thrown him back into the thick of them. You've made the last first. You've made a man's last stage more dangerous than his first. He was crucified to the world and you've plunged him back into it. You've made someone who had decided to look for obscurity in the Lord's house the lord of all. Why? Why did you obstruct the hopes and decisions of a poor, penitent and needy man, a mere beggar? He was getting along quite happily and you blocked his way—turned him round. He's fallen among thieves just as though he had been going down from Jerusalem instead of going up from Jericho. He had escaped the devil's clutches, the grasp of the flesh, and the world's finery, only to fall into your hands, you band of robbers. He didn't leave Pisa only to end up in Rome. Why did you make someone who couldn't endure being second-in-command of a single church, head of the entire Church?

What logic made you attack this peasant as soon as the late Pope was dead, drag him out of his hiding-place, knock his hoe from his hands, stick him on the throne, dress him in fine linen and purple, and give him a sword to wreak vengeance on pagans, curb nations, enchain monarchs, and put princes in leg-irons?

Was there no wise and experienced man among you better suited for these things? It is surely ridiculous to take a man in rags and make him preside over princes, command bishops, and dispose of kingdoms and empires. Ridiculous or miraculous? Either one or the other. I have no doubt that this could be the work of God "who does wonderful things as none else," especially when I hear everyone say that it has been done by the Lord. I have not forgotten the judgments of God in times gone by or what the Scriptures tell us of many men taken from a private and even a rustic life by the will of God, to rule over his people. To mention only one, did he not choose David in rather the same way to be his servant and "take him away from herding sheep, and bid him leave off following the ewes that were in milk"?

And yet I am not happy in my own mind, for his nature is delicate, and his tender diffidence is more accustomed to leisure than to dealing in great affairs. I fear he may not exercise his apostolate with sufficient firmness. What do you think will be the feelings of a man who from the secrets of contemplation and the sweet solitude of his heart, suddenly finds himself snatched from his mother's arms, like a sheep being led to sacrifice and discovering itself in unfamiliar and unwelcome surroundings? Unless the Lord support him with his hand, he must necessarily be overcome and crushed under such an excessive and unaccustomed load, formidable even for a giant, even for the very angels themselves. Nevertheless, because it has been done, and many are saying it has been done by the Lord, it must be your concern, dearest friends, to help and comfort with your fervent support what is clearly the work of your hands. If you have in you any power to console, if there is in you any charity from the Lord, if you have any pity, any compassion, support him in the work to which he has been lifted up by the Lord through you. Whatever things are true, whatever things are seemly, whatever things are of good fame, suggest them to him, persuade him of them, encourage him to do them, and the God of peace will be with you.

Bernard

Going to Trent

St Ignatius Loyola   1546

To two theologians

The founder of the Society of Jesus offers sound advice to anyone attending a conference, together with special recommendations proper to theologians at so momentous a Council as that of Trent, the decisive occasion initiating what has come to be known as the Counter-Reformation.

Dear fellow-Jesuits,

My advice to you is to think hard before saying anything and to do so in a friendly way, especially if a decision is pending on some matter that is up before the Council for consideration or to be discussed by it afterwards. Instead you should reap advantage by listening silently, so that you can assess the speakers' attitudes, feelings and intentions, which should enable you to answer more effectively in your turn, or to keep your peace. When speaking on controversial questions, you should set forth the reasons on both sides so that there is no suspicion of prejudice, and never give anyone an excuse for complaint. Do not cite any authors in your first speech, especially if they are really important, unless you have gone into the question thoroughly beforehand. Remain friendly with everyone and shun favouritism. If the questions discussed are so clearly right and just that you cannot and should not remain silent, offer your opinion with all the composure and humility of which you are capable, and conclude with "*salvo meliori iudicio*" [without offence to better judgment]. Finally, if you want to enter a discussion on a topic such as acquired or infused qualities, it would be better not to think of your own leisure or to hurry because time is short; in other words, don't take your own convenience into account in any way but consider instead the convenience and condition of the individual with whom you are trying to deal, so that you can influence him to the greater glory of God.

Those of our fathers who go to Trent will most effectively promote God's glory among souls by preaching, hearing confessions, lecturing, teaching children, giving a good example, visiting the poor in the hospitals and exhorting their neighbours. When doing these works each father should try according to his special talent to encourage the spirit of prayer and devotion as much as possible, so that everyone begs God mercifully to pour out his Holy Spirit on those taken up with the affairs of the Council. In preaching I would not raise matters of controversy between Protestants and Catholics, but merely exhort people to lead a good life and practise the

Church's devotions. I would stir them to obtain knowledge of their own hearts and a greater awareness and love of their Creator and Lord, appealing to the intellect. When hearing confessions, I would talk to my penitents in words that they could repeat afterwards publicly, and give them as penance some prayers for the Council. When giving the Spiritual Exercises some prayers for the Council should also be recommended. Children should be taught when the opportunity arises, bearing in mind the readiness and attitudes of both master and pupil. It is appropriate to start at the beginning and to develop subjects in a greater or less degree according to the students' abilities, and the lesson or exhortation should be followed by prayers for the Council. The hospitals should be visited at the times of day that are most conducive to health, and you should hear the confessions of the poor, comfort them and take them little presents whenever possible, not forgetting prayers for the Council.

Yours,
   Ignatius Loyola

Problems for Priests

St John Chrysostom   386

To a friend

The "golden-tongued" former lawyer Chrysostom became an even more skilled preacher. The quality of his oratory, evident in his surviving sermons, is echoed in the argument and style of this highly eloquent letter of advice, which draws on classical models but uses vivid imagery to emphasize its main point with verve and immediacy.

My dear Basil,

   . . .

   A priest has to be much more virtuous than a monk, and all the more so because the priest is necessarily exposed to influences which must soil him unless he stops them affecting his soul by remaining ever alert and by firm resolution. It is a fact that delicate features, graceful movement, a set stance, a soft voice, cosmetics used skilfully on eyes and skin, a lot of well tinted hair, good clothes, plenty of gold and shining jewels can ruin a man's passions, unless he has taught himself fierce self-discipline.

   It is not astonishing if this kind of thing is upsetting, but it is more astonishing, quite incredible indeed, that the devil's malice can reach his soul and ruin it by exactly opposite means. Yet some people have avoided the one trap only to be caught in a quite different one. A loose slut with filthy hair and a slouching gait, dressed in filthy rags, friendless and abandoned by everyone, has begun by awakening a man's pity and ended by taking him down with her to utter perdition.

If, then, riches and want, decoration and neglect, elegance and loutishness, in short, everything I have already described, cause a conflict in the heart of the man who encounters them and entrap him on every side, how can he possibly find peace of mind in the midst of so many attacks? Where can he find a place to rest—I shan't say to avoid giving into violence, because that isn't too difficult—but to defend his soul from the relentless effect of impure thoughts?

I shall not stop here to say anything about the compliments paid to priests. They can cause unbelievable trouble. Those from women can be disastrous. As for tributes from men, unless a priest keeps his feet on the ground, they may pull him in two contrary directions: towards servile praise or towards ridiculous self-conceit. He has to bow to the flatterers, their praise turns his head, and straightaway he assumes a high and mighty attitude to everyone lower than him in rank, and is thus dragged down into the bog of arrogant pride. I shall say no more on the subject. Only long experience enables one really to appreciate the vast extent of the evil involved....

Yours ever,

John

I Sent Him Some Trout

St Robert Bellarmine   March 7th 1603

To Cardinal Antoniano

Bellarmine was a great controversialist, who even disputed learnedly with King James VI/I of Scotland and England. This superb report shows that much experience had buttressed his intellectual profundity with a light-hearted subtlety that enabled him to respond to less quick-witted though pompous clerics with an appropriate mixture of due correction and amused kindness.

My Lord Cardinal,

In a sermon my preacher exalted priests to such an extent that he made them out to be greater and more dignified than our Lady, than Christ, and than God himself. He offered very wonderful proofs of this. He said that a priest blessed the consecrated Host in which Christ resides, but that he whose dignity was less was blessed by him whose dignity was greater, and therefore that a priest was greater than Christ. Again, God created creatures but a priest created God himself, and therefore a priest was greater than God, and if he was greater than Christ and God, he must be very much greater than our Lady!

I was very afraid indeed that I would have to stop him preaching after this venture, but when I pointed out in my room what impossible nonsense he had been talking, he edified me with his humility and obedience, and said he was prepared to do whatever I asked of him. Therefore I told him that, on the next day, he was to enter the pulpit and say that the things he had claimed in his sermon were rhetorical exaggerations. He did exactly what I asked and I took the opportunity to reprove him effectively but in a brotherly fashion, reminding him of the rule of St Francis about simplicity in preaching. Then, to sweeten his medicine, I sent him some trout.

Yours,
   Robert Bellarmine

Set Yourself to Learn

St Bernard of Clairvaux   12th century

To the intruded archbishop of Tours

Two parties in the chapter of the See of Tours, France, elected rival candidates to the vacant see. One of them, a young monk called Philip, was chosen quite uncanonically, and removed himself from Tours along with the cathedral treasure. St Bernard was asked by Pope Innocent to inquire into the matter. He annulled Philip's election with the Pope's approval. Philip went to Rome to have his election ratified by the anti-pope Anacletus, returned to Tours and fled the city once again. Eventually he repented, joined the monastery at Clairvaux and was Prior at the time of Bernard's death. This letter was written to the false bishop before the invalid ratification.

My dear Philip,
   You are causing me great sorrow. I beg you not to mock at my grief, because, if you do not see why I should grieve for you, then there is all the more reason why I should do so. Whatever you think of yourself, I think that your condition calls for a whole fount of tears. My grief is no matter

for mockery, but for sympathy. My sorrow has no mere human causes, it is not occasioned by the loss of any fleeting chattels, but by you, Philip. I cannot better describe how great is the cause of my sorrow than by saying Philip is the cause of it. When I have said this I have declared what is a great source of distress for the Church, who once cherished you in her bosom when you were growing like a lily, and blossoming with every heavenly gift. Who would not have said then that you were a youth of fair hopes, a young man with great gifts. But alas! how your blossom has faded. From what great hopes has France fallen who gave you birth and nourished you! If you did but know, even you! If you set yourself to learn, you soon will know grounds for grief; and then in your grief, my grief will bear fruit. I would say more were I to follow my inclination, but I do not wish to say much while I am still uncertain, lest I be like one beating the air. I have written this, so that you should know how greatly I care for you, and that I am always at hand if God should inspire you with the wish to talk to me and afford me the pleasure of your company. I am at Viterbo and you, I hear, are in Rome. Be so good, I pray you, to answer this letter and tell me how it strikes you, so that I may know what to do, whether I should grieve more or less for you. And if you scorn everything I have said and refuse to hear me, I will not lose the fruit of this letter, for it proceeds from charity, but you will have to answer for your contempt before that fearful tribunal.

Yours,
 Bernard

Correcting Luther

Erasmus   November 1519

To the cardinal archbishop and elector of Mainz

Erasmus was well known for his dislike of fanaticism and obscurantism, and abhorred cheap attacks on the biblical commentator, theologian and reformer Martin Luther, instead of dignified argument based on "sound learning." In March 1519 Luther had written to the Catholic thinker and humanist to record his understanding "that my notions [in regard to indulgences] have not only been seen but have also been accepted by you" and that he was "compelled to acknowledge, even though in barbarous style, your noble spirit, which enriches me and all men." Erasmus replied praising Luther's commentaries on the Psalms, but saying in regard to major works: "I neither sanction nor condemn anything you have said." He detected the real root of the problem as the attack of inadequate controversialists and fanatical friars on (Luther's) "sound learning," "for which they cherish the most deadly hatred because they are afraid it will cloud the majesty of their divinity, which many of them prize before Christianity." In May Erasmus wrote to Pope Leo X, enclosing with a copy of a new edition of his New Testament a letter which stated: "I have no acquaintance with Luther, nor have I ever read his books beyond perhaps ten or twelve pages and that only by snatches. From what I then saw, I judged him to be well qualified to expound the Scriptures in the manner of the Fathers, a work greatly needed in an age like this which is greatly given to subleties to the neglect of really important questions. Accordingly, I have favoured his good, not his bad qualities, or rather, I have favoured Christ's glory in him." In the letter of November 1519 reproduced below, Erasmus addresses the "source" of Luther's attack on the sale of Indulgences, for it was the Cardinal-Archbishop's dire need for cash that had started the Indulgence-salesman Tetzel on his rounds and provoked the controversy. The Cardinal had already presented Erasmus with a gold cup in an attempt to win the eminent thinker's friendship. Erasmus was not slow to tell the Cardinal that he blamed all those who "are angry that languages and literature flourish ... and the world is returning to the very fountains of truth. They are trembling for their money-boxes!" Erasmus never changed his views on unworthy attitudes to scholarly discourse, though in later years he engaged in major exchanges with Luther on such fundamental topics as free-will and the nature of God, eventually provoking Luther (though only in conversation with others) to declare that Erasmus was an "enraged viper ... the vainest creature in the world ... to this barefaced scoundrel, God is merely funny."

My Lord Archbishop,

I am neither Luther's accuser, nor advocate, nor judge. His heart I would not presume to judge, for that is always a matter of extreme difficulty, still less would I condemn him. And yet if I were to condemn him, as a good man, which even his enemies admit him to be; as one put upon his trial, a duty which the laws permit even to sworn judges; as one persecuted, which would be only in accordance with the dictates of humanity, and trampled on by the bounden enemies of learning, who merely use him as a handle for the accomplishment of their designs, where would be the blame, so long as I abstained from mixing myself up with his cause? In short, I think it is my duty as a Christian to support Luther in this sense, that if he is innocent, I should not wish him to be crushed by a set of malignant villains; if he is in error I would rather see him put right than destroyed; for thus I should be acting in accordance with the example of Christ, who, as the prophet witnesses, quenches not the smoking flax, nor breaks the bruised reed. I should wish that a mind in which some sparks of evangelical doctrine seem to have fallen should not be extinguished, but be corrected and taught to preach the glory of Christ. As it is, certain divines with whom I am acquainted neither warn Luther nor teach him; they merely traduce him before the people with insane clamours and tear him to pieces with virulent abuse, while they have not a word on their lips save "heresy," "heretics," "heresiarchs," "schism" and "Anti-Christ."

Erasmus

In Defence of Erasmus

St Thomas More   c. 1520

To an anonymous monk

The recipient of this letter from St Thomas (who had considered entering the Charterhouse as a contemplative) was possibly John Batmanson, later Prior of the London Charterhouse. He had expressed his concern at the danger of More's interest in Erasmus leading him to adopt false doctrines and to accept that the early Fathers of the Church had made mistakes. He had also stated his dislike of Erasmus' attacks on monks and friars, and accused him of wasting time as a wandering scholar.

Reverend Father ...

Do you deny that [the early Fathers] ever made mistakes? I put it to you— when Augustine thought that Jerome has mistranslated a passage, and Jerome defended what he had done, was not one of the two mistaken? When Augustine asserted that the Septuagint is to be taken as an indubitably faithful translation, and Jerome denied it, was not one of the two mistaken?

Into what factions, into how many sects, are [monks and friars] divided! Then what tumults, what tragedies arise about little differences in the colour or mode of girding the monastic habit, or some matter of ceremony which, if not altogether despicable, is at all events not so important as to warrant the banishing of all charity. They make more of things that appertain especially to the religious orders than of those very humble things that are in no way peculiar to them but shared by all Christian people, such as the common virtues—faith, hope, charity, the fear of God, humility, and others of the kind. From reflections such as these you may learn the lesson that you should not grow proud of your own order, nothing could be more fatal, nor trust in private observances, and that you should place your hopes rather in the Christian faith than in your own, and not trust in those things that you can do for yourself, but in those that you cannot do without God's help.

I have no doubt that there is no good man to be found anywhere to whom all religious orders are not extremely dear and cherished. Not only have I ever loved them, but intensely venerated them; for I have been wont to honour the poorest person commended by his virtue more than one who is merely ennobled by his riches or illustrious by his birth. I desire, indeed, all men to honour you and your orders, and to regard you with the deepest charity, for your merits deserve it, and I know that by your prayers the misery of the world itself is somewhat diminished. If the assiduous prayer of the just man is of much value, what must be that of the unwearied prayers of so many thousands? Yet, on the other hand, I would wish that you should not with a false zeal be so partial to yourselves, that if anyone ventures to touch on what regards you, you should try, by your way of relating it, to give an evil turn to what he has said well, or that what he at least intended well, you should misinterpret and pervert.

If one looks at [Erasmus'] hard work, he sometimes does more work in one day than your people do in several months. If one judges the value of his work, he sometimes has done more for the whole Church in one month than you have in several years, unless you suppose that anybody's fasting and pious prayers have as deep and wide influence as his brilliant works, which are educating the entire world as to the meaning of true holiness; or unless you suppose he is enjoying himself as he defies stormy seas and savage skies and all the scourges of land travel, provided it furthers the common cause. Possibly, it is not a pleasant experience to endure seasickness and the tortures of tossing waves and the threat of a deadly storm, and to stare at the ever-present menace of a shipwreck. Possibly, it is not a keen delight to plod along through dense forests and wild woodland, over rugged hilltops and steep mountains, along roads beset by bandits, or to be battered by the winds, spattered with mud, drenched by rains, weary of travelling, exhausted from hardships, and then to receive a shabby welcome and be refused the sort of food and bed you yourself are enjoying; and especially since all these many, many troubles, which would soon tire a healthy, sturdy young man, must be encountered and endured with a poor body that is growing old and has lost its strength from hard study and toil.... On these trips, which are the target of your criticisms, he spends his time only with those men approved for learning and goodness, and as a result, his mind is ever nurturing some unborn idea, which eventually will be brought forth to the general profit of scholarship.

Farewell, and if you do not wish to be cloistered in vain, give yourself to the life of the spirit rather than to these squabbles.

T. More

Jesuit Guile

Blaise Pascal   March 20th 1656

Letter to a provincial on the policy of the Jesuits
in establishing a new morality

This is the substance of Letter No. 5 in Pascal's superbly ironic attack on casuistry and other practices inimical to Christianity which he attributed to the Jesuits.

Sir,

You must realize that the intention of the Jesuits is not the corruption of morals. No, indeed, that is certainly not what they are about. Nor do they seek only to reform those same morals. Truly, they would think that a very bad policy indeed. They want something different. Their opinion of themselves is so high that they believe it is useful and even necessary for the well-being of religion that their credit should be extended everywhere, and that they should direct the consciences of all humankind. They are aware, of course, that strict evangelical precepts are necessary to control certain individuals, and they duly apply them wherever they seem fitting. But the way of the world is that most people are not inclined to accept those same precepts, and in such cases our Jesuits overlook them, and act to please everyone. Consequently, since they encounter all sorts and conditions of human being, from very different countries, they have to employ casuists of various types appropriate to the range of human personalities they meet with.

Accordingly, as you must see, if they only had slack casuists, they would foil their own main plan, which is to cover absolutely everyone, for really pious people are determined to behave more rigorously than the mass. Yet, to be sure, such individuals are few and far between, so only a few strict directors are needed to supervise their consciences. The Jesuits have only a few rigorous priests for the few rigorous people there are around. Then the vast number of accommodating casuists can serve the mass of those who need accommodation.

This *obliging and helpful conduct*, as Father Petsu calls it, enables our Jesuits to approach any kind of person. For, if someone comes to them who is intent on making restitution of ill-gotten gains, you may have no fear of their turning him or her away. On the contrary, they will praise such individuals, and confirm them in their holy resolve. But if another one comes along who wants absolution without the inconvenience of restitution, things will be difficult if they do not offer some expedient means of reconciliation that they can also vouch for as the real thing.

In this way they keep all their friends, and defend themselves against all their enemies. If anyone accuses them of extreme negligence, they immediately show the public their austere directors of souls, along with a few books they have written on the strictness of Christian faith; and boobies and those who cannot be bothered to look into the subtleties of things are happy with such proofs.

So they get along with all sorts of people, and answer so well whatever is asked of them, that when they find themselves in countries where the notion of a crucified God seems sheer insanity, they suppress the scandal of the cross and preach only the glorified Christ, and not the suffering Jesus. This was what they did in India and China, where they even allowed Christians to practise idolatry, by recourse to the subtle pretence of getting them to stow beneath their clothes an image of Jesus to which they taught them to direct mentally the worship which publicly they were offering to the idol Cachincoam and to their Keum-fucum, as Gravina the Dominican says of them.

This tendency went so far that the Cardinals of the congregation *Propaganda fide* had to take special measures to forbid the Jesuits, under pain of excommunication, to allow the adoration of idols on any pretext, or to conceal the mystery of the cross from those receiving instruction in religion from them. Furthermore, they were expressly ordered not to accept anyone for baptism unless he or she had that knowledge, and they were expressly ordered to expose the image of Christ crucified in their churches, as is fully laid down in the decrees of the same congregation of July 9th 1646, signed by Cardinal Caponi.

In this way they have spread about the globe, fostering the *doctrine of probabilism*, which is the source and basis of all this disarray. This you must know of them. They hide neither that nor all you have just learnt from anyone, with this single difference, that they conceal their human and tactical prudence under a pretence of divine and Christian prudence; as if faith and the tradition that supports it were not always one and invariable at all times and in all places; as if the law had to relax in order to accommodate the individual who ought to conform to it; and as if all souls had to do to cleanse themselves of their faults, was to alter the law of our heavenly Father, whereas it is the law of the Lord, without stain and all holy, that should change souls and make them conform to its saving precepts!

Go, therefore, and look at those good fathers, and I am sure that you will conclude that their lax notion of morality is the fundamental reason for their doctrine of grace. You will find Christian virtues unrecognizable and devoid of that very love that is their soul and life. You will see a multitude of crimes watered down, and so many errors permitted that you will not find it any more odd when they declare that all people always have sufficient grace to live pious lives as they understand them. Since their morality is wholly pagan, basic human nature is all that is needed to conform to it.

But the separation of the soul from love of the world, the withdrawal of the soul from what it likes best, in order to make it die to itself, to take it and make it cling only and always to God, is the work only of an almighty hand. And it is just as reasonable to suppose that one is always in control, as it would be to deny that these virtues, devoid of divine love, which the good fathers confuse with Christian virtues, are not wholly within our own power.

I am, Sir, your humble and devoted servant,

Blaise Pascal

Evils Resulting from the Disuse of Confession

John Keble   18—

To a friend

One of the principal features of the Tractarian movement in the Church of England was its advocacy of a stronger sacramental life in the church. Keble met with much criticism for his resolute encouragement of the practice of regular confession to a trusted spiritual director.

My dear Friend,

Another reason for my being a worse correspondent than usual is that somehow or other the Parish takes up more and more time; as one gets more acquainted with the people, more and more things occur which make me think a visit worthwhile. This is a reason for which I ought to be very thankful, though it is sad to think, after all, how very little one knows of one's people. We go on working in the dark, and in the dark it will be, until the rule of systematic Confession is revived in our Church.

This is one of the things which make persons like Mr Gladstone, however competent in most respects, yet on the whole incompetent judges of the real working of our English system. They do not, they cannot, unless they were tried as we are, form an adequate notion, how absolutely we are in our parishes like people whose lantern has blown out, and who are feeling their way, and continually stepping in puddles and splotches of mud, which they think are dry stones.

Then the tradition which goes by the name of Justification by Faith, and which in reality means that one who has sinned, and is sorry for it, is as if he had not sinned, blights and benumbs one in every limb, in trying to make people aware of their real state.

These are the sort of things, and not the want of handsome Churches, and respect for Church Authority, and such like comparatively external points, which make me feel at times so disheartened about our system altogether, and cause a suspicion, against one's will, that the life is gone or going out of it.

And this is why I so deprecate the word and the idea of Protestantism, because it seems inseparable to me from "Every man his own absolver;" that is, in other words, the same as "Peace where there is no peace," and mere shadows of Repentance.

Yours,

John Keble

An Aggressive and Insolent Faction

John Henry Newman   January 28th 1870

To Bishop Ullathorne

Before and during the first Vatican Council, Newman had good reason to feel that the extreme supporters of the rumoured definition of Papal Infallibility were using language that, in his biographer Wilfrid Ward's words, "foreshadowed some such definition as could seem called for only to satisfy [an] extravagant devotional feeling towards the Papacy." Newman expressed his dismay in a private letter to the sympathetic Ullathorne, the contents of which some unknown enemy leaked to the Standard *newspaper, which published them in March. The letter was circulated and republished in Rome and elsewhere, and eventually after some controversy about the precise original wording, Newman was compelled to acknowledge and publish the complete text, comforting himself with the thought that it might still help in some small way to avert an undesirable result.*

My dear Lord,

I thank your Lordship very heartily for your most interesting and seasonable letter. Such letters (if they could be circulated) would do much to reassure the many minds which are at present disturbed when they look towards Rome. Rome ought to be a name to lighten the heart at all times, and a Council's proper office is, when some great heresy or other evil impends, to inspire the faithful with hope and confidence. But now we have the greatest meeting which has ever been, and that in Rome, infusing into us by the accredited organs of Rome (such as the *Civiltà*, the *Armonia*, the *Univers*, and the *Tablet*) little else than fear and dismay. Where we are all at rest and have no doubts, and, at least practically, not to say doctrinally, hold the Holy Father to be infallible, suddenly there is thunder in the clear sky, and we are told to prepare for something, we know not what, to try our faith, we know not how. No impending danger is to be averted, but a great difficulty is to be created. Is this the proper work for an Ecumenical Council? As to myself personally, please God, I do not expect any trial at all, but I cannot help suffering with the various souls that are suffering. I look with anxiety at the prospect of having to defend decisions which may not be difficult to my private judgement, but may be most difficult to defend logically in the face of historical facts. What have we done to be treated as the Faithful never were treated before? When has definition of doctrine *de fide* been a luxury of devotion and not a stern painful necessity? Why should an aggressive and insolent faction be allowed to make the hearts of the just to mourn whom the Lord hath not made sorrowful? Why can't we be left alone when we have pursued peace and thought no evil? I assure you, my dear Lord, some of the truest minds are driven one way and another, and do not know where to rest their feet; one day determining to give up all theology as a bad job and recklessly to believe henceforth almost that the Pope is impeccable; at another tempted to believe all the worst that a book like Janus says; at another doubting about the capacity possessed by Bishops drawn from all corners of the earth to judge what is fitting for European society, and then again angry with the Holy See for listening to the flattery of a clique of Jesuits, Redemptorists and Converts. Then again think of the score of Pontifical scandals in the history of eighteen centuries which have partly been poured out, and partly are still to come out. What Murphy inflicted on us in one way, M. Veuillot is indirectly bringing on us in another. And then again the blight which is falling on the multitude of Anglican ritualists, who themselves perhaps, or at least their leaders, may never become Catholics, but who are leavening the various English parties and denominations (far beyond their own range) with principles and sentiments tending towards their ultimate adoption into the Catholic Church.

With these thoughts before me I am continually asking myself whether I ought not to make my feelings public; but all I do is to pray those great early Doctors of the Church, whose intercession would decide the matter,—Augustine and the rest,—to avert so great a calamity. If it is God's Will that the Pope's Infallibility should be defined, then it is His Blessed Will to throw back the times and the moments of that triumph He has designed for His Kingdom; and I shall feel I have but to bow my head to His Adorable Inscrutable Providence. You have not touched on the subject yourself, but I think you will allow me to express to you feelings which for the most part I keep to myself....

John H. Newman

Tyrannousness and Cruelty

John Henry Newman   March 20th 1870

To the bishop of Kerry

Dr Moriarty of Kerry actively opposed the definition of Papal Infallibility. Newman made his sentiments clear to him as he had done to Bishop Ullathorne.

My dear Lord,

I am continually thinking of you and your cause. I look upon you as the special band of confessors, who are doing God's work at this time in a grave crisis; who, I trust, will succeed in your effort, but who cannot really fail— both because you are at the very least diminishing the nature and weight of the blow which is intended by those whom you oppose, and also because your resistance must bear fruit afterwards, even though it fails at the moment. If it be God's will that some definition in favour of the Pope's infallibility is passed, I should then at once submit—but up to that moment I shall pray most heartily and earnestly against it. Anyhow, I cannot bear to think of the tyrannousness and cruelty of its advocates— for tyrannousness and cruelty it will be, though it is successful....

I don't give up hope, till the very end, the bitter end; and am always praying about it to the great doctors of the Church. Anyhow we shall owe you and others a great debt.

My dear Lord, ever yours affectionately in Christ,

John H. Newman

Deposit of Faith

John Henry Newman   March 1871

To Mrs Froude

Newman's correspondence after the first Vatican Council shows him continually engaged in satisfying inquirers with intellectually responsible re-statements and explanations of the definition of Papal Infallibility.

Dear Mrs Froude,

As to your friend's question, certainly the Pope is not infallible beyond the Deposit of Faith originally given—though there is a party of Catholics who, I suppose to frighten away converts, wish to make out that he is giving forth infallible utterances every day. That the Immaculate Conception was in the *depositum* seems to me clear, as soon as it is understood what the doctrine is....

I have no hesitation in saying that, to all appearance, Pius IX wished to say a great deal more (that is that the Council should say a great deal more) than it did, but a greater Power hindered it. A Pope is not inspired; he has not an inherent gift of divine knowledge. When he speaks *ex cathedra*, he may say little or much, but he is simply protected from saying what is untrue....

Yours etc.

John H.Newman

A Christian Country?

John Wesley   1746

To Rev. Thomas Church, Vicar of Battersea, Prebendary of St Paul's

In public controversy and in two long letters, Church had not only defended the Establishment, ecclesiastical and political, but had been fiercely critical and contemptuous of the principles and practice of Methodism. His second letter had attacked Wesley's "Journal" and "Further Papers." Wesley now composed a long letter headed "Principles of a Methodist Further Explained" in which he sought to show the profound connection between his understanding of the social condition of England and its need for spiritual regeneration, while pointing out with dignity but relentless accuracy the culpable darkness of mind of people like Church, whose prejudice and blindness to social misery justified neglect and exacerbated the physical and thus the religious impoverishment of the masses. This extract shows Wesley not only as informed critic and prophet but as one whose compassion and conviction in Jesus Christ allow him to speak as a reproving father in God to a pillar of the Established Church.

Reverend Sir,

Oh that it were possible for you to consider calmly, whether the success of the gospel of Jesus Christ, even as it is preached by us, the least of his servants, be not itself a miracle, never to be forgotten;—one which cannot be denied, as being visible at this day, not in one but an hundred places; one which cannot be accounted for by the ordinary course of any natural cause whatsoever; one which cannot be ascribed with any colour of reason to diabolical agency; and, lastly, one which will bear the infallible test— the trial of the written Word!

But here I am aware of abundance of objections. You object, That to speak anything of myself, of what I have done, or am doing now, is mere boasting and vanity. This charge you frequently repeat. So: "The following page is full of boasting." "You boast very much of the numbers you have converted"; and again, "As to myself, I hope I shall never be led to imitate you in boasting." I think, therefore, it is needful, once for all, to examine this charge thoroughly, and to show distinctly what that good thing is which you disguise under this bad name.

From the year 1725 to 1729 I preached much, but saw no fruit of my labour. Indeed, it could not be that I should: for I neither laid the foundation of repentance nor of believing the gospel; taking it for granted that all to whom I preached were believers and that many of them "needed no repentance." From the year 1729 to 1734, laying a deeper foundation of repentance, I saw a little fruit. But it was only a little; and no wonder: for I did not preach faith in the blood of the covenant. From 1734 to 1738, speaking more of faith in Christ, I saw more fruit of my preaching and visiting from house to house than ever I had done before; though I know not if any of those who were outwardly reformed were inwardly and thoroughly converted to God. From 1738 to this time,—speaking continually of Jesus Christ; laying him only for the foundation of the whole building, making him all in all, the first and the last; preaching only on this plan, "The kingdom of God is at hand; repent ye, and believe the gospel,"—the "word of God ran" as fire among the stubble; it "was glorified" more and more; multitudes crying out, "What must we do to be saved?" and afterwards witnessing, "By grace we are saved through faith." I considered deeply with myself what I ought to do—whether to declare the things I had seen or not. I consulted the most serious friends I had. They all agreed I ought to declare them; that the work itself was of such a kind as ought in no wise to be concealed; and, indeed, that the unusual circumstances now attending it made it impossible that it should. This very difficulty occurred: "Will not my speaking of this be boasting? At least, will it not be accounted so?" They replied: "If you speak of it as your own work, it will be vanity and boasting all over; but if you ascribe it wholly to God, if you give him all the praise, it will not. And if, after this, some will account it so still, you must be content and bear the burden." I yielded, and transcribed my papers for the press; only labouring as far as possible to "render unto God the things which are God's," to give him the praise of his own work.

But this very thing you improve into a fresh objection. If I ascribe anything to God, it is enthusiasm. If I do not (or if I do), it is vanity and boasting, supposing me to mention it at all. What, then, can I do to escape your censure? "Why, be silent; say nothing at all." I cannot, I dare not. Were I thus to please men, I could not be the servant of Christ.

You do not appear to have the least idea or conception of what is in the heart of one whom it pleases him that worketh all in all to employ in a work of this kind. He is in no wise forward to be at all employed therein: he starts back, again and again; not only because he readily foresees what shame, care, sorrow, reproach, what loss of friends, and of that the world accounts dear, will inevitably follow; but much more because he (in some measure) knows himself. This chiefly is it which constrains him to cry out (and that many times in the bitterness of his soul, when no human eye seeth him), "O Lord, send whom thou wilt send, only send not me! What am I? A worm! a dead dog! a man unclean in heart and lips!" And when he dares no longer gainsay or resist, when he is at last "thrust out into the harvest," he looketh on the right hand and on the left, he takes every step with fear and trembling, and with the deepest sense (such as words cannot express) of "Who is sufficient for these things?" Every gift which he has received of God for the furtherance of his word, whether of nature or grace, heightens this fear and increases his jealousy over himself; knowing that so much the stricter must the inquiry be when he gives an account of his stewardship. He is most of all jealous over himself when the work of the Lord prospers in his hand. He is then amazed and confounded before God. Shame covers his face. Yet, when he sees that he ought "to praise the Lord for his goodness and to declare the wonders which he doeth for the children of men," he is in a strait between two; he knows not which way to turn: he cannot speak; he dares not be silent. It may be for a time he "keeps his mouth with a bridle; he holds his peace even from good. But his heart is hot within him," and constrains him at length to declare what God hath wrought. And this he then doeth in all simplicity, with "great plainness of speech"; desiring only to commend himself to him who "searcheth the heart and trieth the reins," and (whether his words are the savour of life or of death to others) to have that witness in himself, "As of sincerity, as of God, in the sight of God, speak we in Christ." If any man counts this boasting, he cannot help it. It is enough that a higher Judge standeth at the door.

But you may say, "Why do you talk of the success of the gospel in England, which was a Christian country before you were born?" Was it indeed? Is it so at this day? I would explain myself a little on this head also.

And: No one can deny that the people of England in general are called Christians. They are called so, a few only excepted, by others as well as themselves. But I presume no man will say that the name makes the thing, that men are Christians barely because they are called so. It must be allowed that the people of England, generally speaking, have been christened or baptized. But neither can we infer, "These were once baptized; therefore they are Christians now." It is allowed that many of those who were once baptized, and are called Christians to this day, hear the word of God, attend public prayers, and partake of the Lord's Supper. But neither does this prove that they are Christians. For, notwithstanding this, some of them live in open sin; and others, though not conscious to themselves of hypocrisy, yet are utter strangers to the religion of the heart; are full of pride, vanity, covetousness, ambition; of hatred, anger, malice, or envy; and consequently are no more scriptural Christians than the open drunkard or common swearer.

Now, these being removed, where are the Christians, from whom we may properly term England a Christian country? The men who have the mind which was in Christ, and who walk as he also walked, whose inmost soul is renewed after the image of God, and who are outwardly holy, as he who hath called them is holy? There are doubtless a few such to be found. To deny this would be want of candour. But how few! How thinly scattered up and down! And as for a Christian visible Church, or a body of Christians visibly united together, where is this to be seen?

> Ye different sects, who all declare
> Lo, here is Christ! or, Christ is there!
> Your stronger proofs divinely give,
> And show me where the *Christians* live!

And what use is it, of what good end does it serve, to term England a

Christian country? (Although it is true most of the natives are called Christians, have been baptized, frequent the ordinances; and although a real Christian is here and there to be found, "as a light shining in a dark place.") Does it do any honour to our great Master among those who are not called by his name? Does it recommend Christianity to the Jews, the Mahometans, or the avowed heathens? Surely no one can conceive it does. It only makes Christianity stink in their nostrils. Does it answer any good end with regard to those on whom this worthy name is called? I fear not; but rather an exceeding bad one. For does it not keep multitudes easy in their heathen practice? Does it not make or keep still greater numbers satisfied with their heathen tempers? Does it not directly tend to make both the one and the other imagine that they are what indeed they are not—that they are Christians while they are utterly without Christ and without God in the world? If men are not Christians till they are renewed after the image of Christ, and if the people of England in general are not thus renewed, why do we term them so? The god of this world hath long blinded their hearts. Let us do nothing to increase that blindness, but rather labour to recover them from that strong delusion, that they may no longer believe a lie.

Let us labour to convince all mankind that to be a real Christian is to love the Lord our God with all our heart and to serve him with all our strength, to love our neighbour as ourselves, and therefore to do unto every man as we would he would do unto us....

Your friend and servant for Christ's sake,

John Wesley

Persons

Dietrich Bonhoeffer

August 7th 1928
To Helmut Roessler

At an early stage in his career, Bonhoeffer reveals his ability to see the real issues.

Dear Roessler,

...

I'm getting to know new people every day, at least, their circumstances; and sometimes one also gets a glimpse of them as persons, behind their stories. One thing strikes me again and again: here one meets people as they are, away from the "masquerade" of the Christian world, people with passions, criminal types, little people with little ambitions, little desires and little sins, all in all people who feel homeless in both senses of the word, who loosen up if one talks to them in a friendly way, real people; I can only say that I have gained the impression that it is just these people who are much more under grace than under wrath, and that it is the Christian world that is more under wrath than under grace....

For a long time I thought that there was a central point in preaching, which, once one touched on it, could move anyone, or confront them with a decision. I don't believe that any more. First, preaching can never apprehend this central point but can only be apprehended by it, by Christ. So Christ becomes flesh as much in the words of the pietists as in those of the churchmen or the Religious Socialists, and these empirical restrictions do not mean relative, but in fact absolute difficulties for preaching; men are not the same even at the deepest level, but they are individuals, totally different and only "united" by the Word in the church. I have noticed that the most effective sermons were those in which I spoke enticingly of the Gospel, like someone telling children a story of a strange country....

D.B.

CHAPTER 10

True Belief and
True Religion

The Love of the Beautiful

George Macdonald   1847

To his father

The young George Macdonald became a tutor to some very spoiled children. He wished to be a minister but was unsure of his suitability for holy orders, not only because he wanted his own mind and behaviour to be wholly in accordance with God's will, but because he was increasingly suspicious of the claims to exclusivity of any denomination.

My very dear Father,

... I did not wish you to understand me as having finally made up my mind as to the ministry. 'Tis true this feeling has been gradually gaining ground on me. What a mercy I was not allowed to follow out Chemistry! But, on the other hand, I fear myself—I have so much vanity, so much pride.... I have not prayed much about it, for it has seemed so far in the distance, as if it was scarcely time to think of it yet.... I love my Bible more—I am always finding out something new in it. All my teaching in youth seems useless to me. I must get it all from the Bible again.... If the gospel of Jesus be not true, I can only pray my maker to annihilate me, for nothing in the universe is glorious, except sin.... One of my greatest difficulties in consenting to think of religion was that I thought I should have to give up my beautiful thoughts and my love for the things God had made. But I find that the happiness springing from all things not in themselves sinful is much increased by religion. God is the God of the beautiful, Religion the love of the Beautiful, and Heaven the home of the Beautiful, Nature is tenfold brighter in the sun of Righteousness, and my love of Nature is more intense since I became a Christian—if indeed I am one. God has not given me such thoughts and forbidden me to enjoy them....

To answer another question. I have smoked a good deal since I came to London, though not much lately. When I am well it is a great enjoyment to me. Mr R— is a smoker. He gave me a beautiful pipe. But I should not have much right to claim much love for you, if I would not give it up at your request. I was almost sorry it was not a greater sacrifice. And yet I would not have you think it was not a greater sacrifice. And yet I would not have you think it no sacrifice. So I promise you never in this world to smoke again. That is settled now.

I should have much to say to you if I were with you, and many a long conversation I trust we may have before very long. May I never cause you a thought of pain, as I have so often done in years that are past.... Give my love to Johnny; to grandmama too....

Your very affectionate son,

George

Praise be to God!

St Maximilian Kolbe
c. 1913

To his mother

Throughout his life St Maximilian, the future martyr of Auschwitz, had a special devotion to Our Lady. Here the young Franciscan records an unusual event with characteristic simplicity.

Dear Mother,

I nearly lost my right thumb. An abscess had formed. Though the doctor treated it, the infection wouldn't stop. The doctor was already speaking of amputating the thumb, because the bone had been eaten into. I told him that I had a better idea. When our doctor heard that I had some Lourdes water, he was quite ready to use it for a dressing. The next morning the doctor at the hospital said the case was improving. He could forget the amputation. After this short treatment, my thumb healed up. Praise be to God and thanks to the Immaculata!

Your

Maximilian

Return to the True Faith

St Joan of Arc   March 23rd 1430

To the Hussites of Bohemia

When the campaign seemed to be turning against the English, Father Pasquerel, Joan's confessor, wrote and signed this letter to the Hussite heretics of Bohemia, perhaps one of many instances over the centuries in which the Saint's reputation was invoked for ecclesiastical and political reasons. Important authorities have accepted it as authentic, but it is debatable to what extent these are Joan's own words. The statement that she might abandon the campaign against the English to purge Bohemia of heresy seems uncharacteristic, for she was single-minded in her mission. Since all Joan's letters were dictated, it is possible that she was aware of the general intention but did not sanction the exact phrasing of a letter that exists in French and German versions, but must have been composed originally in Latin.

JESUS MARY

For some time now it has been rumoured, but recently the undoubted voice of the people has told me, Joan the Maid, that you have turned from being Christian heretics and have become blind pagans and Saracens; that you have put an end to the true faith and all that is edifying in the service of God; that you have exchanged all that for a repellent superstition, which you defend and seek to spread by means of terror and devastation; and that you destroy holy images, and reduce holy buildings to ashes and ruins! Are you so completely enraged? What crazy fury possesses you? You seek to persecute sublime belief, to undermine and even extirpate what Almighty God, the Son and the Holy Spirit have created, instituted, raised up, and sealed by the supreme sacrifice, which they have fortified with thousands of miracles. Those deprived of vision and of the light of the eyes see luminously compared with you, the blindest of all. Do you think to escape unpunished? Do you not know that God will allow your crimes to increase, your errors to grow, your darkness to thicken, your murderous swords to prevail, only, once you have reached the heights of impiety, quite abruptly to cast you into the depths?

I, Joan the Maid, in order to tell you the truth truly, would long ago have visited my vengeful wrath upon you, if the war against the English had not kept me here constantly. But if I do not soon hear that you have mended your ways and have returned to the bosom of the Church, I may leave the English and turn against you in order to extirpate your frightful superstition with the iron blade and take either your heresy or your life away from you. But if you return to the light that still shines, to the bosom of the

Catholic faith, send me your envoys. I shall tell you what you must do. But if you persist in your contrariness, then may the darkness of the evil that you have done, and the crimes with which you have sullied yourselves, destroy your determination. Await me, supported by the most steadfast human and divine power and ready to repay you with like for like.

Given at Sully on March 3rd.

In the Wrong

Søren Kierkegaard   1843

From "Judge William" to the young man and author "A"

In the assumed identity of the letter-writer of his pseudonymously published "Either/ Or", Kierkegaard stresses the edification implied in the thought that as against God we are always in the wrong, which is necessary on the road to faith, "not to lull, not to win a metaphysical view, but to clear for action," so that "the labouring thoughts, the restless mind, the fearful heart may there find rest where alone it is to be found."

Dear Friend,

I am sending you a Jutland pastor's sermon in order that it may make its impression on you in a quiet hour:

"It is painful to be in the wrong, and the more painful the more frequently it occurs; it is edifying to be in the wrong, and the more edifying the more frequently it occurs.... Why was it you wished to be in the wrong with respect to a person? Because you loved. Why did you find this edifying? Because you loved. The more you loved, the less time you had to deliberate whether you were in the right or not; your love had only one wish, that you might constantly be in the wrong. So also in your relation to God. You loved God, and hence your soul could find repose and joy only in the thought that you must always be in the wrong. It was not by the toil of thought you attained this recognition, neither was it forced upon you, for it is in love that you find yourself in freedom. So if thought convinced you that such was the case, that it could not be otherwise than that you must always be in the wrong, or that God must always be in the right, then this recognition followed as a logical consequence—but in fact you did not attain the certainty that you were in the wrong as a deduction from the knowledge that God was always in the right; but from love's dearest and only wish, that you might always be in the wrong, you reached the apprehension that God was always in the right.... But this wish is the affair of love, hence, of freedom, and you were not in any way compelled to recognize that you were always in the wrong. So it was not by reflection you became certain that you were always in the wrong, but the certainty was due to the fact that you were edified by the thought. So it is an edifying thought that against God we are always in the wrong....

... one may have known a thing many times and acknowledged it, one may have willed a thing many times and attempted it; and yet it is only by the deep inward movements, only by the indescribable emotions of the heart, that for the first time you are convinced that what you have known belongs to you, that no power can take it from you; for only the truth which edifies is truth for you."

Yours sincerely,

Judge William

The Lord Himself

George Macdonald   February 8th 1855

To his father

In a letter essentially called forth by the news that his sister was suffering from lung disease, Macdonald memorably summarizes his conviction that not dry-as-dust theology but the living Christ makes the most direct appeal to the human heart.

My dear Father,

Will you allow me to tell you one thing founded on the deepest conviction—that in Scotland especially, and indeed in all dissenting modes of teaching in England, a thousand times too much is said about faith.... I would never speak about faith, but speak about the Lord himself—not theologically, as to the why and wherefore of his death—but as he showed himself in his life on earth, full of grace, love, beauty, tenderness and truth. Then the needy heart cannot help hoping and trusting in him, and having faith, without ever thinking about faith. How a human heart with human feelings and necessities is ever to put confidence in the theological phantom which is commonly called Christ in our pulpits, I do not know. It is commonly a miserable representation of him who spent thirty-three years on our Earth, living himself into the hearts and souls of men, and thus manifesting God to them. Can anyone fear the wrath of God, who really believes that he is one with that only Saviour? If your suffering friend could but see in her fear how full of love God's heart is to her, by seeing his real nature expressed in the most tender-hearted helpful man that ever lived, while he would not yield one hair's breadth from the will of God, surely fear would go, and love would come.

Your affectionate son,

George

Out of Sin

Dietrich Bonhoeffer

June 30th 1944
To a friend

Having made the ultimate commitment to truth in the face of evil, Bonhoeffer points out the necessity of seeing the "whole of human life, in all its manifestations" as the central concern of Christian theology.

Dear Friend,

...

God is being increasingly edged out of the world, now that it has come of age. Knowledge and life are thought to be perfectly possible without him. Ever since Kant, he has been relegated to the realm beyond experience.

Theology has endeavoured to produce an apologetics to meet this development, engaging in futile rearguard actions against Darwinism, etc. At other times it has accommodated itself to this development by restricting God to the so-called last questions as a kind of "Deus ex machina." God thus became the answer to life's problems, the solution of its distresses and conflicts.... As a result, if anyone had no such difficulties, if he refused to identify himself in sympathy with those who had, it was no good trying to win him for God. The only way of getting at him was to show that he had all these problems, needs and conflicts without being aware of it or owning up to it.... If, however, a man won't see that his happiness is really damnation, his health sickness, his vigour and vitality despair, if he won't call them what they really are, the theologian is at his wits' end. He must be a hardened sinner of a particularly vicious type. If not, he is a case of bourgeois complacency, and the one is as far from salvation as the other.

You see, this is the attitude I am contending against. When Jesus blessed sinners, they were real sinners, but Jesus did not make every man a sinner first. He called them out of their sin, not into their sin.... Of course Jesus took to himself the dregs of human society, harlots and publicans, but never them alone, for he sought to take to himself man as such. Never did Jesus throw any doubt on a man's health, vigour or fortune, regarded in themselves, or look on them as evil fruits. Why else did he heal the sick and restore strength to the weak? Jesus claims for himself and the kingdom of God the whole of human life in all its manifestations....

Good-bye,

Dietrich

Divine Light and Power

George Fox   June 7th 1677

To Princess Elizabeth of the Rhine

In 1677 the indefatigable Fox made a continental visit to existing Friends and members of other denominations who were interested in their religious way. While at Amsterdam, after the departure of William Penn and others for Germany and before making his way there, Fox wrote to encourage the already lively sympathies of Elizabeth, Princess of the Rhine, the eldest daughter of Frederick V, Elector Palatine. Her mother was a daughter of James VI/I of Scotland and England. Fox sent the letter by his daughter-in-law. This is a notably polite but direct exhortation from the homely Fox, who travelled by open waggon and slept on straw. It elicited a refreshingly straightforward and sincere if cautious reply: "Dear Friend: I cannot but have a tender love to those that love the Lord Jesus Christ, and to whom it is given, not only to believe in him, but also to suffer for him; therefore your letter and your friends' visit have both been very welcome to me. I shall follow their and your counsel as far as God will afford me light and unction; remaining still your loving friend, Elizabeth."

Princess Elizabeth,

I have heard of thy tenderness towards the Lord and his holy truth, by some Friends that have visited thee, and also by some of thy letters which I have seen. It is indeed a great thing for a person of thy quality to have such a tender mind after the Lord and his precious truth, seeing so many are swallowed up with voluptuousness and the pleasures of this world; yet all make an outward profession of God and Christ in one way or other, but without any deep, inward sense and feeling of him. For it is not many mighty, nor wise of the world, that can become fools for Christ's sake, or can become low in the humility of Christ Jesus from their mighty state, through which they might receive a mightier estate, and a mightier kingdom through the inward Holy Spirit—the divine light and power of God; and a mightier wisdom which is from above, pure and peaceable. This wisdom is above that which is below; that is earthly, sensual and devilish by which men destroy one another, yea, about their religions, ways and worships, and churches; but this they have not from God nor Christ. But the wisdom which is from above, by which all things were made and created, which the holy fear of God in the heart is the beginning of, keeps the heart clean: and by and with this wisdom are all God's children to be ordered, and with it come to order all things to God's glory. This is the wisdom that is justified of her children. And in this fear of God and wisdom, my desire is, that thou may be preserved to God's glory. For the Lord is come to teach his people himself, and to set up his ensign, that the nations may flow unto it.

. . .

O therefore, feel the grace and truth in thy heart, that is come by Jesus Christ, that will teach thee how to live, and what to deny. It will establish thy heart, and season thy words, and bring thy salvation; it will be a teacher unto thee at all times. By it thou mayest receive Christ from whence it comes; and as many as receive him, to them he gives power, not only to stand against sin and evil; but to become the sons of God; if sons, then heirs of a life, a world, and kingdom, without end, and of the eternal riches and treasures thereof.

So in haste, with my love in the Lord Jesus Christ, that has tasted death for every man, and bruises the serpent's head, that is betwixt man and God, that through Christ man may come to God again, and so can praise him through Jesus Christ, the Amen; who is the spiritual and heavenly rock and foundation for all God's people to build upon, to the praise and glory of God, who is over all blessed for evermore.

George Fox

True Religion

John Wesley

March 29th 1737

To Mrs Chapman

In spite of all his preaching, administrative duties and other writing, Wesley composed a vast number of letters of spiritual direction, never over-hortatory yet judiciously corrective, always with a positive goal in view, and nicely attuned to the mind and character of the recipient. The following, written from Savannah, during his ultimately unsuccessful missionary venture in North America, to the mother of

Robert Chapman, a Methodist of Pembroke College, Oxford, is a good instance of his plain style, selective metaphors, use of examples from his own life, and care for right-minded but never "nice" distinctions in self-examination. We must remember that the slowness of the mails in the mid-eighteenth century made this transatlantic direction of souls a long-drawn-out business. "Mr Law" is William Law, the devotional writer and mystic (see Biographical Notes). Wesley's sermon on love was a touchstone piece for him; he preached it in Savannah in 1736, and in London in 1738; it includes a moving description of his father's death.

My dear Friend,

True friendship is doubtless stronger than death, else yours could never have subsisted still in spite of all opposition, and even after thousands of miles are interposed between us. In the last proof you gave of it there are a few things which I think it lies on me to mention: as for the rest, my brother is the proper person to clear them up, as I suppose he has done long ago.

You seem to apprehend that I believe religion to be inconsistent with cheerfulness and with a sociable, friendly temper. So far from it, that I am convinced, as true religion or holiness cannot be without cheerfulness, so steady cheerfulness, on the other hand, cannot be without holiness or true religion. And I am equally convinced that true religion has nothing sour, austere, unsociable, unfriendly in it; but on the contrary, implies the most winning sweetness, the most amiable softness and gentleness. Are you for having as much cheerfulness as you can? So am I. Do you endeavour to keep alive your taste for all the truly innocent pleasures of life? So do I likewise. Do you refuse no pleasure but what is an hindrance to some greater good or has a tendency to some evil? It is my very rule; and I know no other by which a sincere, reasonable Christian can be guided. In particular, I pursue this rule in eating, which I seldom do without much pleasure. And this I know is the will of God concerning me: that I should enjoy every pleasure that leads to my taking pleasure in him, and in such a measure as most leads to it. I know that, as to every action which is naturally pleasing, it is his will that it should be so; therefore, in taking that pleasure so far as it tends to this end (of taking pleasure in God), I do his will. Though, therefore, that pleasure be in some sense distinct from the love of God, yet is the taking of it by no means distinct from his will. No; you say yourself it is his will I should take it. And here, indeed, is the hinge of the question, which I had once occasion to state in a letter to you, and more largely in a sermon on the love of God. If you will read over those, I believe you will find you differ from Mr Law and me in words only. You say the pleasures you plead for are distinct from the love of God, as the cause from the effect. Why, then they tend to it; and those which are only thus distinct from it no one excepts against. The whole of what he affirms, and that not only on the authority of men but from the words and example of God incarnate, is: There is one thing needful—to do the will of God; and his will is our sanctification: our renewal in the image of God, in faith and love, in all holiness and happiness. On this we are to fix our single eye at all times and in all places; for so did our Lord. This one thing we are to do; for so did our fellow servant, Paul, after His example: "Whether we eat or drink, or whatsoever we do, we are to do all to the glory of God". In other words, we are to do nothing but what directly or indirectly leads to our holiness, which is His glory; and to do every such thing with this design, and in such a measure as may most promote it.

I am not mad, my dear friend, for asserting these to be the words of truth and soberness; neither are any of those, either in England or here, who have hitherto attempted to follow me. I am, and must be, an example to my flock; not, indeed, in my prudential rules, but in some measure (if, giving God the glory, I may dare to say so) in my spirit and life and conversation. Yet all of them are, in your sense of the word, unlearned, and most of them of low understanding; and still, not one of them has been as yet entangled in any case of conscience which was not solved. And as to the nice distinctions you speak of, it is you my friend, it is the wise, the learned, the disputers of this world, who are lost in them, and bewildered more and more, the more they strive to extricate themselves. We have no need of nice distinctions; for I exhort all, dispute with none. I feed my brethren in Christ, as he giveth me power, with the pure, unmixed milk of his word. And those who are as little children receive it, not as the word of man, but as the word of God. Some grow thereby, and advance apace in peace and holiness: they grieve, it is true, for those who did run well, but are now turned back; and they fear for themselves, lest they also be tempted; yet, through the mercy of God, they despair not, but have still a good hope that they shall endure to the end. Not that this hope has any resemblance to enthusiasm, which is an hope to attain the end without the means: this they know is impossible, and therefore ground their hope on a constant, careful use of all the means. And if they keep in this way, with lowliness, patience, and meekness or resignation, they cannot carry the principle of pressing toward perfection too far. Oh may you and I carry it far enough! Be fervent in spirit. "Rejoice evermore; pray without ceasing; in everything give thanks." Do everything in the name of the Lord Jesus. Abound more and more in all holiness, and in zeal for every good word and work.

Your friend,

John Wesley

Our Own Umbrellas

John Donne   c. 1609

To Sir Henry Goodyer

A superb meditation on the state and relation of humanity to God and the universe written when Donne was a frequent visitor to the house of Lady Bedford at Twickenham, and addressed to his friend Henry Goodyer, then staying with the Countess of Huntingdon (who was married to a cousin of Lady Bedford). Goodyer had suggested that Donne should send a poetic tribute to the Countess.

Sir,

It should be no interruption to your pleasures, to hear me often say that I love you, and that you are as much my meditations as my self: I often compare not you and me, but the sphere in which your resolutions are, and my wheel; both I hope concentric to God: for methinks the new astronomy is this appliable well, that we which are a little earth, should rather move towards God, than that he which is fulfilling, and can come no whither, should move towards us. To your life full of variety, nothing is old, nor new to mine; and as to that life, all stickings and hesitations seem stupid and stony, so to this, all fluid slipperinesses, and transitory migrations seem giddy and feathery. In that life one is ever in the porch or postern, going in or out, never within his house himself: It is a garment made of remnants, a life revalled [pulled] out into ends, a line discontinued, and a number of small wretched points, useless, because they concur not: A life built of past and future, not purposing any constant present; they have more pleasures than we, but not more pleasure; they joy oftener, we longer; and no man but of so much understanding as may deliver him from being a fool, would change with a mad-man, which had a better proportion of wit in his often *Lucidis.*

You know, they which dwell farthest from the sun, if in any convenient distance, have longer days, better appetites, better digestion, better growth, and longer life; And all these advantages have their minds who are well removed from the scorchings, and dazzlings, and exhalings of the world's glory: but neither of our lives are in such extremes; for you living at Court without ambition, which would burn you, or envy, which would divest others, live in the sun, not in the fire: And I which live in the country without stupefying, am not in darkness, but in shadow, which is not no light, but a pallid, waterish, and diluted one. As all shadows are of one colour, if you respect the body from which they are cast (for our shadows upon clay will be dirty, and in a garden green, and flowery), so all retirings into a shadowy life are alike from all causes, and alike subject to the barbarousness and insipid dullness of the country: only the employments, and that upon which you cast and bestow your pleasure, business, or books, give it the tincture, and beauty. But truly wheresoever we are, if we can but tell ourselves truly we are so composed, that if abundance, or glory scorch and melt us, we have an earthly cave, our bodies, to go into by consideration, and cool ourselves: and if we be frozen, and contracted with lower and dark fortunes, we have within us a torch, a soul, lighter and warmer than any without: we are therefore our own umbrellas, and our own suns.

These, Sir, are the salads and onions of Mitcham, sent to you with as wholesome affection as your other friends send melons and quelquechoses from Court and London. If I present you not as good diet as they, I would say grace to theirs, and bid much good do it you. I send you, with this, a letter which I sent to the Countess. It is not my use nor duty to do so, but for your having of it, there were but two consents, and I am sure you have mine, and you are sure you have hers. I also writ to her Ladyship for the verses she showed in the garden, which I did, not only to extort them, nor only to keep my promise of writing, for that I had done in the other letter, and perchance she hath forgotten the promise; nor only because I think my letters just good enough for a progress, but because I would write apace to her, whilst it is possible to express that which I yet know of her, for by this growth I see how soon she will be ineffable.

Your &c

J. Donne

Christ's Deep Sayings

George Macdonald

April 29th 1853

To his father

Macdonald eventually became a Congregational minister but found that his deacons treated him as "their servant instead of Christ's." He was suspected of heresy not only because of his unacceptably broad-minded views on the beneficence of the Creator (he maintained that some provision would be made for the heathen after death), the keeping of the Sabbath-day, the redemption not only of humankind but of the animal kingdom and all creation, but because of his mystical yet inquiring cast of mind—he was said to be tainted with German theology. His stipend was reduced in the hope that he would leave, but he accepted the privation. He resigned in May 1853.

My dear Father,

... But indeed my way of thinking and feeling would not help to make you more sad. I grow deeper and happier.... I know a little now, and only a little, what Christ's deep sayings mean, about becoming like a little child, about leaving all for him, about service, and truth and love. God is our loving, true, self-forgetting friend. All delight, all hope and beauty are in God. My dear and honoured father—if I might say so to you—will you think me presumptuous if I say?—leave the Epistles and ponder the Gospel—the story about Christ. Infinitely are the Epistles mistaken because the Gospels are not understood and felt in the heart: because the readers of the Epistles too often possess nothing of that sympathy with Christ's thoughts and feelings and desires which moved and glorified the writers of the Epistles. The Epistles are very different from the Apostles' preaching; they are mostly written for a peculiar end and aim, and are not intended as expositions of the central truth....

God has provided for us very lovingly. Our salary is reduced—but not so much as we feared, and our sister's boarding with us has helped much to take us through....

Your very affectionate son,

George

Christ's Great Heart

George Macdonald   May 20th 1853

To his father

In his many letters to his father, Macdonald expounded his developing understanding of Christianity, not as some dry-as-dust reflection of German Higher Theology, but as the message that he expounded thus in the article referred to in the letter below: "As a mathematical theorem is to be proved only by the demonstration of that theorem itself, not by talking about it; so Christ must prove himself to the human soul through being beheld. The only proof of Christ's divinity is his humanity. Because his humanity is not comprehended, his divinity is doubted.... There are thoughts and feelings that cannot be called up in the mind by any power of will or force of imagination; which, being spiritual, must arise in the soul when in its highest spiritual condition; when the mind, indeed, like a smooth lake, reflects only heavenly images...."

My dear Father,

... I am always finding out meaning which I did not see before, and which I now cannot see perfectly—for, of course, till my heart is like Christ's great heart, I cannot fully know what he meant. The great thing for understanding what he said is to have a living sense of the reality that a young man of poor birth appeared unexpectedly in the country of Judaea and uttered most unwelcome truths, setting at nought all the respectabilities of the time, and calling bad, bad, and good, good, in the face of all religious perversions and false honourings. The first thing is to know Jesus as a man, and any theory about him that makes less of him as a man—with the foolish notion of exalting his divinity—I refuse at once. Far rather would I be such a Unitarian as Dr Channing than such a Christian as by far the greater number of those that talk about his Divinity, are. The former truly believes in Christ—believes in him far more than the so-called orthodox. You will find some thoughts of mine on this matter (though the Editor begged leave to omit the most important portion) in the "Christian Spectator" for May. They are in an article headed "Browning's Christmas Eve." The life, thoughts, deeds, aims, beliefs of Jesus have to be fresh expounded every age, for all the depth of Eternity lies in them, and they have to be seen into more profoundly in every new era of the world's spiritual history....

You must not be surprised if you hear that I am not what is called getting on. Time will show what the Father will make of me. I desire to be his— entirely—so sure am I that therein lie all things. If less than this were my hope, I should die.

I expect to find a few whom I can help in Manchester. The few young who are here and not [adversely] influenced by their parents, the simple, honest and poor, are much attached to me—at least most of them—and that means but a very few. If I were in a large town I do not think that I should yield to them and leave—but it is better for me to be driven away than to break up such ties as may be supposed to exist between a true pastor and true people for the sake of getting a larger salary....

Your very affectionate son,

George

Worldliness

Dietrich Bonhoeffer

July 21st 1944
To a friend

Facing death for his unflinching dedication to truth and justice, Bonhoeffer gives one of his most poignant explanations of committed Christianity in the modern world.

Dear Friend,

...

During the last year or so I have come to appreciate the "worldliness" of Christianity as never before. The Christian is not a homo religiosus [*religious man*], but a man, pure and simple, just as Jesus was a man, compared with John the Baptist anyhow. I don't mean the shallow this-worldliness of the enlightened, of the busy, the comfortable or the lascivious. It's something much more profound than that, something in the knowledge of death and resurrection as ever present. I believe Luther lived a this-worldly life in this sense. I remember talking to a young French pastor at A. thirteen years ago. We were discussing what our real purpose was in life. He said he would like to become a saint. I think it is quite likely he did become one. At the time I was very much impressed, though I disagreed with him, and said I would prefer to have faith, or words to that effect. For a long time I did not realize how far we were apart.

I thought I could acquire faith by trying to live a holy life, or something like that....

Later I discovered and am still discovering up to this moment that it is only by living completely in this world that one learns to believe. One must abandon every attempt to make something of oneself, whether it be a saint, a converted sinner, a churchman (the priestly type, so called!) a righteous man or an unrighteous one, a sick man or a healthy one. This is what I mean by worldliness: taking life in one's stride, with all its duties and problems, its successes and failures, its experiences and helplessness. It is in such a life that we throw ourselves utterly into the arms of God and participate in his sufferings in the world and watch with Christ in Gethsemane....

Good-bye,

Dietrich

Camphor Lumps and Camphor Scent

Friedrich von Hügel   May 5th 1919

To his niece, Gwendolen Greene, in Salisbury

Here the Baron, who hated rigorism ("... it's all wrong. Our Lord was never a rigorist. He loved publicans and sinners. How he loved all the beauties of nature, the family—children! His parables are full of these homely things. God nearly always teaches us through a person, he teaches us through individuals ..."), explains the relation of the institutional Church to religion with his usual simplicity and directness.

My very dear Gwen,

Here I am writing to you, in your new temporary home, looking out of your window, I expect, upon how much of past history recorded in gloriously beautiful monuments, poems in stone!

Sit on a footstool here, by me, Daughter; and I will try and give you— not exterior things, but interior things—things that cost one a lot to get, a lot to keep. They are things, indeed, that also cost one a good deal to give—and I can clearly tell you why, my Gwen. Look you, Dear: there is simply *nothing* that one soul can transfer to another soul—even at those souls' best—with the particular connotations, the particular experiences of heart and heart, of blood and breeding, of sex and age, etc., yet it is these particularities which incarnate the convictions of any one soul for that soul. Any one soul can be fully impressive for another soul only if that first soul comes out, to the second soul, with its convictions clothed and coloured by those its particularities. And yet the second soul, even if thus impressed—even if it thus wakes up to great spiritual facts and laws,—this second soul will at once, quite spontaneously, most rightly, clothe and colour these its new convictions with its own special qualities and habits and experiences of thought, feeling, imagination, memory, volition; and so—most really—to try and help on the life of another soul means, Dear, a specially large double death to self on the part of the life-bringing soul. For it means death to self before and in the communication—the life-bringing soul must already, then, discriminate within itself between the essence of what it has to say and the accidents, the particularities, which clothe the utterance of this essence; and it must peacefully anticipate the acceptance *at most* of that essence, and not of these accidents. And then, after the communication, this soul must be ready actually to back the other soul in the non-acceptance even of the essence of the messsage, if there is evidence that the other soul is not really helped, but is hindered, at least for the time being, by this essence now offered to it. And, as already said, at best, *only that essence* can and should be taken over by this other soul, and the light-bearing soul, even then, must at once be busy helping the less experienced soul to clothe the newly won essence in clothing from the wardrobe of this other soul.

My Gwen, you see, this now, as follows, is the point which, with the sendings of books which I begin today, I hope you may end by seeing clearly, steadily, in your quite individual manner and degree. You see, I see, how deep, and dear, how precious, is your faith in God and in Christ. I thank God for [it], and if to the end you cannot acquire, without really distracting or weakening that faith, a strong and serene insight and instinct concerning the great occasions and means by which those great faiths have been, and still are conveyed to, and articulated and steadied among mankind—why then, to the end, I must, and will, actually defend you against the sheer distraction of such instincts and insights not actually possible to you. But it is plain that you would be a much richer, wiser, more developed and grateful soul if you could and did permanently develop the insights and instincts that I mean. And certainly the things I am thinking of—their perception—constitutes just the difference between a fully awake, a fully educated mind, and a mind that is awake only as to results, not as to the processes; as to what it holds, and not as to who it is to whom it owes that it has anything large and definite to hold at all.

You see, my Gwen, how vulgar, lumpy, material, appear great lumps of camphor in a drawer; and how ethereal seems the camphor smell all about in the drawer. How delicious, too, is the sense of bounding health, as one races along some down on a balmy spring morning; and how utterly vulgar, rather improper indeed, is the solid breakfast, are the processes of digestion that went before. Yet the camphor lumps, and the porridge, and its digestion: they had their share, had they not? in the ethereal camphor scent, in the bounding along upon that sunlight down? And a person who would both enjoy camphor scent and disdain camphor lumps; a person who would revel in that liberal open air and contemn porridge and digestion: such a person would be ungrateful, would she not?—would have an unreal, a superfine refinement? The institutional, the Church is, in religion, especially in Christianity, the camphor lump, the porridge etc.; and the "detached" believers would have no camphor scent, no open air, bounding liberty, had there not been, from ancient times, those concrete, "heavy," "clumsy," "oppressive" things—lumps, porridge, Church.

The main point to consider is, not the harm done by churchmen at their worst, but the special function and work of the Church at its best. You see, Gwen, this is but the same principle which comes continually into everything. So with the State, so with Art, so with Science, so with all that the hands of men touch at all—hands which so readily soil even what they most need, what is most sacred. But notice how Church, State, Family, Children, the Marriage Tie, these, and other right and good things, not only possess each its Ideal, unattained outside of and above it. No, no: they each possess within them more or less of that Ideal become real—they each and all live on at all because, at bottom, they are necessary, they are good, they come from God and lead to Him, and really in part effect what they were made for.

I trust the Salisbury time will refresh and rest you, my Gwen Niece.

Uncle H.

People are like Sheep

Henri de Tourville   c. 1880

To a penitent

The Abbé de Tourville was an invalid for the last twenty-two years of his life yet remained a lively and optimistic spiritual adviser. He was especially acute in his ability to comfort those disturbed by transition and change, and to show them in direct, commonsense language that essential things remain even when conventions are upset. As he said elsewhere: "The best travellers are never tidy and timid. We must go our own way and not worry about the puddles we fall into, lest we stop moving ahead altogether. The journey itself puts right the accidents it has led us into. We must dry ourselves, give ourselves a good shake, and continue on our way."

My dear ...,

The present-day world isn't really so bad as we imagine, even though the ideas we learned when we were young stay with us and make us see progress as if it were only a force turning everything upside down and inside out. Most good people and saints indulge in the bad habit of always complaining inwardly about everything under the sun. I don't know what earthly paradise they are dreaming of, the memory of which makes them so disappointed. Such a paradise certainly doesn't exist. In this world we make a great number of attempts at various good enterprises which to all intents and purposes just don't succeed. At any rate, their success is very small in proportion to what they cost. Yet the results for which they pave the way are vast. You have only to think of an event like the Roman Empire becoming Christian the morning after the most ghastly persecutions, because everywhere all kinds of little seeds had been germinating in the dark. Things go wrong to show us that God wants us to change them. That's the real truth.

As far as I can see, God keeps the world moving ahead in order to shake us out of our clinging old ways and moulds and bring us back to more natural behaviour. That happens now and again in history. I think the present time is very good and very interesting. Don't groan about the state things are in, as if all that was good had gone for ever. What is actually happening is a clash between old and new. This causes a lot of noise because what is old suddenly realizes how very old it truly is, and abruptly realizes exactly why no one can put up with things like that any longer. The outcome is never in doubt. What is coming to be is victorious in the great struggle over what has been.

Progress is the same in all sectors. In the world, in the Church, and in the religious life. Ways that were acceptable in the past conflict with what is new, and with what different needs demand. Most people are like sheep; they are content to follow old methods and tradition, even though they draw scant personal benefit from them. A small minority hesitantly emerges to face the contradictions, in the midst of a vast amount of talk. Yet, if God has put you there as far as natural ability and inclination are concerned, you are one of that minority and have to accept the fact.

Yours ever,

De Tourville

A New Language

Blaise Pascal

November 5th 1656

To Mademoiselle de Roannez

Pascal affirms the importance of the religion of the heart and of the living God to whom he had dedicated himself: not the "God of the philosophers," but "the God of Abraham, Isaac and Jacob, who is "to be found only as the Gospel teaches us."

Dear Mlle de Roannez,

A new language usually introduces a new heart.

In his Gospel Jesus gave us a sign by which to recognize those who have faith. They will speak a new language. What happens is that a renewal of thoughts and desires brings about a renewal of language. Renewal is a constant necessity, for this particular novelty, which cannot fail to please God as much as the old creature could not fail to displease him, differs from what is new in the world. Earthly things, you see, however new they are, grow old even as they endure, whereas this new spirit renews itself all the more the longer it lasts. The old man in us dies away, says St Paul, and is renewed each day, and will only be perfectly new in eternity, where we shall sing without ceasing the new song that David speaks of in the psalms: the song, that is, that springs from the new spirit of love.

It is certain that the graces God grants in this life are a sign of the glory which he prepares for us in the next. Moreover, when I contemplate the end and the crowning of his work in their first-fruits as they appear in the devout, I am filled with awe and thus with respect for those whom he seems to have chosen as his elect. I seem indeed to see them already on one of those thrones from which those who have forsaken everything will judge the world together with Jesus Christ, according to the promise he made. But when I think that the same persons can fall, and be counted instead among the unfortunate company of those who are judged, and that there will be so many of those who will fall from their glory, and by their negligence allow others to assume the crown that God offered to them, I find this thought insufferable; and the horror that I would feel on seeing them in this condition of everlasting wretchedness, after having so reasonably imagined them in that other state, makes me cease entertaining this notion. Then I have recourse once again to God, and ask him not to abandon these his weak creatures. "Blessed is the man that fears the Lord."
 Yours,
  Blaise Pascal

Essential Truth
George Macdonald   c. 1855

To his father

Macdonald's father feared that his son might be over-presumptuous in refusing to accept the criticisms of the elders of his congregation, who found upsetting the speculative and generous approach of a man who said that God was easy to please but hard to satisfy. In this letter George sweetly, passionately yet directly and logically justifies his individual stand against sectarianism and outward conformism, and asserts the inevitability of doubts and inward questioning. This was the cast of mind that, as G. K. Chesterton remarked, enabled him to escape from the bias of environment and evolve "out of his own mystical meditations a complete alternative theology leading to a completely contrary mood."

My dear Father,
 I am sorry that you should feel any uneasiness about me and my position. It is unavoidable that the friends of any public man who cannot go with the tide, should be more or less anxious about him.... But your faith in God, and the faith of individual good men in me, should quiet your fears.

As to the congregational meetings and my absence from them, perhaps if you saw a little behind the scenes, you would care less for both. I will not go where I have not the slightest interest in going, and where my contempt would be excited to a degree very injurious to myself. Of course, when I disclaim all favour for their public assemblies, I do not deny individual goodness. I have no love for any sect of Christians as such—as little for Independents as any. One thing is good about them—which is continually being violated—that is the Independency. And independent I mean to be, in the real sense of the word.... There is a numerous, daily increasing party to whom the charge of heterodoxy is as great a recommendation, in the hope of finding something genuine, as orthodoxy is to the other, in the hope of finding the traditions of the elders sustained and enforced. For popular rumour surely you need not care—as if it could be true, and were not the greatest liar under the sun! And from all its lies God can keep his own. For my part I do not at all expect to become minister of any existing Church, but I hope to gather a few around me soon—and the love I have from the few richly repays me for the abuse of some and the neglect of the many.

But does not all history teach us that the forms in which truth has been taught, after being held heartily for a time, have by degrees come to be held merely traditionally and have died out and other forms arisen which new forms have always been abused at first? There never was Reformation but it came in a way people did not expect and was cried down and refused by the greater part of the generation amongst whom it began. There are some in every age who can see the essential truth through the form, and hold by that, and who are not alarmed at a change; but others, and they the most by far, cannot see this, and think all is rejected by one who rejects the forms of a truth which they count essential, while he sees that it teaches error as well as truth, and is less fitted for men now than it was at another period of history and stage of mental development....

But why be troubled because your son is not like other people? Perhaps it is impossible for him to be. Does not the spirit of God lead men and generations continually on to new truths? And to be even actually more correct in creed with less love to God and less desire for truth, surely is INFINITELY less worthy! But if you believe in the spirit of God—why fear? Paul, I think, could trust in God in these things and cared very little about orthodoxy, as it is now understood. "If in anything ye be otherwise minded, God shall reveal even this unto you" are words of his about the highest Christian condition. And Jesus said: "If any man is willing to do the will of the Father, he shall know of the doctrine." Now real earnestness is scarcely to be attained in a high degree without doubts and inward questionings and certainly divine teachings; and if you add to this the presumption that God must have more to reveal to every age, you will not be sorry that your son cannot go with the many. . . . If there is to be advance, it must begin with a few, and it is possible (I cannot say more, nor does modesty forbid my saying this) I may be one of the few.

Increase of truth will always in greater or lesser degree look like error at first. But to suffer in this cause is only to be like the Master; and even to be a martyr to a newer development of truth (which certainly I do not expect to be required of me) is infinitely nobler than success in the commoner use of the word. . . . I believe there is much more religion in the world than ever, but it is not so much in the churches, or religious communities in proportion, as it was at one time. Your Huntly young men would not refuse me, however the be-titled and pompous doctors of the law would set me down—and better men than I—with the terms of "German" and "new view." If this seems like glorying, I will venture to take Paul's defence, of being compelled thereto! For if it be alleged against me that some condemn me, what have I to say but that others, and they to my mind far more estimable, justify and receive me? Your own Troup would be cast out by many. But I will not write more about it, sure that one day, either in this world or the next, my father and I will hold sweet sympathetic communion with each other about God and Jesus and Truth.

A few young men in Manchester are wishing to meet together in some room, and have me for their minister. That is what I have wished from the first; and if they give what they can to support me, I will be content and try to make it up in other ways. But it does not seem very improbable that if I had a beginning once, I should by and by have a tolerable congregation.

Your son,

    George

CHAPTER 11

Persecution, Torture and Imprisonment

By Fire Resolved

St Robert Southwell   c. 1587

To his fellow-Catholics persecuted and in prison

From a series of letters written originally to Philip Howard, imprisoned in the Tower. Southwell, while chaplain to Howard's wife, and living at Arundel House in the Strand, later recast these to form "An Epistle of Comfort," intended to console and encourage those under persecution for their faith. Here he presents the challenge of the Christian life in terms of the familiar notion of the holy war.

Dear Friends,

When we come to the service of Christ, we come to a rough profession, that is found to have a continual defiance and enmity with the pleasures, vanities and praises of this world, and therefore we can look for nothing else at their hands who are friends to the same, but only trouble, hatred and persecution.

Christianity is a warfare, and Christians spiritual soldiers. In its beginning, our faith was planted in the poverty, infamy, persecution and death of Christ; in its progress it was watered by the blood of God's saints; and it cannot come to the full growth unless it be fostered with the showers of the martyrs' blood. Our flowers, that foreshow the happy calm of our felicity, grow out of thorns, and of briars must we reap our fruit. But if the stalk wound, the flowers heal; if the gathering be troublesome, the fruit is the more delightsome. We know that the flower of Jesse gave its most pleasant scent, and came to its full growth upon the cross; we know that the fruit of life was not gathered without thorns. We must now ascend to the mount of myrrh, which is in taste bitter, and to the hill of frankincense,

which giveth no sweet savour but when it is by fire resolved. Now comes
the winnower with his fan to see who is blown away like light chaff, and
who resists the blasts like massy wheat. That which lies hid in the young
blade of corn is displayed in the ripe ear; and that which is concealed in
the flower is uttered in the fruit. The cunning of the pilot is not known
till the tempest rises; nor the courage of the captain till the war begins; nor
the constancy of the Catholic till the persecutor rages.

Now must it be known whether we be vessels of honour or reproach;
whether we be signed with the seal of the lamb, or branded with the mark
of the beast; whether we be of the wheat or of the tares; and, finally,
whether we belong to the flock of Christ or to the herd of Belial.

Yours &c,

R. Southwell

Bought and Sold

St Vincent de Paul   July 24th 1607

To a lawyer

*St Vincent, one of whose many evangelical interests later in life was catechizing the
galley-slaves of the Royal fleet, writes to Monsieur Comet, advocate at the presidential
court of Dax, to describe his own extraordinary experiences as a captive. His wry
asides reveal the knowledge of the vagaries of human nature for which he was noted.*

Dear Friend,

Two years ago my affairs were going so well that you might have thought
that Fortune, contrary to what I deserved, was only trying to find out how
to make me more enviable than imitable. Unfortunately she was only
trying to use me as an example of her inconstancy and fickleness, turning
her favour to disfavour, her kindness to unkindness.

You probably knew, for you were kept only too well informed of what
I was doing, how I found, on my return from Bordeaux, that a will had been
made in my favour by a kind old lady of Toulouse. Her property consisted
of some movable goods and lands which had been granted to her by the
Castres court as compensation for a debt of three or four hundred crowns
owed to her by a good-for-nothing, worthless scamp. In order to recover
some of it, I set out for Toulouse with the intention of selling the property.
I did so on the advice of my best friends, because I not only needed money
to settle some debts I had contracted, but also because I knew that I was

going to be caused great expense for something I can't talk about now.

On my arrival, I learned that my fine fellow had decamped, because a warrant had been taken out for his arrest by my good old friend to whom he owed the money. I was told that he was doing very well at Marseilles, and was quite well off. Whereupon my lawyer said (as the case in fact required) that I ought to go to Marseilles, for he believed that if I had the fellow arrested, I might recover two or three hundred crowns. As I had no money to do what he advised, I sold the horse I had hired in Toulouse, intending to pay for it on my return, which has been so unfortunately delayed that I am deeply dishonoured at having left my affairs in such confusion. It would never have happened if God had let my concerns turn out as fortunately as appearances deserved.

Acting on this advice, therefore, I went to Marseilles, captured my man, had him thrown into prison, and settled with him for three hundred crowns which he paid cash down. As I was about to return to my home by land, I was persuaded by a gentleman with whom I was lodging to set sail with him for Narbonne because the weather was favourable. I did so in order to arrive there sooner and spare expense, or, to put it more accurately, never to reach there at all and to lose everything.

The wind was so favourable that it would have taken us in a day to Narbonne, fifty leagues distant, if God had not allowed three Turkish brigantines, which were cruising about in the Gulf of Lyons, on the look-out for ships from Beaucaire—where a fair was being held which is thought of as one of the finest in the Christian world—to bear down on us and attack us so fiercely that two or three of our men were killed and all the rest wounded, including myself, who received an arrow-wound that will serve me as a clock for the rest of my life.

We were forced to surrender to these ruffians, worse than tigers, who, in the first fury of their rage, cut our pilot into a hundred thousand pieces, because they had lost one of their own leaders, as well as four or five other scoundrels slain by our men. Then—having roughly committed a thousand robberies on the way, but releasing all who had surrendered without a fight, after plundering them—at last, laden with booty, at the end of seven or eight days, they made for Barbary, which is, without the authorization of the Grand Turk, a lair and den of thieves. On our arrival there we were exposed for sale, with a proclamation to the effect that we had been captured on a Spanish vessel, because, but for this lie, we would have been released by the Consul, whom the King maintains there to protect trade with France.

This is how we were sold. They stripped us stark naked, and gave each of us a pair of drawers, a linen jacket and a cap. They then marched us through the streets of Tunis, to which they had come expressly to sell us. After making us parade five or six times through the city, they brought us back to the ship, so that the merchants could see the difference between the hearty eaters and the others, and be sure that our wounds were not mortal. They then took us back to the market-place, where the merchants came to examine us, just as one does when buying a horse or an ox. They made us open our mouths and show our teeth, felt our sides, examined our wounds, and made us walk, trot and run. They then forced us to carry loads and wrestle, so that they could judge the strength of each individual, besides a thousand other brutalities.

I was sold to a fisherman, who very soon had to part with me because I could not stand the sea. I was bought by an old man, a Stagirite physician and a first-class extractor of quintessences. He was a very humane and kindly fellow. As he told me, he had laboured for fifty years seeking to discover the philosopher's stone, but all in vain as far as the stone was concerned, though most successfully as regards another method of transmuting metals. I have often seen him melt down equal quantitites of gold and silver, first arranging them in thin layers, over which he put a layer of some powders, then another layer of the metals, and finally another layer of powders. Thereupon he placed the lot in a melting-pot or goldsmith's crucible and set it all in a furnace for twenty-four hours. When he opened it the silver had become gold. I have also seen him, very frequently, freeze, or fix, quicksilver into pure silver, which he sold to give alms to the poor. It was my duty to keep the furnaces going and, thanks be to God, this gave me both pleasure and pain. He was very fond of me, and enjoyed talking to me about alchemy and still more about his religion, doing everything he could to convert me to it, promising me great riches and all his knowledge.

God always encouraged a firm belief in me that one day I would escape through the constant prayers I offered up to him and to the Blessed Virgin Mary, to whose sole intercession I firmly believe I owe my deliverance. My hope and resolute conviction that I would see you again made me constantly beg my owner to teach me to cure gall-stones, which I saw him do every day quite miraculously. He showed me his method, and even allowed me to prepare and administer the ingredients.

How often since then I have wished I was a slave before the death of your brother who was, with you, a co-Maecenas in doing good to me, and that I knew then the secret which I now send you. Death would not have triumphed over him (at least in the way it did), even though it is said that human days are reckoned in the sight of God. That is true, not because God had reckoned the number of one's days as so many, but because the number had been reckoned in the sight of God since things have been like that; or, to put it more clearly, he did not die when he actually did because God had so foreseen it, or calculated the number of his days as being so and so, but because God had foreseen his death and the number of his days to be what they were, since he died when he actually did.

I remained with this old man from September 1605 until the following August, when he was taken away and carried off to the Grand Sultan to work for him; but in vain, for he died of grief on the journey. He bequeathed me to one of his nephews, who at once resold me, after his uncle's death, because he had heard a rumour that Monsieur de Brèves, the King's Ambassador to Turkey, was coming with authentic and formal instructions from the Grand Turk, for the recovery of Christian slaves.

I was bought by a renegade Christian, from Nice in Savoy, a natural enemy, who carried me off to his "temat," the name given to land held by feu from the Grand Sultan, for the people do not own anything; everything belongs to the Sultan. This man's "temat" was in the mountains where the country is excessively hot and sandy. One of his three wives (a Greek-Christian, but a schismatic) was a very intelligent woman who liked me very much. Towards the end, another wife, a born Turk, was the instrument of God's boundless mercy in withdrawing her husband from apostasy, restoring him to the bosom of the Church and rescuing me from slavery. As she was curious to know our manner of life, she said she would come daily to the fields where I was digging. She did so and ordered me to sing the praises of my God. I recalled the "How shall we sing the Lord's song in a strange land?" of the captive children of Israel in Babylon and this prompted me to start reciting, with tears in my eyes, the psalm "By the waters of Babylon." Then I sang the "Hail, Holy Queen," and several other prayers. It was quite splendid to see how delighted she was by all this.

She did not fail to tell her husband in the evening that he had done wrong to abandon his religion, which she considered an extremely good one, from what I had told her of our God, as also from some of his praises which I had sung in her presence. She said that she experienced such heavenly delight in hearing them that she did not believe the paradise of her ancestors, for which she hoped, was so glorious, or gave her so much pleasure as she had felt when I was praising my God, and she concluded by saying that what she had heard from me was really marvellous.

This other Caiphas, or Balaam's ass, was the cause of her husband's saying to me, the next day, that he was only waiting for the next opportunity for us to make our escape to France, and that God would be glorified by what he would do. But this short delay lasted ten months, during which he encouraged me in vain hopes, which were nevertheless realized in the end, for we escaped in a little skiff and arrived at Aigues-Mortes on June 15th. Shortly afterwards we reached Avignon, where his Lordship the Vice-Legate, with tears in his eyes, and a voice shaken with sobs, reconciled the renegade in St Peter's church, to the honour of God and the edification of the onlookers. His Lordship has kept both of us near him. He intends to take us to Rome, as soon as his term of office, which ends on St John's day, has expired. He has assured the penitent that he will have him admitted to the austere monastery of Fate bene fratelli, which the man had vowed to enter, and he has promised to provide me with a good benefice. He does me the honour of loving and tenderly cherishing me, on account of some secrets of alchemy which I have taught him, and which he values more highly, he says, than if I had given him a mountain of gold, because he has been working at alchemy all his life and nothing gives him so much pleasure.

As my Lord is aware that I am an ecclesiastic, he has ordered me to procure my letters of ordination, assuring me that he will provide well for me, and find me a really good benefice. I was worrying how to find a truly efficient messenger for this purpose, when a friend of mine, one of his Lordship's household, introduced me to Monsieur Canterelle, the bearer of this letter, who was setting out for Toulouse. I have asked him to be kind enough to push on to Dax, in order to give this letter to you, and to obtain my own letter of ordination, as well as the certificate of my baccalaureate in theology, which I gained at Toulouse, and I beg you to let him have them. I am sending you a receipt for this purpose.

I brought two turquoises with me, which are naturally diamond-shaped, and I am sending you one with the request that you will as generously accept it as I humbly offer it.

Yours ever,

Vincent de Paul

Persecution rages

St Edmund Campion

October 1581

To his superior

After five months on the English mission, St Edmund describes the state of things in a country where persecution is hot and his boldly announced presence makes him a special quarry of the pursuivants. He foresees his capture but is as resolved as ever to continue his work.

Reverend Father,

Well, I came to London, and my good angel guided me into the same house that had harboured Father Robert Persons before, whither young gentlemen came to me on every hand. They embrace me, reapparel me, furnish me, weapon me, and convey me out of the city. I ride about some piece of the country every day. The harvest is wonderful great. On horseback I meditate my sermon; when I come to the house, I polish it. Then I talk with such as come to speak with me, or hear their confessions. In the morning, after Mass, I preach; they hear with exceeding greediness, and very often receive the sacrament, for the administration whereof we are ever well assisted by priests, whom we find in every place, whereby both the people is well served, and we much eased in our charge. The priests of our country themselves being most excellent for virtue and learning, yet have raised so great an opinion of our Society, that I dare scarcely touch the exceeding reverence all Catholics do unto us. How much more is it requisite that such as hereafter are to be sent for supply, whereof we have great need, be such as may answer all men's expectation of them! Specially let them be well rationed for the pulpit.

I cannot long escape the hands of the heretics; the enemies have so many eyes, so many tongues, so many scouts and crafts. I am in apparel to myself very ridiculous; I often change it, and my name also. I read letters sometimes myself that in the first front tell news that Campion is taken, which, noised in every place where I come, so filleth my ears with the sound therof, that fear itself hath taken away all fear. My soul is in mine own hands ever. Let such as you send for supply premeditate and make count of this always.

Marry, the solaces that are ever intermingled with the miseries are so great, that they do not only countervail the fear of what punishment temporal soever, but by infinite sweetness make all worldly pains, be they never so great, seem nothing. A conscience pure, a courage invincible, zeal incredible, a work so worthy the number innumerable, of high degree, of mean calling, of the inferior sort, of every age and sex.

A certain matter fell out these days unlooked for. I had set down in writing by several articles the causes of my coming in and made certain demands most reasonable. I professed myself to be a priest of the Society; that I returned to enlarge the Catholic faith, to teach the Gospel, to minister the sacraments, humbly asking audience of the queen and the nobility of the realm, and proffering disputations to the adversaries. One copy of this writing I determined to keep with me, that if it should fall into the officers' hands, it might go with me; another copy I laid in a friend's hand, that when myself with the other should be seized, another might thereupon straight be dispersed. But my said friend kept it not close long, but divulged it, and it was read greedily; whereat the adversaries were made answering out of the pulpit, that themselves certesse would not refuse to dispute, but the queen's pleasure was not that matters should be called in question being already established. In the meanwhile they tear and sting us with their venomous tongues, calling us seditious, hypocrites, yea, heretics too, which is much laughed at. The people hereupon is ours, and that error of spreading abroad this writing hath much advanced the cause. If we be commanded, and may have safe conduct, we will unto the court.

But they mean nothing less, for they have filled all the old prisons with Catholics, and now make new; and, in fine, plainly affirm that it were better so to make a few traitors away than that so many souls should be lost.

At the very writing hereof, the persecution rages most cruelly. The house where I am is sad; no other talk but of death, flight, prison, or spoil of their friends; nevertheless they proceed with courage. Very many, even at this present, being restored to the Church, new soldiers give up their names, while the old offer up their blood; by which holy hosts and oblations God will be pleased, and we shall no question by Him overcome.

You see now, reverend father, how much need we have of your prayers and sacrifices, and other heavenly help, to go through with these things. There will never want in England men that will have care of their own salvation, nor such as shall advance other men's; neither shall this Church here ever fail so long as priests and pastors shall be found for their sheep, rage man or devil never so much. But the rumour of present peril causeth me here to make an end. Arise God, his enemies avoid.

Fare you well.

E. C.

Edifying Things

John Gerard, SJ 1589-90

To Fr Claude Aquaviva, general of the Society of Jesus

Gerard well conveys the atmosphere of danger suffered not only by hunted priests on the English mission but their patrons.

Dear Father Aquaviva,

That solemn meeting of ours was fixed for the three days that precede the feast of St Luke [October 18th]. The house we had chosen for the purpose of our assembly was that which we had almost always employed on former occasions. It was the house of two sisters, one a widow, and the other a virgin, both of them illustrious for goodness and holiness, whom in my own mind I often compare to the two women who received our Lord.

Of a sudden there arrives a Queen's messenger. Rosaries, chalices, sacred vestments, all other signs of piety are, with the men, thrown into a cavern; the mistress of the house is hidden away in another hiding-place. On this occasion, as often enough on others when the pursuivant came, the younger sister, the unmarried one, passed herself off for the mistress of the house. To all the other discomforts this is to be added, that in cases like this it is necessary to contend with men who are hard to satisfy. This the young lady did with such skill and prudence as to be able to control their pertinacity and talkativeness. She was remarkable at all times for her virginal modesty and shamefacedness, but in the cause of God and the defence of his servants the *virgo* became *virago*. She is almost always ill, but we have seen her when so weakened as to be scarce able to utter three words without pain, on the arrival of the pursuivants become so strong as to spend three or four hours in contest with them. When she has no priest in the house she feels afraid; but the simple presence of a priest so animates her that then she makes sure that no devil has any power over her house. This was proved to be true in this cruel search in particular. For, quite miraculously, one pursuivant who took into his hand a silver pyx which was used for carrying the Blessed Sacrament from place to place, straightway put it down again, as if he had never seen it. Before the eyes of another lay a precious dalmatic folded up. He unfolded everything else, but that he did not touch. I should never stop if I were to write down all the edifying things that have happened in this or other searches.

John Gerard SJ

In a Strange Land

St Isaac Jogues   August 5th 1643

To the Jesuit provincial

St Isaac, a future martyr of North America, writes to his Superior to describe the harsh life and sufferings that awaited resolute missionaries among the native Americans/Canadians whom they tried to evangelize, and who often saw them as representatives of the alien powers, religiously divided as well as warring, that had disrupted their way of life.

Dear Father in God,

On August 1st, after an expedition, we embarked for the territory of the Hurons. On the second day of the journey back we met seventy Mohawks with twelve canoes hidden in the grass and trees. Suddenly they surrounded us. Terrified, the Hurons left their canoes and many of them made for the dense woods. We were left alone. The Mohawks turned on me with their fists and knotted sticks. They left me lying there almost dead. Later they tore out my nails and bit off my two forefingers. It was unbelievably painful.

They took us prisoner into their lands, and on the afternoon of the tenth day of travelling we abandoned the canoes and made the rest of the four days' journey on foot. We were constantly hungry. For three days we ate nothing but then we found some wild fruit. Eventually we came to the first Iroquois village, on the eve of the feast of the Assumption. The Huron slaves waiting with the Iroquois on both banks of the river warned us to escape because if we did not we would be burned to death. The Iroquois beat us with sticks, fists and stones which they threw with particular vehemence at my head, because they hate shaven heads. I had only two nails left from previous ill-treatment; they ripped them out with their teeth and used their own razor-sharp nails to tear away the flesh down to the bone. They then took us to a village on another hill. Before we got there we had to run the gauntlet between lines of young men with sticks. But we who knew that "He scourges every son whom he receives" offered ourselves voluntarily to God, who was acting with paternal strictness so that he might be well-pleased with his sons. We went forward one by one. First went a naked Frenchman; then René Goupil, another Frenchman; then I, wearing a shirt and breeches. The wicked Iroquois beat my back cruelly and for a long time with their sticks and with iron rods they had got from the Dutch. René could not get out of the way and was beaten so much, especially in the face, that all you could see of him was the whites of his eyes, which stood out all the more because he already looked like one who was like a "leper and struck by God, neither beautiful nor comely." We had hardly had time to get our breath back when they struck us three times with a heavy rod on the bare shoulders, and then started taking out their knives to cut off our remaining fingers. They started on me as I was the most eminent and it was clear that the French and the Hurons respected me. An old man and a woman approached me. He told her to chop off my thumb. At first she refused, but when he had threatened her three or four times, she did what he said. Then I remembered the sacrifices I had offered you, Lord, in your Church. I grasped the amputated thumb with my other hand and offered it to you, the living and true God. But one of the others warned me and I let the thumb drop, in case they followed their usual custom and put it in my mouth and forced me to swallow it. Thank God, they left me the thumb of my right hand. That made it possible for me to write this letter and beg my fathers and brothers to pray for us in the holy Church of God, which is accustomed to pray for the "afflicted and captives."

The next day, the feast of the Blessed Virgin, they took us to another village five or six miles distant from the first. My pagan guard stole my shirt and left me merely a rag which even he allowed me for decency's sake.

Otherwise I was allowed no more than a piece of sacking which I begged him to give me to cover my shoulders, but I was beaten so often that I could not stand its roughness and weight, especially when the unrelenting sun had roasted my skin as if in an oven, so that it came off my neck, shoulders and arms in flakes.

On the way into the village they beat us again, striking us mainly on the leg bones. At night we lay there naked on the bare ground, in chains, and they threw coals and red-hot embers on us. We were conducted all over the place to satisfy the general curiosity. In the third village we met four more Hurons who had just been captured and mutilated like us. I managed to instruct and baptize them: two with the dew of which there was so much in the tall leaves of Turkish corn on the stalks they let us chew, and the other two in a stream we passed on our way to another village. At night they took us into a cabin and told us to sing. We had no choice, but sang the canticles of the Lord in a strange land. They soon exchanged singing for torture. They chose René and me especially. They burned me with live coals, especially on the chest. They then tied me upright between two wooden stakes with bark-thongs—I imagined they were going to set me on fire. But even if I managed to suffer the rest with strength and patience, that was through no merit of mine, but by the power of him who gives strength to the weary. They left me almost entirely alone while this torture was in progress, and I wept. "I shall glory only in my infirmities." Thank you, Lord, for teaching me through this trifling experience what you willingly bore for my sake on the cross, where your most holy body was not even supported by cords, but hung from hands and feet pierced by cruel nails. We spent the remainder of the night fixed to the ground with stakes. They did and tried to do many things to us, but you, Lord whom I thank, spared me the impure hands of the barbarians.

After all that they left me and René together to lead the life of what one might call free slaves. On our Lady's birthday, one of the leading Dutchmen from the colony some forty miles distant came over to bargain for our ransom. Though he remained for some days, and offered them a large sum, he got nothing. We were warned that danger threatened, and went over to a hill to pray. We offered our lives to God and began to say the rosary. We had reached the fourth decade when two young men told us to go back to the village. I told René that this did not look too good and that it was time to commend ourselves to God and our Lady. At the village gate, one of the men took out a hatchet which he had hidden and aimed a blow at René's head. He fell down half-dead but remembered to call out, as we had agreed, the holy name of Jesus. I expected the same attack and bared my neck and fell on my knees to receive it. But after a while the young pagan told me to get up. He had no permission to kill me, he said.

I stood up and absolved my friend who was still breathing. The pagan finally killed him with two more blows. René was not over thirty-five, and a very unassuming and innocent person, whose patience was constant and who always followed God's will. The next day I risked my life in looking for his body so that I could bury it. They had tied a rope around his neck, dragged him half naked through the entire village, and then thrown him into the river some way off. I found him by the river bank. His body was half-eaten by dogs. I covered it with stones in a dried-up river bed, thinking to return the next day with a pick-axe to bury him more securely. When I came back with tools, they had taken him away. I looked everywhere, even wading into the water to look for his body with my hands and feet, but they told me that the torrent had borne it away. I held a memorial service for him by singing the pre-scribed psalms and prayers from the Ritual. I sobbed and wailed, and my tears were mixed with the waters. When the snows melted in the spring, I heard of his remains, for the young men of the region told me that they had seen his bones on the river bank. I kissed them reverently, put them with his head, and buried them as best I could.

Yours,

Isaac Jogues

Trials of a Missionary

Bd Théophane Vénard   May 10th 1860

To a friend (a priest)

Before his eventual capture in November 1860, Vénard often came close to the martyrdom he had desired from childhood onwards. Here he describes vividly the conditions of persecution under which he had to live in Tonkin, in north-eastern Indo-China, which eventually became a French colony and is now part of Vietnam.

Reverend and dear Father,

I write to you from Tonkin, from a dark little hole where the only light comes through the crack of a partially-opened door, which just makes it possible for me to trace these lines, and now and then to read a few pages of a book. One has to be ever watchful. If the dog barks, or any stranger passes, the door is instantly closed, and I prepare to hide myself in a still lower hole, which has been excavated in my temporary retreat. This is how I have lived for three months, sometimes alone, sometimes together with my dear old friend, Mgr Theurel. The convent which sheltered us before has been destroyed by the pagans, who got wind of our being there. We just had time to escape through two double walls about a foot wide. We saw through the chinks the band of persecutors, with the mayor at their head, garotting five or six of the oldest nuns, who had been left behind when the younger ones took flight. They beat these poor women with rods, and we heard them howling like very demons, threatening to kill and burn everybody and everything, unless they were given a large sum of money. This agreeable visit lasted for four hours, till they were invited by the principal people of the village to go and eat and to get drunk with them. We could not escape until cock-crow, and took our refuge in a smoky dung-heap belonging to a pious old Christian widow, where we were joined by another missionary.

What do you think of our position? Three missionaries, one of whom is a bishop, lying side by side, day and night, in a space about a yard and a half square, our only light and means of breathing being three holes, the size of a little finger, made in the mud wall, which our poor old woman is obliged to conceal by some faggots thrown down outside. Under our feet is a brick cellar, constructed in the dead of night with great skill by one of our catechists. In this cellar there are three bamboo tubes which are cleverly contrived to open on to the borders of the neighbouring lake with its fresh air.

You might well ask: Why don't you go mad? Always shut up in the thickness of two walls, with a roof one can touch with one's hand, our companions spiders, rats and toads, always obliged to speak in a low voice, "like the wind," as the Annamites say, receiving every day the most terrible news of the torture and death of our fellow-missionaries, and worse still, of their occasional apostasy under torture. It requires, I must admit, a special grace not to be utterly discouraged and dejected. As to our health, we are like poor plants in cellars. One of my brethren writes to me today to say that for eighteen months he has not seen the sun. He dates his letter from the "land of the moles." As for me, I live on without being too bilious. My weakness is my nerves. I need something strengthening such as wine, but we have barely enough to say Mass, so one must not think of it. Not many days ago I managed to get into an adjoining house, and was very much astonished to find myself tottering like a drunken man. The fact was that I had lost the habit and almost the power of walking and the daylight made me feel giddy.

As a result of the destruction of our College, upwards of 1200 young men are on the wide world, without homes or occupations, not daring to return to their families, and wandering from one Chinese mission to another until they almost inevitably fall into the hands of their persecutors. Scarcely one has yielded to the cruelty or blandishments of their tormentors and the Church may indeed be proud of having produced such noble confessors of the faith. But you see how impossible it is for us, pastors of the flock, to console or break the bread of life for our poor suffering children. We are compelled to hide and to leave our lambs to the wolves. Before this terrible persecution our mission was so flourishing. And now I feel like Jeremiah groaning over the ruins of Jerusalem. Will they ever be rebuilt?...

Your friend,

Théophane Vénard

A New Life at Hand

St Ignatius of Antioch   107

To the Romans

A victim of the persecution of Christians under the Emperor Trajan, and despatched to Rome to die, the aged St Ignatius wrote letters to St Polycarp (whom he met at Smyrna) and to various churches to predict the martyrdom that he devoutly anticipated.

To the Church in the territory of the Romans,

...

I write to all the churches, and I am quite willing to die for God if you do not prevent me in any way. I beg you not to be unhelpfully kind. Let the wild beasts have me, for that is how I shall reach God. I am wheat for God and the teeth of wild beasts will grind me until I become the pure bread of Christ. You must coax the wild animals to give me a tomb and leave no fragment of my body behind. Then, as I sleep in death, I shall not be a burden to anyone. I shall be a true disciple of Jesus Christ, though the world will be unable to see even my body. Ask the Lord to ensure that these creatures allow me to become an acceptable sacrifice to him. I am not trying to lay down the law for you as Peter or Paul might have done. They were apostles and I am condemned to death. They were free and I am now a slave. But, even if I do suffer, I shall do so as a freedman of Christ. In Christ I shall rise again, a free man. Now, in my bondage, I must learn to forget all my desires.

I fight with wild beasts all the way from Syria to Rome. I fight by land and by sea, day and night, tied fast to ten leopards, the soldiers in my bodyguard. They are even worse when bribed. Yet I learn all the more, the more unjustly they treat me. But that is not how I am justified in this condition. I intend to enjoy the wild beasts that are ready for me. I pray that they will finish me off quickly. By flattery I shall persuade them to eat me as speedily as possible, and not treat me like some other victims whom they have been afraid to touch. If they are reluctant and refuse to rend me, I shall make them do so by force. You must understand that I am the best judge of what is good for me. At last I am beginning to be a disciple. May nothing visible or invisible prevent me through jealousy from reaching Jesus Christ. Whether I suffer by fire or cross, entire herds of wild animals, drawing and quartering, scattering of bones, severed limbs, a crushed body, and all the devil's vile attacks, I welcome all these things if they bring me to Jesus Christ.

Neither the most distant realms of the earth nor the kingdoms of this world will bring me any profit. It is more noble to die for Jesus Christ than to rule the uttermost ends of the earth. I seek Jesus who died for us. I desire Jesus who rose again for us. My birth into a new life is at hand. Bear with me, brethren. Do not come between me and life. Do not desire my death. I want to belong to God, so do not give me to the world. Do not tempt me with earthly goods. Let me find true illumination. Once I have that I shall be a man. Let me imitate the passion of my God. The man in whom He dwells will understand my longing and sympathize with me, for he will realize the difficulties that face me.

The ruler of this world wants to capture me and to turn me from my purpose, which aims at God. None of you on my side must help the rule of the world. Become God's defenders by being mine. Do not have Jesus Christ on your lips and the world in your hearts. Throw envy out. If I ask for your help when I am with you, do not believe me. Believe what I am writing to you now. I write to you as a living person who longs to die. My earthly emotions are crucified and all the fire of bodily passion is put out in me. But a fountain of living water speaks within me, saying: "Come to the Father." I desire the Bread of God, the flesh of Christ, born years past from the seed of David. I long to drink his Blood, a pure love-feast.

I no longer desire to live as men think of living, and my wish will be granted if only you wish it too. Let that be your desire, so that your wishes and mine may come to pass. I beg you in these few words. Believe me: Jesus Christ will show you unmistakably that I am speaking the truth. He is God's unerring mouth through whom the Father has spoken truly. Pray for me so that I may reach my end through the Holy Spirit. What I write to you does not accord with human feelings but with the mind of God. If I suffer you will have wished me well, but if I am rejected that will mean that you hated me.

. . .

Ignatius

A Letter from Prison

St Théophane Vénard   January 20th 1861

To his family

The village schoolmaster's son who had worked heroically on the Indo-Chinese mission writes to his family from the cage in which he had been imprisoned for some months. In little more than a week he was to suffer a cruel death intended to frighten not only other missioners but the many thousands of Christian converts in the country.

My dear family,

I write to you at the start of this year which will be my last in this world. I hope you received the short note announcing my capture on the feast of St Andrew, when God allowed me to be betrayed by a traitor, against whom I bear no grudge.... The mandarin treated me very well. His brothers visited me at least ten times to try to persuade me to trample on the cross rather than see me die so young. After a couple of days I arrive at Kechoo, the ancient capital of the Tonkinese dynasty. You must picture me sitting peacefully in my wooden cage carried by eight soldiers, besieged on every side by a vast crowd that almost stopped the soldiers from passing. "What a lovely little fellow that Westerner is!" some of them declared. "He is as jolly and cheerful as someone travelling to a feast. He doesn't seem at all afraid!" My catechist Khang, bearing his terrible wooden yoke, walked behind my cage. I asked God's Spirit to strengthen us both, and I begged the Queen of Martyrs to help her loyal child.

To begin with the judge gave me a cup of tea which I drank without ceremony in my cage. Then, after the usual interrogation: "Trample on the cross and you will be spared!"

"What! Have I preached the religion of the cross all my life until now and you expect me to desert it? I do not treasure the things of this world so highly that I wish to buy them by apostasy."

The mandarins then questioned my catechist, and gave him ten strokes of the knout which he suffered without flinching. God never failed to give him the strength to confess the faith gloriously.

Since then I have been put in my cage at the door of the prefect's house, guarded by a band of Cochin-Chinese soldiers. I am patiently awaiting the day when God will let me offer him the sacrifice of my own blood. I am not sorry to leave this world. My soul thirsts for the waters of eternal life. My exile is at an end. I am approaching the soil of my own true land. Earth fades and heaven opens. I am on my way to God. Farewell, dearest father, sister, brothers, do not mourn for me, do not shed tears for me, live the years you have left in unity and love. One day we shall meet again in heaven. Three long and wearisome years have passed since I had news of you and I do not know who is dead and who is living. Jesus Christ's prisoner greets you. The sacrifice will soon be made. May God keep you always. Amen.

I send my sister and friend, Melanie, a special word of love and farewell.... It is midnight. Round my wooden cage I can see only banners and swords. In the corner of the hall where my cage is placed some soldiers are playing cards. Another group are playing draughts. Occasionally the sentries strike the hour of the night on their gongs. Two feet or so from my cage a faint oil-lamp throws a wavering gleam on this sheet of Chinese paper and allows me to trace these few lines. Every day I await my sentence—tomorrow perhaps. I shall probably be beheaded. You will weep when you hear the news, sister dear, but they must be tears of joy you shed. Think of your brother in a halo of martyrdom, with the palm of victory in his hand. In a few short hours my soul will leave this earth, my exile will be at an end and the battle will be won. I shall rise upwards and enter into our true home. There I shall be among God's elect and see what no human eye can imagine. I shall listen to unheard-of melodies, enjoy a happiness the heart cannot in the least understand. But first the grain of wheat has to be ground and the bunch of grapes must be trodden in the wine-press. May I become pure bread and wine quite fit to serve the Master! I hope that this will be so through the mercies of my Redeemer and Saviour and under the protection of his Immaculate Mother. Therefore, even while I stand in the arena in the thick of the fray, I dare to sing a triumphant hymn as if the victory were already mine. Now I leave you, dearest sister, to till the field of virtue and good works. Reap a rich harvest for the everlasting life which awaits us both. Take up faith, hope, charity, patience, tenderness, sweetness, perseverance and a holy death, and thus we shall go forward, hand in hand, now and for evermore.

Farewell, Melanie! Goodbye, dear sister.

Farewell again,

Your brother

Théophane

A Message from Auschwitz

St Maximilian Kolbe   June 15th 1941

To his mother

Some prisoners in the "work-camp," or slave-labour, section of the Auschwitz concentration and mass-extermination camp, the scene of probably the most appalling crimes ever committed by human beings against one another, were allowed to write a few words in German on post-cards. These messages, which could contain nothing critical of the place or its organization, represented a minimal attempt to hide the real horror from the Polish population, who were already well aware of the German occupiers' capacity for cruelty. Even within the compass of the few words allowed him Maxmilian conveyed the quality of the extraordinary faith that enabled him to offer his life for another man two months later. This pencilled letter is one of the shortest yet most poignant written by any saint.

My dear Mother,

I was consigned to Auschwitz (Oswiecim) Camp at the end of the month.

I am all right. Dear Mother, don't worry about me and my health, because the good God is with me everywhere, and thinks with great love of everyone and everything.

It would be good to wait a while before writing another letter in answer to mine, as I don't know how long I shall be staying here.

With all loving wishes and kisses,

Kolbe Rajmund

A New Language

Dietrich Bonhoeffer   1945

To a young friend

Before his execution by an evil regime, Bonhoeffer leaves a message for the future and offers perhaps the most succinct summary yet of the Church's failure to witness to truth in the most testing years of the twentieth century.

Dear D ...,

... During these years the Church has fought for self-preservation as though it were an end in itself, and has thereby lost its chance to speak a word of reconciliation to humanity and the world at large. So our traditional language must perforce become powerless and remain silent, and our Christianity today will be confined to praying for and doing right by our human brothers and sisters. Christian thinking, speaking and organization must be reborn out of this praying and this action. By the time you are grown up the shape of the Church will be changed beyond all recognition. We are not yet out of the melting pot and every attempt to hasten matters will only delay the Church's conversion and purgation. It is not for us to prophesy the day, but the day will come when people will be called again to utter the word of God with such power as will change and renew the world. It will be a new language, which will horrify human beings, and yet overwhelm them by its power. It will be the language of a new righteousness and truth, a language which proclaims the peace of God with humankind and the advent of his kingdom....

Dietrich

CHAPTER 12

Suffering, Death and Beyond

Self-Denial

Charles de Foucauld

December 1st 1916

To Olivier de Bondy

Charles de Foucauld wrote 734 letters to his cousin Olivier de Bondy between 1889 and 1916. This is the last letter. It was written on the day of his death, which occurred while he was waiting for the postman (an Arab soldier), who eventually arrived the next day. He was tied up by a band of Touareg raiders, including someone whom he had once helped and who pretended to be the courier. They probably intended to carry him off and demand a ransom for his return to the French authorities. While the rest of the raiding party pillaged the hermitage, his fifteen-year-old guard panicked and shot Charles when he made an instinctive movement to warn two approaching Arab soldiers of the danger they were in.

Dear Cousin,

Your sufferings, the worrying uncertainties in the past and more recently, received with good will and offered to God in union with and for the intentions of the sufferings of Jesus, these are not the only thing, but they are the most valuable that God gives to you in order that you come before him with full hands. Self-abnegation is the best of all ways of uniting oneself with Jesus and of bringing good to others: as St John of the Cross keeps on saying: "To suffer and to love is the greatest thing that can be done in this world. We know when we suffer, we do not always know when we love, and that is one suffering the more; but we can will to love, and to will it is to do it." We think that we do not love enough, and that is true, for one can never love enough; but God, who knows of what clay we are made, who loves us far more than any mother is able to love her child, who never

247

dies, God has told us that he will not spurn those who come to him....
Your cousin,

Charles de Foucauld

Suffering

Friedrich von Hügel   19—

To a friend in his last illness

Von Hügel did not shirk the daunting task of offering spiritual counsel in situations of "the bitterest anguish." In letters such as the following he reveals the qualities that allowed the Swedish Archbishop Söderblom to describe him as penetrating into "the vast mysteries of the human heart and religion, that universal teacher and blessed saint."

My Friend,

I keep your case, and its necessities and possible helps, well in my mind and in my prayers. And since you continue to press me, so gently yet so firmly, to propose to you whatsoever I may believe will or might help you to deepen your spiritual life and fully to utilize the suffering that God himself is now sending you, I will suggest the two following closer practices and self-examinations. I need not say, that they are both intended simply as rough material, or approximate suggestions for your own experimenting and hewing into shape. I do not even want to hear your impressions upon them—it all aims solely at the depths of your heart and conscience, to help the fullest awakening and purification that God may call you to. Certain it is, that only such growing, deepening (even if interiorly painful at first) can and will anchor your soul in a peace which not all the possible hurricanes of pain, or oppressions of physical weakness can break you away from, really, at all.

I would, then, first, get my imagination and reason into the habit, not simply of looking at, and looking for, sin as an offence against God, but of realizing and picturing it as always (except with hardened grave sinners) chiefly a shirking of some effort, or loneliness or pain, etc., attached to a light or commandment as it offered itself to us, or a seeking of some pleasure, relaxation, vanity, etc., attached to the contrary course. Now the cure, the only cure, for such shirking of right pain, and for such seeking of wrong pleasure, is precisely the recovering (more and more deliberately) of that mean shirking and mean seeking. Pain—most real pain, which comes ready to our hand for turning into right pain—gets offered us by God. Try more and more at the moment itself, without any delay or evasion, without any fixed form, as simply, as spontaneously as possible, to cry out to God, to Christ our Lord, in any way that comes most handy, and the more variously the better: "Oh! Oh! this is real: oh! deign to accept it, as a little real atonement for real sin!" "Oh, help me to move on, from finding pain so real, to discovering sin to be far more real." "Oh, may this pang deepen me, may it help to make me real, real—really humble, really loving, really ready to live or die with my soul in your hands...." And so on, and so on. You could end by such ejaculations costing your brains practically nothing. The all-important point is to make them at the time and with pain well mixed up into the prayer.

The second thoroughly concrete matter I would quietly watch in myself is, whether I had not been hard and absolute, "so far and no further," "I have done with so and so", "I have washed my hands of him," etc. I have had to fight this in myself for many years; and since God in his goodness has (through suffering, saintly advice, etc.) wakened me up to a tiny bit more of his love, I have come to find that I cannot be too watchful about this.... Of course, this does not mean any indiscriminate acceptance of anyone, least of all to the possible or real weakness or fantastic notions of priests or others who may have wandered far afield from sobriety, or from what we cannot help feeling to be so. Only the absoluteness, the hardness, the dryness, etc., of finality in such states of soul is here meant; and such characteristics will, where not offences against the soul's own light, be presumably indications for its still largely dormant condition. Also, if any of the persons thus felt about by such a soul have happened first to have treated the soul unkindly or woundingly: oh, there is a fine opportunity for the discrimination between the impulses of our poor untrained naturalness and the inspiration of God's supernatural Spirit. I would then do my poor best to oust from my heart all such hardness; astonishing sweetness and elasticity of growth in the midst of the bitterest anguish would be the infallible result.

Friedrich von Hügel

A Familiar Guest

St Robert Southwell   September 30th 1591

To Thomas Howard

A year before his betrayal and arrest, and while still chaplain to the wife of the imprisoned Philip Howard, Southwell writes to his friend Thomas Howard, Earl of Suffolk, to console him on the death of his sister, Lady Margaret Sackville. This letter is one of the most sonorous and moving pieces of Elizabethan prose, and put by some commentators in an even higher category of achievement than St Robert's poetry.

Dear Friend,

Death is too ordinary a thing to seem any novelty, being a familiar guest in every house. Since his coming is expected and his errand not unknown, neither should his presence be feared nor his effects lamented. What wonder is it to see the fuel burned, the spice pounded or the snow melted? And as little fear it is to see those dead, that were born upon condition once to die. Night and sleep are perpetual mirrors, figuring in their darkness, their silence, and the shutting up of the senses, the final end of our mortal bodies; and for this some have entitled sleep the eldest brother of death: but with no less convenience it might be called one of death's tenants, near unto him in affinity of condition, yet far inferior in right, being but the tenant for a time of that, of which death is the inheritor: for, by virtue of the conveyance made unto him in Paradise, that dust we are, and to dust we must return, he has hitherto shown his seigniority over all, exacting of us not only the yearly, but hourly reverence of time, which ever by minutes we defray unto him: so that our very life is not only a memory, but a part of our death, since the longer we have lived, the less we have to live. What is the daily lessening of our life, but a continual dying? Not the quantity but the quality commends our life; the ordinary gain of long livers being only a greater burden of sin.

Our life is but lent; a good whereof to make, during the loan, our best commodity. It is a debt due to a more certain owner than ourselves, and therefore so long as we have it, we receive a benefit; when we are deprived of it, we suffer no wrong. We are tenants at will of this clayey farm, not for any term of years; when we are warned out we must be ready to remove, having no other title but the owner's pleasure. It is but an inn, not a home; we came but to bait, not to dwell; and the condition of our entrance was finally to depart. If the departure be grievous, it is also common—this today to me, tomorrow for thee; and the case equally affecting all, leaves none any cause to complain of injurious usage. Some are taken in their first step into this life, receiving at once their welcome and farewell, as though they had been born only to be buried. Some live till they be weary of life, to give proof of their good hap that had a kindlier passage; yet though the date be diverse, the debt is all one, equally to be answered of all, as their time expires: for who is the man that shall live and not see death, since we all die, and like water slide into the earth?

In paradise we received the sentence of death; and here as prisoners we are kept immured, tarrying but our time till the gaoler call us to our execution. Whom has any virtue eternized, or desert commended to posterity, that has not mourned in life and been mourned after death? Even the Blessed Virgin, the mother of God, was thrown down as deep in temporal miseries, as she was advanced high in spiritual honours; none amongst all mortal creatures finding in life more proof than she of her mortality. For though she had the noblest son that ever woman was mother of, not only above the condition of men, but above the glory of angels; being her son only, without temporal father, and thereby doubling the love of both parents in her breast; yes, though he was God, and she the nearest creature to God's perfections, no prerogative either acquitted her from mourning, or him from dying; and though they surmounted the highest angels in all preeminences, yet were they equal with the meanest men in the sentence of death.

Seeing therefore that death spares none, let us spare our tears for better uses, it being an idol-sacrifice to this deaf and implacable executioner. And for this, nature did promise us a weeping life, exacting tears for custom at our first entrance, and suiting our whole course to this doleful beginning; therefore they must be used with measure that must be used so often, and since we cannot end our tears, let us at the least reserve them. Learn to give sorrow no long dominion over you. Some are so obstinate in their own will, that even time, the natural remedy of the most violent agonies, cannot by any delays assuage their grief. They entertain their sorrow with solitary musings, and feed their sighs and tears; they pine their bodies, nursing their heaviness with a melancholy humour, as though they had vowed themselves to sadness; unwilling it should end till it had ended them, that being true which Solomon observed, "that as a moth the garment, and a worm the wood, so does sadness pervade the heart." But this impotent softness does not fit sober minds. It is for the most part the fault, not of all, but of the silliest women who, next to the funeral of their friends, deem it a second widowhood to force their tears, and make it their happiness to seem most unhappy; as though they had only been left alive, to be a perpetual map of dead folks' misfortunes. Much sorrow for the dead is either the child of self-love or rash judgment. If we shed our tears for the death of others as a means to our contentment, we show but our wound—perfect lovers of ourselves: if we lament their decease as their hard destiny, we attach them of evil deserving with too peremptory a censure, as though their life had been a rise, and their death a leap into final perdition; for otherwise, a good departure craves small condoling, being but a harbour from storms, and an entrance into felicity.

It could not displease you to see your friend removed out of a ruinous house, and the house destroyed or pulled down, if you knew it were to be built in statelier form, and to transfer the inhabitant with more joy into a fairer lodging. Let then your sister's soul depart without grief; let her body also be altered into dust; withdraw your eyes from the ruin of this cottage, and cast them upon the majesty of the second building, which St Paul says shall be incorruptible, glorious, strange, spiritual and immortal. Think it no injury that she is now taken from you, but a favour that she was lent you so long ago; and show no unwillingness to restore God his own, since hitherto you have paid no usury for it. Consider not how much longer you might have enjoyed her, but how much sooner you might have lost her, and take our Sovereign's right for a sufficient reason for her death. Let him, with good leave, gather the grape of his own vine, and pluck the fruit of his own planting, and think such curious works ever safest in the artificer's hand, who is likeliest to love them, and best able to preserve them. Since God was well pleased to call her, she not displeased to go, and you the third twist to make a triple cord, saying, our Lord gave, and our Lord took away, as it has pleased our Lord, so has it fallen out: the name of the Lord be blessed.

Robert

The Divine Sweetness

St John of the Cross   April 14th 1589

To a religious

St John writes to a penitent who has described his great desire to occupy his will with God alone and to love him above all things, and encourages him with typical intensity.

Your Reverence,
  The peace of Jesus Christ, son, be ever in your soul. . . .

He would be very ignorant who should think that, because spiritual delight and sweetness are failing him, God is failing him, and should rejoice and be glad if he should have them and think that for this reason he has been having God. And still more ignorant would he be if he went after God in search of this sweetness, and rejoiced and rested in it; for in this case he would not be seeking God with his will grounded in the emptiness of faith and charity, but with spiritual sweetness and pleasure, which is of creature, following his taste and desire; and thus he would not then love God purely, above all things (which means to set the whole strength of the will upon Him), for, if he seizes hold upon that creature and clings to it with the desire, his will rises not above it to God, who is inaccessible; for it is impossible that the will can rise to the sweetness and delight of divine union, or embrace God or experience his sweet and loving embraces, save in detachment and emptying of the desire with respect to every particular pleasure whether from above or from below....

It must be known, then, that the desire is the mouth of the will, which opens wide when it is not impeded or filled with any morsel—that is, with any pleasure; for, when the desire is set upon anything, it becomes constrained, and apart from God everything is constraint. And therefore, in order for the soul to succeed in reaching God and to become united with him, it must have the mouth of its will opened to God alone and freed from any morsel of desire, to the end that God may satisfy it and fill it with his love and sweetness, and it may still have that hunger and thirst for God alone and refuse to be satisfied with aught else, since here on earth it cannot taste God as he is, and furthermore, that which it can taste, if it so desire, as I say, impedes it. This was taught by Isaiah when he said: "All you that thirst, come to the waters", etc. (Isaiah. 55:1). Here he invites those that thirst for God alone to the fullness of the divine waters of union with God, though they have no money—that is, no desire.

Very meet it is, then, if your Reverence would enjoy great peace in your soul and achieve perfection, that you should surrender your whole will to God, so that it may thus be united with Him, and that you should not employ it in the vile and base things of earth.

May his Majesty make you as spiritual and holy as I desire.

John

The Everlasting Kingdom

St Aelred of Rievaulx   c. 1160

To his sister

The Cistercian Abbot Aelred was an understanding counsellor, known as "friendship's child." This scripturally based letter of comfort nicely combines a formal presentation of the future life with personal touches.

My dear sister,

May the glorious procession enter the high city of Jerusalem, the eternal heavenly city. Christ himself will lead it, and all the members of his Body assembled in him will follow him. There the King of glory will reign in them and they in him. They will receive the kingdom of everlasting happiness as the inheritance prepared for them even before the creation of the world. We have no idea what that kingdom will be like, so how can we write about it? But one thing I know, and I shall declare it boldly, is that you will have all you desire, and you will have nothing that you would rather not have. There will be no weeping or wailing, no sorrow and no fear, no discord or envy, no troubles or temptations. There will be no corruption, suspicion or ambition. There will be no sickness of old age, death or poverty. There will be not the slightest need or tiredness or faintness. Where none of these things exists, there must be perfect joy and gladness and peace, perfect security, and unspoiled love and charity; perfect riches, beauty and rest; health and strength and the perfect vision of God. In that eternal and perpetual life there is nothing more that you could want. God our creator will be clearly seen, known and loved. He will be seen in himself reigning in perfect bliss. He will be perceived in his creatures governing and ruling all things without any trouble or difficulty, caring for all things without growing weary, and giving himself to all things to the extent that they are able to receive him, without any reduction of his divinity. The divine countenance that the angels long to see will be seen in all its sweetness, loving-kindness and desirability. But who may speak of the clarity and luminance of that vision?

There we shall see the Father in the Son, the Son in the Father, and the Holy Spirit in them both. There God who made us will be seen not as in a glass darkly but face to face, as the Gospel says. There God will be seen as he is, when his gospel promise will be fulfilled: "Who loves me will be loved by my Father and I shall love him and show him my own self." From this clear vision of God arises that happy knowledge which Christ describes in the Gospel: "This is everlasting life, that they may know Thee, the one

true God, and Jesus Christ whom you sent." This knowledge gives rise to
so great an outburst of happy longing, to so much fulness of love, to such
sweetness of charity, that the completion of bliss cannot reduce the joyful
longing nor desire bar the way to fulness. How can we summarize all this?
Surely, sister, we can put it thus: "The eye has not seen, nor the ear heard,
what God has prepared for those who love him".

    Your brother,

     Aelred

Beauteous and Lovely

St Robert Southwell   c. 1587

To other members of his faith persecuted or in prison

*In this vision of ultimate bliss the individual lyricism of Southwell the poet is more
restrained, and scriptural and liturgical echoes are to the fore, though metaphors and
examples such as that of the behaviour to be expected from a new ruler directly evoke
Elizabethan experience. The first version of this letter was one of a series sent to Philip
Howard in the Tower. These were later reworked as the letters that made up "An
Epistle of Comfort," addressed to all those who in penal times faced suffering, and
possibly imprisonment, torture and a cruel death.*

Dear fellow-Catholics,

    What a glorious dignity it is, how great a felicity, to fight under God as
a ruler, and to be crowned by Christ as the judge of the combat! The time
is come for you to take repose, and enjoy the felicity of the land of promise.
You have been on Mount Sinai, when thunders began to be heard,
lightnings to flash, and a thick cloud to cover the mount. Now you are
called unto Mount Tabor where, enjoying his glory you may say, with St
Peter, "It is good for us to be here!" Our country is heaven, our parents
the patriarchs. There a great multitude of our friends expect us, a vast
number desire our coming—secure and certain of their own salvation, and
only solicitous for ours. What unspeakable comfort it is to come to the
sight and embraces of them. How great is the contentment of their abode,
without fear of dying, and with eternity of living. There is the glorious
choir of apostles, the company of rejoicing prophets, the innumerable
multitude of martyrs, there are the troops of fair virgins.

    If God can make such mighty emperors and worthies, as we read to have
been in times past, from a child that comes naked out of his mother's womb

and has no more to help himself than the poorest brat that is born in the world, how much more able is he to advance the most impotent wretch to a greater dignity in heaven? God esteems not the toys that men account of, his judgment only searches every man's deserts. On the death of a prince and the accession of a new one, they that were in authority are then deposed; those that were base and abject before are then advanced; and the prince that is newly created regards little whom his predecessor favoured, but who seems to him best worthy of preferment: even so when we die little esteems God what account the world has made of us, but how well we have deserved to be well thought of, and worthily rewarded.

Besides men, we shall have the company of many choirs of angels, of our Blessed Lady, Christ and the most Blessed Trinity; and these as beautiful to see and so amiable and loving to converse with that we shall have no less joy of our company than of our own glory. Everyone's wish shall be fulfilled in himself, in all other creatures, yes and in almighty God. And so shall all be absolute kings, because everyone's pleasure and will shall be fully accomplished.

In the sight of God we shall have the fulness of felicity, which neither eye has seen, nor ear heard, nor man's heart achieved. The understanding shall be without error, the memory without forgetfulness, the will without evil desires, the thoughts pure and comfortable, the affection ordinate and measurable, all the passions governed by reason and settled in a perfect calm. No fear shall affright us, no presumption puff us up, no love disquiet us, no anger incense us, no envy gnaw us, no pusillanimity quail us; but courage, constancy, charity, peace and security shall replenish and establish our hearts. It shall be lawful to love whatsoever we like, and whatsoever we love we shall perfectly enjoy; and not only love, but be also loved so much as we ourselves will desire. Our knowledge shall comprise whatsoever may be to our comfort, not only one thing at once but all things together: so that the multitude of the objects shall delight us, not confound us; fill our desire of knowledge, not hinder the perfect intelligence of them all.

And as for our bodies, they shall be of most comely and gracious feature; beauteous and lovely; healthful, without all weakness; always in youth, and in the flower and prime of their force; personable of shape, as nimble as our thought, subject to no penal impression, incapable of grief, as clear as crystal, as bright as the sun, and as able to find passage through heaven, earth or any other material stop as is the liquid and yielding air.

There plenty cloys not; there, satiety offends not; there, continuance annoys not; there, hunger is satisfied, yet not diminished; there, desire is accomplished, but not sated: so that their mind is quieted by having their desire, and annoyance avoided by desiring what they have. Neither is their joy contained in their own persons; for each by loving others as himself, delights in the happiness of others as much as in his own, and what he has not in himself, he possesses in the society he is in; so that he has as many joys as he has fellows in felicity; and the several joys of all are of as great comfort to every saint as his own peculiar joys: and because all love God more than themselves, they take more pleasure in his bliss than of all their joys besides....

Yours,
Robert Southwell

For Ever and Ever

St Peter Damian   1065

To a dying friend

Peter Damian, Doctor of the Church, was a rigorous ecclesiastical disciplinarian but also wrote some of the most treasured hymns of the Latin church. This letter in which he commits his dying friend to his Creator was used in the Church's liturgy for many centuries until the reforms of recent years, and survives only in an attenuated form. The original Latin has been used and echoed by many writers, most notably by James Joyce, who incorporated the beautiful sound-play of such phrases as "liliata rutilantium turba confessorum te circumdet" (surrounded by the lily-white throng, etc.) into his own work as touchstones of emotional evocation.

Dear Brother,

I commend you to almighty God, and consign you to the care of him who created you, praying that when, by dying, you shall have paid the debt of humankind, you may return to your Maker, who formed you out of earthly clay.

May your spirit, as it leaves the body, be met by the noble company of angels. May it be greeted by the apostles at their judgment-seat, welcomed by the victorious army of white-robed martyrs, surrounded by the lily-white throng of glorious confessors, hailed by the exultant choir of virgins, and enfolded in the bosom of the patriarchs in blessed peace. May Christ Jesus show himself to you with smiling and gentle aspect, and appoint a place for you in his presence for all eternity.

Far from you be all the terror of darkness, the hiss of flames, the anguish of torment. Begone the loathsome fiend and his accomplices; when you draw near with your angelic escort, let him shrink abashed into the vast chaos of eternal night.

"Let God arise, and let his enemies be scattered; let them also that hate him flee before him. Like as the smoke vanisheth, so shalt thou drive them away; and like as wax melteth at the fire, so let the ungodly perish before God" (Ps. 68).

Shame and confusion light upon the whole array of hell. Let no minister of Satan dare to bar your way.

May Christ, who for your sake was crucified, deliver you from torment: Christ, who stooped to die for you, deliver you from everlasting death. May he, the Christ, Son of the living God, grant you a place within that paradise of his where winter never comes; he, the true shepherd, own you for one of his flock. May he absolve you from all your sins, and place you among the elect at his right hand.

May you see your Redeemer face to face, and standing ever in his presence gaze with delighted eyes on Truth itself made manifest. There take your place in the ranks of the blessed and enjoy the blissful vision of your God for ever.

Your friend,
    Peter Damian

The Parting of the Ways
Alfred Delp, SJ

January 1945

To his fellow-Jesuits

Alfred Delp was a courageous and clear-thinking man, with an unusually precise understanding of the lessons of history. Unlike many of his fellow-Christians, he never doubted the evil of the regime that plunged his people into moral chaos and eventually the same devastation that it brought to so many other countries. In the few years allowed him he worked selflessly for the democratic recovery of his nation and against what he tellingly defined as the essence of totalitarianism: the "determination to destroy," for the recognition of which he was condemned to death.

Dear Brothers,

Here I am at the parting of the ways and I must take the other road after all. The death sentence has been passed and the atmosphere is so charged with enmity and hatred that no appeal has any hope of succeeding.

I thank the Order and my brethren for all their goodness and loyalty and help, especially during these last weeks. I ask pardon for much that was untrue and unjust; and I beg that a little help and care may be given to my aged, sick parents.

The actual reason for my condemnation was that I happened to be, and chose to remain, a Jesuit. There was nothing to show that I had any connection with the attempt on Hitler's life, so I was acquitted on that count. The rest of the accusations were far less serious and more factual. There was one underlying theme—a Jesuit is *a priori* an enemy and betrayer of the Reich. So the whole proceedings turned into a sort of comedy developing a theme. It was not justice—it was simply the carrying out of the determination to destroy.

May God shield you all. I ask for your prayers. And I will do my best to catch up, on the other side, with all that I have left undone here on earth.

Towards noon I will celebrate Mass once more and then in God's name take the road under his providence and guidance.

In God's blessing and protection,

Your grateful,

Alfred Delp, SJ

Biographical Notes

AELRED OF RIEVAULX (St) (1110-1167)

Aelred was born in the north of England in 1100. He became a Cistercian monk at Rievaulx in 1133, then Abbot of Revesby, Lincolnshire, and eventually Abbot of Rievaulx. He was also master of the household to King St David of Scotland. He wrote various works of spiritual guidance and lives of the saints. Though reportedly of an austere character, he was known for his gentleness towards his monks.

AQUINAS, (St) Thomas (c. 1225-1274)

Thomas Aquinas was born near Aquino, Italy. He was educated by the Benedictines and became a Dominican in 1244. He taught in France and Italy, was a major devotional and liturgical poet and is most celebrated as a great theologian, the Universal Teacher of the Church, and above all as the author of the *Summa contra Gentiles* and the *Summa Theologica*. He died while travelling to the fourteenth ecumenical Council at Lyons. In 1880 he was made patron saint of universities and schools.

AUGUSTINE OF HIPPO (St) (354-430)

Augustine was born at Thagaste in North Africa. The influence of his mother, St Monica, eventually predominated in his life and work and he became the leading Latin Father of the Church, but until his thirty-second year he lived a dissolute life and was captivated by a version of the Manichaean heresy whose principal opponent he later became. At Milan he underwent a major conversion experience that involved him in much inner debate and torment of spirit. He was baptized by St Ambrose and returned to Africa. He was appointed Bishop of Hippo in 396. Augustine founded many religious communities. He was a noted preacher, and a pre-eminent controversialist. His *Confessions* remains a great classic of the spiritual life and of autobiography and his *City of God* is still a key work on the nature of Church and State.

BELLARMINE, (St) Robert (1542-1621)

Bellarmine was born at Montepulciano, Italy and became a Jesuit in 1560. He taught theology at Louvain and in Rome, and worked for many years on the Vulgate, or Latin version of the Bible, which for centuries remained the basic text of Scripture in the Roman Catholic Church. He was made a cardinal in 1598. He became Archbishop of Capua then director of the Vatican Library. He was a great controversial theologian and one of the major figures of the Counter-Reformation. He wrote many anti-Protestant disputations, an influential catechism and various devotional works. In 1931 he was declared a Doctor of the Church.

BERNADETTE OF LOURDES (St) (1844-1879)

Bernadette was a French miller's daughter. When fourteen, in 1858, she underwent an intense religious experience, and, after some years of strong official opposition, her visions of our Lady proved immensely influential throughout the Church and beyond. The spot at Lourdes where she saw Mary became one of the world's great healing shrines and places of pilgrimage. She became a Sister of Notre Dame in 1866 and tried to lead a life of pious obscurity. Bernadette was a person of immense spiritual assurance and strength of conviction which have lasted in spite of contemporary manipulation of her legend in the struggle of the French church against nineteenth- and twentieth-century anti-clericalism, and the usual tawdry manifestations of popular piety encouraged not only by ecclesiastical politics but by financial interests.

BERNARD OF CLAIRVAUX (St) (1090-1153)

Bernard was born near Dijon, France. He entered Cîteaux monastery when twenty-two. He founded and became Abbot of the monastery of Clairvaux, and established sixty-eight Cistercian monasteries. He was an indefatigable controversialist, took part in various councils, confuted Abelard, preached a crusade, opposed monarchs, advised popes, joined missions against the Albigensians, wrote devotional treatises and conducted an immense correspondence. He was declared a Doctor of the Church in 1830.

BONHOEFFER, Dietrich (1906-1945)

Dietrich Bonhoeffer was born in Breslau, Germany (now Wroclaw, Poland). He studied theology, became a pastor in the Confessing Church and travelled widely. In 1931 he was appointed Profesor of Systematic Theology at Berlin University. He was an undaunted critic of the Third Reich, of anti-Semitism, and of "Nazi Christianity." In 1935 he was made director of a seminary which was closed by the Nazis. He became involved with a group dedicated to the removal of Hitler and his regime. He visited the United States in 1939 but returned to Germany where he worked clandestinely for the church, in the anti-Nazi Kreisau Group's preparations for Hitler's overthrow, and in its discussions about the nature of a democratic post-war Germany. In 1943 he was arrested, sent to a concentration camp, and hanged shortly before Allied forces arrived in 1945. Bonhoeffer was an extraordinarily devout, courageous and clear-headed patriot and thinker in a time of intellectual muddle, moral duplicity and devotion to self-preservation in the churches. He wrote a number of key works on ethics, theology, the relations between Christianity and humanism, politics and religion, and a "religionless Christanity" that seemed more appropriate to "humankind come of age" than most forms of traditional supernaturalism. His *Letters and Papers from Prison* is his best-known work. Bonhoeffer's thought and example have been deeply and widely influential throughout the churches.

BOSCO, (St) John (1815-1888)

Don Bosco was born into a peasant family in Piedmont, Italy. He became a priest and an impressive preacher, but distinguished himself above all in the service of youth, establishing boys' clubs and schools, and founding the Salesian order to help boys and the Daughters of Our Lady Help of Christians for girls, as well as lay organizations to assist the work among young people. He was an immensely charismatic person who worked unceasingly and to the detriment of his own health to persuade people from all walks of life to give money and devote some part of their efforts to the welfare of the young.

CABRINI, (St) Frances Xavier (1850-1917)

Frances Cabrini was born in Italy and in 1880 founded the Missionary Sisters of the Sacred Heart in Lombardy. In 1889 she went to North America to work among Italian immigrants. She established an orphanage and hospitals, and extended her work to Latin America in spite of considerable opposition. She was a woman of tough character and great holiness of life. She was the first United States citizen to be canonized.

CAMPION, (St) Edmund (c. 1540-1581)

Campion was one of the foremost students at Oxford University. He became a Catholic and then went to Rome to join the Jesuits. He was sent first to Bohemia and then on the English mission in 1580. After a year of hard and successful work he was betrayed to the authorities and sent to the Tower of London, tortured in an attempt to force him to reveal the names of other Catholics, and made to engage in controversial debate in which he displayed his usual brilliance. He was hanged, drawn and quartered at Tyburn.

CATHERINE DEI RICCI (St) (1522-1590)

Catherine dei Ricci was born at Florence, Italy and became a Dominican tertiary in 1535, and eventually novice-mistress and prioress. She experienced unusually intense ecstatic visions, many of which centred on our Lord's passion. She is said to have received the stigmata.

CHRYSOSTOM, (St) John (c. 347-407)

Chrysostom (or "Golden Mouth") was born at Antioch. He became a priest in 386 and Archbishop of Constantinople in 398, and was one of the great Greek Doctors of the Church. He was an exceedingly eloquent and indefatigable but sometimes harshly if justifiably outspoken preacher who also established hospitals and homes for the sick and poor. He was a dexterous churchman but his enemies had him banished from his see in 403. He was recalled, offended Empress Eudoxia by plain speaking, and was exiled to Armenia and beyond.

DAMIAN, (St) Peter (1007-1072)

Peter Damian was born at Ravenna, Italy. He was an unwanted child and made to work at pig herding but one of his brothers sent him to school. He became a hermit monk and eventually an abbot and, in 1057, Cardinal-Bishop of Ostia. He constantly preached against and criticized clerical abuses. He was declared a Doctor of the Church in 1828.

DE BREBEUF, (St) John (16?-1649)

He was sent to Quebec with two other Jesuits in 1615, where he became the Apostle of the Hurons, working among Native Americans for thirty-four years with great understanding and sympathy for their language and culture. He was tortured and executed by the Iroquois.

DE CHANTAL, (St) Jane Frances (1572-1641)

Jeanne de Chantal was born in Dijon, France. In 1592 she married the Baron de Chantal and had four children. After the Baron's death, with the help of St Francis de Sales she established the Order of the Visitation of the Virgin Mary, and despite much opposition founded sixty-six convents in her own lifetime. The order welcomed widows and women whom other orders rejected because of ill-health. St Jane was a very sensitive person yet firm and unyielding in pursuit of her charitable ideals and the needs of her order.

DE FOUCAULD, Charles (1858-1916)

Charles de Foucauld was born in Strasbourg, France. He joined the army and served in North Africa where he became interested in Islamic spirituality and practice. He stayed in Trappist monasteries, led a life of prayer, self-negation and poverty, then studied theology in Rome. He spent three years with the Poor Clares in Nazareth and was ordained priest in France in 1901. He founded a hermitage in the Sahara and later lived in great poverty and isolation at Tamanrasset in Algeria, studying the local dialect and various aspects of effective, that is, charitable, Christian witness in an alien yet religious environment. He was killed by a band of marauding Arabs. The Little Brothers of Jesus and the Little Sisters of Jesus in various countries, and the Catholic Worker movement in the USA, owe their foundation to his writings. The simplicity and tenderness of de Foucauld's example have borne much fruit in circumstances such as those of poverty-stricken Latin America, and have justifiably obscured some problematical aspects of his attachment to the notion of the civilizing mission of French colonialism.

DELP, Alfred (1907-1945)

Alfred Delp was born in Mannheim, Germany. He was converted to Catholicism while at school and in 1926 joined the Society of Jesus. He became a religious journalist and a historian with a strong interest in sociology. He was a dedicated opponent of the Nazi regime and from spring 1942 he worked closely with Bonhoeffer and others in the Moltke or Kreisau Circle involved in preparing the structure of a future democratic Germany. Delp was particularly concerned with the planning of a Christian social order for post-war Germany. He was imprisoned in 1944 and hanged in Berlin shortly before the end of the war. He published works on Christian responsibility, existence and history, and while in gaol wrote a number of profound meditations issued after his death. Delp was a courageous and loving man with a strong sense of social and political responsibility. He stressed the importance of freedom of conscience and openness to the Spirit; he opposed all forms of totalitarianism, not only those of the unjust State and the undue constrictions of the inner self, but those of middle-class respectability and a bureaucratic Church.

DE PAUL, (St) Vincent (1580-1660)

Vincent de Paul became a priest when twenty years of age. He is said to have been a "worldly" and even arrogant cleric initially. He later came under the influence of the Oratorians and decided to devote himself to the spiritual welfare of the French peasantry, but his concern for the poor and destitute extended to all sorts and conditions of people from galley-slaves to the war-wounded. He became noted for his loving character, humility and extreme tenderness. He founded the Congregation of the Mission, or Vincentians, in 1625 and later the Sisters of Charity. He is the patron saint of charitable societies and institutions.

DE SALES, (St) Francis (1567-1622)

Francis de Sales was born in Savoy. He studied law at Paris and Padua but was ordained in 1593. He was sent as a missionary priest among Protestants and in his work of conversion stressed charity and good example rather than controversy. In 1602 he became Bishop of Geneva. He helped to reform preaching style and catechetical instruction, replacing floridity and obfuscation with simplicity and clarity. Together with St Jane Frances de Chantal he founded the Visitation Order of nuns in 1604. He wrote devotional treatises of lasting effect, such as the *Treatise on the Love of God* and the *Introduction to the Devout Life*. He was declared a Doctor of the Church in 1877.

DE TOURVILLE, Henri (1842-1903)

Henri de Tourville (often known as "the Abbé de Tourville"), was a lawyer's son born in Paris. He read law but became a priest in 1873 and won a reputation as a remarkable confessor and spiritual adviser. He resigned because of ill-health and retired to the country where he studied what would now be known as sociology. Over a period of twenty years he wrote a number of deeply loving and sympathetic letters of spiritual direction.

DONNE, John (1573-1631)

John Donne was raised as a Roman Catholic and entered the University of Oxford at an early age to avoid taking an anti-Catholic oath. He was admitted as a lawyer, joined Essex's expedition to Cadiz, became a civil servant, and was imprisoned for eloping with and marrying the Lord Chancellor's niece. He prepared for the Anglican priesthood and was ordained in 1615 and appointed chaplain to James VI/I. He then became a country rector, and eventually Dean of St Paul's Cathedral. Donne was a religious controversialist and an eminent preacher, but he is best-known as one of the greatest of English poets. In his "metaphysical" verse he engaged in unrelenting self-scrutiny and represented the relations and contradictions between spiritual, emotional and physical inclinations and achievements. Sexuality is one of the central emphases in his highly-nuanced devotional works; and religion in his equally intricate love poems. Sin, death, judgment and responsibility before God are major considerations in even his most passionate writings. Donne's profound awareness of the complexity of human nature, and of the problems that result from simultaneous awareness of the paradoxes of the human psyche and experience, and of the divine vocation of humanity, have made him a major influence on twentieth-century writers.

DUCHESNE, (Bd) Philippine (1769-1852)

Philippine Duchesne was born in Grenoble, France, and entered the Visitandine Order. She became a Sacred Heart nun after the Revolution and in 1818 was sent to the United States with four other religious. She founded a free school in Missouri and became a courageous frontierswoman for the Society of the Sacred Heart, even establishing a free school for Native American children in Kansas in her seventies.

ENGLISH MYSTIC, An unknown (c. 1380)

The anonymous author of the *Cloud of Unknowing* and *A Letter of Private Direction* is thought to have been a Dominican spiritual director in the East Midlands who had studied Dionysius the Areopagite and the Rhineland mystics. He addresses his works especially to those who wish to lead a solitary, contemplative life, and must teach themselves the way of self-forgetting, oblivion to mundane reality and orientation to God alone.

ERASMUS, DESIDERIUS (c. 1466-1536)

Erasmus was the illegitimate son of a Dutch priest. He eventually entered a monastery but left it when appointed secretary to the Bishop of Cambrai. He studied in Paris, visited England and met the humanist John Colet and the More circle. He studied the history of the early Church, biblical texts and scholarship, and promoted many of the same interests as contemporary humanists and the Reformers. He settled in Basle, Switerland, which became one of the centres of the Reformation. He left the city for Freiburg, Germany, at the height of the influence of the Reform, but returned there to die. Erasmus was a prolific, immensely popular but critically responsible author. He published satirical works, a critical edition of the New Testament stressing the original Greek texts, editions of the Fathers, and a major work on freedom of will that attacked some of Luther's notions yet acknowledged their importance. He was an opponent of "fundamentalism." Erasmus' stress on the primacy of Jesus' own words and on critical scholarship, and his sense of truth, fairness and toleration, earned him the respect of Protestants and Catholics, but also the distrust of both parties in an age when taking the appropriate side seemed a criterion of eternal salvation and could be a matter of life and death.

EUDES, (St) John (1601-80)

St John Eudes was a Norman farmer's son. He founded the Sisters of Our Lady of Charity of the Refuge (who gave rise to the Good Shepherd nuns), and an Order for the sanctification of the clergy and aspiring priests—the Congregation of Jesus and Mary, now known as the Eudists. He was a missionary spirit of unusual persistence in a great era of renewal of the Christian life. He was a member of the French Oratory for twenty years, a missioner with a special devotion to the Sacred Heart, and a noted scholar. His practical works of mercy included caring for victims of the plague. His many letters stress his constant desire to discover the will of God in an atmosphere of Christ-centred love. Devotion to Jesus is the watchword of the instruction he offers in his simple, direct prose.

FENELON, François de Salignac de la Motte (1651-1715)

François Fénelon was born in the Périgord, France, into a poor but aristocratic family. He was ordained priest in Paris in 1675 and appointed Superior of a community of converts. He became a missioner among French Protestants. In 1688 he met the Quietist mystic Madame Guyon and thereafter was strongly, though far from uncritically, influenced by her thinking. Later, when she was condemned, he defended her views. In 1689 he was appointed tutor to Louis XIV's grandson, the Duke of Burgundy, for whom he wrote an instructional "novel," *The Adventures of Télémaque*, in which he outlined the responsibilities of monarchs, and affirmed their subjection and that of States to the moral law. He became spiritual adviser to a number of devout people at court. He was made Archbishop of Cambrai in 1695. In 1697 he wrote a work on mystical spirituality, and was attacked by the anti-mystical Bishop Bossuet, who had previously recommended him. Part of his book was condemned by the Holy See in 1699 and he retracted some of his views. In the same year, however, he published *Télémaque* surreptitiously and was exiled from court to his diocese, more for his views on statecraft than for those on religion. Fénelon defended orthodox thinking against the Huguenots and the Jansenists and wrote a number of theological and spiritual works. He was a valued spiritual counsellor, a man of great personal charity, and a firm critic of political absolutism.

FOX, George (1624-1691)

George Fox was a Leicestershire weaver's son. He had no schooling, was apprenticed to a shoemaker and became agent to a wool-dealer. He was self-educated and this experience of self-dependence for enlightenment influenced his attitude to religious truth and his stress on inward and silent devotion. He spent two years wandering about the country seeking truth. In 1646, after perceiving the "inner light of the living Christ," he started popular preaching, when he sometimes entered a trance-like state. He avoided formal church services and religious debate, but was gaoled in 1649 for "brawling" in church, when he interrupted a service with an appeal to the Holy Spirit for guidance. Fox founded the Society of the Friends of Truth, or Quakers (a nickname said to have originated with his demand that a judge should "tremble at the word of the Lord"), with yearly meetings from 1669. He made missionary visits to Scotland, Ireland, North America, the West Indies and the Netherlands; was often imprisoned in England (spending altogether six years in various gaols under harsh conditions), and spoke and worked to improve prison conditions, education, and the state of the disadvantaged and labouring classes from which, initially, he drew most of his followers. He died in London. Fox emphasized the "inner light," and God's direct communication with the individual soul. Among his many writings on the Gospel and Christian life, his *Journal* remains a classic of religious literature.

FRY, Elizabeth (1780-1845)

Elizabeth Fry was born Elizabeth Gurney, the daughter of a Quaker banker, in Norwich. She married a London merchant and had several children. She founded a girls' school and, when twenty-nine, became a Quaker "minister" and preacher. Her social position helped her to gain access to people in important positions. She was a dedicated evangelist but concerned above all with practical charity and social reform. In 1813 she began her lifelong and often successful campaign for prison reform (including the separation of the sexes, women warders for female prisoners, and religious and other education in gaols) at home and abroad, and for improved conditions for urban vagrants and beggars. In 1839 she started a society for the rehabilitation of criminals. She was received by foreign monarchs and founded an order of nursing sisters. Fry was responsible for an influential report on social conditions in Ireland and helped to institute libraries at coastguard stations and in naval hospitals and elsewhere. After her husband's bankruptcy in 1828 her efforts were necessarily less effective.

GERARD, John (1564-1637)

John Gerard, SJ, was the second son of Sir Thomas Gerard. He was born into a recusant family at New Bryn, Lancashire, England. When fifteen he entered Exeter College, Oxford. Four years later he went to Reims, and spent three years there before joining the Society of Jesus in Paris. He was imprisoned for a year in the Marshalsea, London, and went to Rome in 1586. He was ordained priest in 1587 and was sent on the English mission in 1588. He was watched by spies even in Rome, betrayed and imprisoned in England, and tortured in the Tower. He escaped and continued his mission in hiding for some years, was sought for in connection with the Gunpowder Plot, yet, unlike so many of his martyred associates, escaped from England and survived for thirty years. He spent the last ten years of his life as "the spiritual father of aspirants to the English mission," the trials of which he knew so well. Gerard is an example of endurance and determination in times of extreme persecution.

GREGORY THE GREAT (St) (c. 550-604)

Gregory was born in Rome. He was the son of a patrician and of St Sylvia. He became papal legate at Constantinople and was elected Pope (the first monk to reach that office) in 590. He sent St Augustine and other monks to convert the English, defended central Italy against the Lombard incursions, worked to establish and strengthen monastic orders, constantly promoted the primacy of the See of Rome, and wrote many scholarly and homiletic works, such as his *Dialogues*. He was one of the great Doctors of the Western Church.

HERBERT, George (1593-1633)

George Herbert was educated at Cambridge University, where he became public orator. He became a deacon and prebendary of Lincoln in 1626. He was ordained priest in 1630 and appointed rector of Bemerton, near Salisbury. He was strongly influenced by Nicholas Ferrar's semi-monastic religious community at Little Gidding. Herbert was a devoted parish priest, and wrote fine prose works such as *A Priest to the Temple,* based on his pastoral experience. He was one of the finest English devotional poets. Herbert's verse emphasizes church experience and liturgical life, but above all, under the influence of Donne, the vagaries of the inner life and the various stages and complexities of true piety.

HOPKINS, Gerard Manley (1844-1889)

Gerard Manley Hopkins was born at Stratford, Essex, and studied at Balliol College, Oxford. He became a Roman Catholic in 1866 and entered the Society of Jesus. He was eventually appointed to the chair of Greek at the Catholic

University of Ireland. He went through agonies of body and mind when in such teaching posts and when assisting in slum parishes. He destroyed his early verse and started writing poetry again when his superior asked for a poem on the "Wreck of the Deutschland" in which four refugee German nuns were killed. The Jesuit *The Month* rejected the poem because of its unconventional style, and possibly its concern with problems of (Hopkins' own) spiritual development. Following the theologian Duns Scotus, then regarded as something of a maverick, Hopkins was interested in the individuality of people and things. He evolved a highly flexible use of language and poetic form to express multiple aspects of observation and experience, including his lifelong struggle to accommodate his sexual inclinations and his poetic vocation to the discipline of the religious life. Then his poems reach a near-tragic intensity. His verses were not published until after his death—by his friend, the poet Robert Bridges. Hopkins' journals and sermons are also writings of great power. He was a major influence on such leading twentieth-century writers as James Joyce.

HOWARD, (St) Philip (1557-1595)

Philip Howard was Earl of Arundel and Surrey. For some time he led a wayward life, neglecting religion, wife and duties. He eventually reformed his life and, together with his wife, was reconciled to the Catholic Church but imprisoned in the Tower of London in 1585. He was condemned to death in 1589 but the sentence was suspended and he died in the Tower.

IGNATIUS OF ANTIOCH (St) (died c. 107)

Ignatius was Bishop of Antioch and was said to have been a disciple of St John the Evangelist. When very old he was sent to Rome to be executed during the persecution of the Christians, and was eventually thrown to the lions. On the way he wrote seven letters to different churches which are among the main surviving documents of early Christianity. He was a staunch defender of the humanity of Christ and his letters are invaluable for the light they cast on major intellectual influences on Christianity in its first years of development.

IGNATIUS OF LOYOLA (St) (1491-1556)

Ignatius was born the son of a nobleman at Loyola Castle, Spain. He was wounded when fighting the French, went on pilgrimage to the Holy land, and became a priest. He applied the precision and necessary obedience of his military years to the training of a company of spiritual soldiers of the Counter-Reformation, dedicated to the greater glory of God, and ever ready to obey their instructions as missionaries in any part of the globe. His straightforward but rigorous *Spiritual Exercises* have been immensely influential even outside the Society of Jesus, which he established. Even before his death his Order was at work from South America through Africa to the East Indies, and is now to be found throughout the world.

JOAN OF ARC (St) (1412-1431)

Joan was a farmer's daughter born at Domrémy, France. She was a fascinating mixture of holiness of life and purpose, courage and simplicity, belief in the right of the self-determination of nations and the divine mission of rulers, and an extraordinarily unswerving assurance of right and justice. During and after her lifetime, her faith was misused by venal and less justifiably nationalist interests. When she was seventeen, "voices" told her of her mission to free France from the English and restore Charles VII to his throne. She convinced the future king of her proficiency, and her campaign enabled him to be crowned at Reims. The Burgundians captured her in 1430 and sold her to the English. They and the Bishop of Beauvais put her before an ecclesiastical court which declared her a heretic and the instrument of diabolical forces. The English burnt her at Rouen. In 1486 a posthumous retrial found her innocent. She was canonized in 1920.

JEROME (St) (c. 342-420)

Eusebius Hieronymus (or Jerome) Sophronius was born at Stridon, Dalmatia. He became a scholar and travelled widely. In 385 he retired to Bethlehem with St Paula and other devout and scholarly women, and he set about his major work of revising the Latin Bible, or Vulgate. He was a very strong critic of his many opponents (especially in biblical criticism), but also of his own failings.

JOGUES, (St) Isaac (16?-1646)

Isaac Jogues was a Jesuit sent with others to Canada in 1636. He worked among Native Americans and, while travelling to assist the distressed Hurons, was captured by the Mohawks, tortured, escaped, and continued his work. He died after being tomahawked by the Iroquois.

JOHN OF THE CROSS (St) (1542-1591)

Juan de Yepes was a weaver's son born in Old Castile, Spain. He entered the Carmelite order in 1563. St Teresa chose him as the first member of a new friary of the reformed observance. His work to establish this reform met with much opposition and he was imprisoned at Toledo, one of many indignities he suffered at the hands of obscurantist, envious and uncomprehending opponents. John of the Cross was a wholly original mystic of great power and literary brilliance who wrote six major treatises, and some poems and letters, arising from his own fascinating and extraordinary spiritual experiences. His writings remain universally influential inside and outside the Church. He was declared a Doctor of the Church in 1926.

KEBLE, John (1792-1866)

John Keble was educated at Oxford University and became a fellow of Oriel College, and, after taking orders and acting as a country curate, Professor of Poetry at Oxford in 1841. He was later appointed a vicar in Hampshire and was a noted parish priest distinguished for the quality of his spiritual guidance and pastoral care. His *The Christian Year* was a very popular book of devotional verse for many years after its publication in 1827. It is as hymns, however, that his compositions have survived. Keble was a leading Tractarian and one of the main forerunners of the Anglo-Catholic movement in the Church of England. His Oxford Assize sermon of 1833 on national apostasy is taken as the start of the Oxford Movement and he remained one of its leaders when its best-known member, John Henry Newman, became a Roman Catholic.

KIERKEGAARD, Søren (1813-1855)

Søren Aabye Kierkegaard, the son of a very successful, "self-made" man, was born in Copenhagen. His father's rejection of God imbued the young Kierkegaard with a lifelong sense of guilt and doom, and a feeling of the remoteness of the Creator, which he found appropriate to the actual human condition. He missed this awareness in the then very influential works of Hegel, which he spent much time in refuting. Kierkegaard tried to reinstate the importance of the individual and to find the right balance between God's nearness and personality and his otherness and transcendence. He stressed the importance of human freedom, and of faith as the only way of knowing the hidden Christ in a confusing world where bureaucratically religious, political, ethical and philosophical systems obfuscate the real issues. He wove his inability to accept the married state into his polemical and other writings. His works, both positive, on the struggle of the individual person to assert his or her true self, and negative, on the shortcomings of institutional religion, have remained major influences on twentieth-century religious and philosophical thinking.

KOLBE, (St) Maximilian (1894-1941)

Maximilian Kolbe, the son of Franciscan tertiaries, was born near Lodz, in Russian Poland. He became a Franciscan in 1910. Maximilian had a strong devotion to our Lady, started a Marian sodality and communities in Japan and Poland. He was appointed Superior of the friars of Niepokalonow. St Maximilian was a man of great courage, tenderness and selflessness. His community sheltered Jews and other refugees from persecution during the German invasion of Poland and published articles criticizing the injustice and behaviour of the occupying forces. He was imprisoned at the infamous concentration and extermination camp of Auschwitz during the concerted German attempt to exterminate the educated classes of the country. Maximilian volunteered to take the place of an innocent man, a parent, condemned to death in reprisal for an escape. After two weeks in a vile hole, he was murdered with a phenol injection.

LIGUORI, (St) Alphonsus (1696-1787)

Alphonsus de' Liguori was born near Naples, Italy. He was a lawyer but became a priest in 1696. He set up the first convent of Redemptoristine nuns and in 1732, with great difficulty, founded a new Order to work among the peasantry: the Redemptorists. St Alphonsus was Bishop of St Agata dei Goti from 1762 to 1775. He was unjustly condemned by Pope Pius VI and had to surrender control of his congregation. He wrote many works of moral theology in spite of great practical and spiritual trials. He was declared a Doctor of the Church in 1871.

MACDONALD, George (1824-1905)

George Macdonald was born at Huntly, Aberdeenshire, Scotland. He studied at King's College, Aberdeen University, and at a London theological college. In 1850 he was appointed to the Congregational ministry in Sussex. His salary was reduced and he eventually resigned because of his liberal views on the eternal damnation of non-Christians. He became a prolific novelist and writer of books for children as well as sermons and verse, and a lay preacher, but lived in relative poverty. Macdonald was a friend of Ruskin, Morris, Tennyson, Carlyle and other great Victorians, whose high seriousness he shared, but with the addition of a uniquely childlike cheerfulness. All his works are marked by a spiritual and mystical cast of mind, by sympathy for the emotionally and socially disadvantaged and, indeed, for all humble people and things, and by an unshakable faith in the security of a loving God's unremitting concern for his creatures. Twentieth-century critics, especially C. S. Lewis, have assessed Macdonald's children's books and works of fantasy, such as *At the Back of the North Wind* and *Phantastes*, as great achievements of Victorian literature.

MORE, (St) Thomas (1478-1535)

Thomas More was born in Cheapside, London. He was educated at Oxford and became a lawyer. He was twice married and his household was celebrated as a centre of culture, learning, religious discourse and Christian concord. He made sure that his children profited from the ethos of his home and his intellectual circle. More was acquainted with many famous European thinkers of his day. He wrote a number of important works on justice, government and statecraft, among which his "novel" *Utopia* is still the best-known. In 1529 Henry VIII made him Lord Chancellor in succession to Cardinal Wolsey. One of his duties was to arraign heretics, and he did so conscientiously, fairly by the criteria of the time and in accordance with his finely honed notions of truth and justice, but with a rigour that seems repellent outside the sixteenth-century context. More refused to approve the King's divorce and resigned his post. He would not take an oath recognizing the Act of Succession, and rejected the Act of Supremacy making Henry supreme governor of the Church in England. He was sent to the Tower for fifteen months and eventually beheaded. More remains one of the greatest models of unshakable moral justice and integrity coupled with a superlative justness of thought and expression.

NEWMAN, (Cardinal) John Henry (1801-1890)

John Henry Newman was born to Evangelical parents and was educated at Oxford University. He became a fellow of Oriel College and a curate at St Clement's, tutor at Oriel, then vicar of St Mary's. He preached and wrote in defence of the apostolic succession and the catholic essence of the Church of England. Together with Pusey and others he started the Tractarian or Oxford Movement for reform of the church and its return to universal catholic order. His Tract XC offered a catholic interpretation of the Thirty-nine Articles of the Church of England which called forth an official ban on Tractarianism. He retired to Littlemore in 1842 and spent three years in study and meditation before resigning his living and becoming a Roman Catholic. He was ordained priest at Rome in 1846, founded the Birmingham Oratory in 1847, became rector of the short-lived first Catholic University at Dublin in 1854, and was made a Cardinal in 1879. He published some of the fundamental works of nineteenth-century thought, including *An Essay on the Development of Christian Doctrine* (an epoch-making exposition of the gradual unfolding of truth), the *Idea of a University* (still a major work on education), a *Grammar of Assent* (on the nature of belief), and *Apologia pro Vita Sua* (one of the world's most penetrating autobiographies). "Ultramontanes" and fanatical supporters of papal infallibility found Newman's acceptance of an infallible Church as ambivalent as his earlier notion of Anglicanism as a "via media" had seemed to such Anglicans as Charles Kingsley, who later accused him of not considering truth to be a necessary virtue. Truth, however, was Newman's principal concern. He wrote with a delicate exactitude on the various stages of his many-sided thinking on history, faith and belief. Newman's ideas on the nature of doctrine and the Church were powerfully influential at Vatican II and beyond. He engaged in an immense correspondence.

PASCAL, Blaise (1623-1662)

Blaise Pascal, the son of a magistrate and amateur scientist, was born in Clermont-Ferrand, France. He was a brilliant mathematician from an early age and probably invented the calculating-machine. In 1646 he was seriously influenced by Jansenism. He led a somewhat profligate life but went through a deeply meditative period and experienced a mystical conversion in 1654. From 1655 he lived near the Jansenist centre of Port-Royal. His best-known works are his *Thoughts* and *Provincial Letters*. The former are notes toward an apology for the Christian religion that will elevate faith above reason, for the paradoxes of human life can be explained only by the Fall and Redemption. Certainty is impossible, but the wager of faith, ultimately obtained only through grace and discipline, is that the only truly reasonable course for anguished humankind is to seek happiness in the afterlife; God is apparent to the heart and not to reason. The *Letters* contain an impassioned defence of the Jansenist teaching on divine grace and an ironic attack on Jesuit opposition to Jansenism, and on the casuistry and moral decadence of the Society's self-interested polemicists. Pascal remains one of the most profound and sympathetic religious thinkers of all time. In the latter part of the twentieth century, mistrust of reason and progress has made his acute analysis of human psychology all the more relevant. His *Letters* was put on the former Index of Forbidden Books of the Catholic Church, and in 1660 the authorities ordered it to be publicly burnt, but in the present century Pascal has been a major influence on leading Catholic and other Christian writers.

SOUTHWELL, (St) Robert (1561-1595)

Robert Southwell was born in Norfolk. He entered the Society of Jesus in Rome when seventeen and was sent on the English mission in 1586. He was a largely devotional poet of considerable skill and elegance but his well-tuned prose is often equally delightful. He was betrayed in 1592 and spent three years in prison before he was tried, tortured and eventually hanged, drawn and quartered as a priest at Tyburn.

TEN BOOM, Corrie (1892-1983)

Corrie ten Boom was a humble and loving Dutchwoman of Haarlem whose family, led by her eighty-four-year-old father, defied the anti-Semitic inhumanity of the German authorities and their Dutch collaborators during the occupation of the Netherlands in World War II. When it became clear that the Germans intended to deport the entire Jewish population to the East (where almost all of them were exterminated in purpose-built camps), her father said that it would be an honour to give his life for God's ancient people. Until their betrayal and imprisonment, Corrie and her family saved as many Jews as possible by hiding them. Thirty-five of these good Christians were arrested. Corrie was kept in solitary confinement at Scheveningen and later at Vught concentration camp, then sent to the appallingly cruel concentration camp for women at Ravensbruck, where her sister died. Her father had already perished. Corrie ten Boom's letters bear witness to her deep faith "in Jesus Christ in the midst of the deepest human evil."

TERESA OF AVILA (St) (1515-1582)

Teresa was born in Avila, Spain. She became a Carmelite nun as Teresa de Jesús. In spite of considerable opposition, she founded a new convent in 1562, and later sixteen others in Spain, because she considered that the discipline of the order ought to be reformed in accordance with her notions of primitive observance. Together with St John of the Cross she introduced similar reforms among the friars. She was an astute and resourceful governor of and provider for her houses, and a great mystic able to convey her experiences in highly nuanced literary works which mix humour with profundity, tenderness, realism and psychological penetration and have remained influential. They include a superb autobiography and a voluminous correspondence.

THERESE OF LISIEUX, (St) (1873-1897)

Thérèse Jesus was born at Alençon, France. She became a Carmelite nun at Lisieux taking the name "of the Child Jesus," when she was fifteen. She was made novice-mistress of her convent but suffered from extreme ill-health. In spite of the obscurity of her short life, her "little way" and her approach to the execution of everyday tasks and duties with care and humility were soon immensely influential among all sorts and conditions of people. Her superiors asked her to write an autobiography which they "improved" considerably. It became and remains extraordinarily popular.

VENARD, (St) Théophane (1829-1861)

Théophane Vénard was a teacher's son, born at St Loup, France. He joined the French Foreign Missions in 1850, was ordained priest, and in 1852 was sent first to Hong Kong and then to Western Tonkin, where he looked after some ten thousand Christians for five years, while suffering ill-health and cruel persecution. He was imprisoned in 1860 and kept in a cage until his savage execution.

VON HÜGEL, (Baron) Friedrich (1852-1925)

Friedrich von Hügel was a Baron of the Holy Roman Empire. The son of an Austrian diplomat and a Scottish mother, he was born in Florence, Italy, and lived in England from 1873 onward. He was a scholar of philosophy, history and religion, and sympathetic to the Modernist views of Loisy, Tyrrell and others, especially in biblical criticism, though he preferred a more spiritual emphasis. His interest in religion extended well beyond the bounds of his denomination, and his thinking on mysticism and the human encounter with God, as well as his uniquely open-hearted spirituality, permeated his various writings and especially his correspondence, which contains superb examples of his seemingly unorthodox spiritual direction.

WEIL, Simone (1909-1943)

Simone Weil was a Frenchwoman of Jewish origins who studied philosophy and became a teacher. She was interested in sociology and politics, and worked as a labourer at a motor factory for a year and then joined the International Brigade to fight for the Republicans in Spain. When Jews were forbidden to teach after the German occupation of France, she worked on a farm in the unoccupied zone. In 1942 she escaped to New York with her family, then went to London to work for the Free French government in exile. She followed the diet typical of wartime France and died of tuberculosis. For many years Weil remained an agnostic but in later life developed a non-dogmatic, even anti-clerical, but deeply inquiring and near-mystical Christianity. She continued to identify with the industrial labourer as the ideal type of suffering humanity in a world bent on dehumanization. She was opposed to all forms of dominative authority and injustice, and believed that the self should be destroyed by love within, not by degradation without. Her posthumously published works are filled with profound religious insights, in the tradition of Pascal.

WESLEY, Charles (1707-1788)

Charles Wesley studied at Christ Church, Oxford. With other students he started a circle for religious discussion and devotion of so strict an observance that they were nicknamed "Methodists." He was ordained priest in 1735. On Whitsunday 1838 he underwent a conversion experience, rejoicing "in hope of loving Christ." Charles became a travelling evangelist and settled in London in 1771. Though he shared many of his brother's and others' Methodist views, and was an enthusiastic preacher with an unshakable concern to affect the souls of the humble and disadvantaged, prisoners and other marginal people, he was reluctant to separate as surely as other Methodists from the Church of England, and did not accept John's ordinations of Methodist ministers after 1784. He was an extraordinarily prolific writer of often quite sweetly perfect hymns. Hundreds of the many thousands he wrote are still sung throughout the churches.

WESLEY, John (1703-1791)

The grandson of puritan Nonconformists, but the son of the Church of England rector of Epworth, Wesley was educated at Christ Church, Oxford. He was ordained priest in 1728. He taught at Oxford and conducted Charles' "Methodist" society for spiritual improvement. He was influenced by German Moravianism while an unsuccessful missionary in the USA. He returned to England and in May 1738 underwent a conversion experience when his heart was "strangely warmed" while reading Luther's preface to Romans. He began field preaching, founded Methodist chapels, and started the "United Society." In the 1740s he became the overseer of rapidly spreading missions. After 1755 he acknowledged the rift between his lay-preachers and the Anglican ministry, but did not ordain presbyters capable of ordination and administration of the sacraments until 1784. Wesley was fired by apostolic zeal to convert nation and Church to scriptural holiness of life. He preferred direct open-air preaching to ordinary people with whom he established an extraordinary rapport. His saintliness changed the lives of millions. He had a special love for the common people of Britain, was aware of the cruel constraints of their social conditions, and brought a conviction of Christian truth to multitudes. He has often been credited with preventing a revolution in England.

Sources and Further Reading

The sources of letters are identified by page references in I below. To help the reader, additional page references are sometimes given to reprints of the original text, or to other translations. If the work from which the letter is taken does not appear in the acknowledgements under III below, and it was not originally written in English, the present editor has translated the letter from the original, or revised an out-of-date version while comparing it with the original text. In a number of instances, parts of the original letter have been omitted for the sake of clarity or emphasis, or because they have little or nothing to do with the main burden of the letter. In some cases letters in a connected series, or those related by theme, have been conflated. To make the texts more accessible, the spelling and punctuation, and very occasionally the vocabulary, of pre-nineteenth-century English letters have been modernized, and introductory or closing phrases have been modified or new ones inserted. Some writings (including collections and selections of letters) other than direct sources, as well as biographies and other works on the authors, are listed, but the following makes no claim to be exhaustive or to offer details of the most scholarly or up-to-date works in each case.

I. Individuals

AELRED OF RIEVAULX, ST
Patrologia Latina (J. P. Migne), cxcv, cols. 337-422; *A Letter to his Sister*, ed. G. Webb & A. Walker (London, 1957): p. 60. *Aelred of Rievaulx: A Study*, by A. Squire, OP (London, 1969).

AQUINAS, ST THOMAS
Sexdecim Monita Sancti Thomae de Aquino pro Acquirendo Scientiae Thesauro (Paris, 1921): p. 6 *et seq.*; *Opuscula Omnia necnon Opera Minora*, ed. J. Perrier (Paris, 1949); *The Life of Thomas Aquinas*, by K. Foster, OP (London, 1959).

AUGUSTINE, ST

Patrologia Latina (J. P. Migne), xxxii-xlvii; clviii, col. 1068; *Augustine of Hippo: A Biography*, by P. Brown (London, 1967).

BELLARMINE, ST ROBERT

The Life and Works of Blessed Cardinal Robert Bellarmine, J. Brodrick, SJ, 2 vols (London, 1928): Vol. I, pp. 422-5, Vol. II, p. 108; *Robert Bellarmine, Saint and Scholar*, by J. Brodrick, SJ (London & Westminster, Md, 1961).

BERNADETTE, ST

Lourdes, Documents authentiques, ed. R. Laurentin, B. Billet & P. Galland (Paris, 1958 ff); *Les Ecrits de Sainte Bernadette et sa voie spirituelle*, ed. A. Ravier (Paris, 1961); *La Confidante de L'Immaculée* (Paris, 1925): p. 243; *Bernadette of Lourdes*, by F. P. Keyes (London, 1953); *Bernadette Soubirous*, by A. Ravier (Paris, 1979).

BERNARD OF CLAIRVAUX, ST

Patrologia Latina (J. P. Migne), clxxxii-clxxxv; *The Letters of St Bernard of Clairvaux*, tr. & ed. B. S. James (London, 1953): pp. 227, 433-4, 364-6, 385-6, 436, 452, 465-6, 504, 506-7, 510-1, 511, 514, 520; *St Bernard of Clairvaux*, by B. S. James (London, 1957); *S. Bernard*, by J. Leclercq (Paris, 1966).

BONHOEFFER, DIETRICH

Gesammelte Schriften, ed. E. Bethge, 4 vols (Munich, 1958-61): Vol. I, pp. 51-3, Vol. II, pp. 205-16; *Letters and Papers from Prison* (London, 1953): pp. 114-5, 124-5, 160; *No Rusty Swords: Letters, Lectures and Notes from the Collected Works*, Vol. I, ed. E. H. Robertson, rev. ed. (London, 1970): pp. 33-5, 296-302; *Dietrich Bonhoeffer*, by E. Bethge (London, 1970).

BOSCO, ST JOHN

Epistolario di S. Giovanni Bosco, ed. E. Ceria (Turin, 1955 ff): pp. 71-4; *Don Bosco*, by L. C. Sheppard (London, 1957).

CABRINI, ST FRANCES XAVIER

The Travels of Mother Frances Xavier Cabrini, Foundress of the Missionary Sisters of the Sacred Heart of Jesus, as related in several of her letters (Streatham Hall, Exeter, 1925): pp. 172-4, 252-6; *Immigrant Saint: The Life of Mother Cabrini*, by Pietro di Donato (New York, 1960).

CAMPION, ST EDMUND

Edmund Campion by Richard Simpson (London, 1896): pp. 97-9, 174-6, 246-50; *Edmund Campion*, by Evelyn Waugh (London, 1935; New York, 1959).

CHRYSOSTOM, ST JOHN

Patrologia Graeca (J. P. Migne) xlvii-lxiv: lii, I, col. 549; xlvii; lvii; *St John Chrysostom*, by C. Baur, 2 vols (London & Westminster, Md, 1959-60); *Golden Mouth*, by J. N. D. Kelly (London, 1995).

DAMIAN, ST PETER

Patrologia Latina (J. P. Migne), cxliv, cxlv; cxliv, col. 497 and the traditional Roman Ritual, as a prayer in the rite for a departing soul; *Selected Writings on the Spiritual Life*, ed. P. McNulty (London, 1959).

DE BREBEUF, ST JOHN

Jesuit Relations, ed. R. G. Thwaites (London, 1897-1901), Vol. 39: pp. 175-7.

DE CHANTAL, ST JANE

Sainte J. F. Frémyot de Chantal: Sa vie et ses oeuvres, ed. F.-M. de Chaugy, 8 vols (Paris, 1874-9); *The Spirit of St Jane de Chantal,* tr. Sisters of the Visitation (London, 1933): pp. 57-9; *Saint Jane Frances de Chantal*, by E. Stopp (London, 1962).

DE FOUCAULD, CHARLES

Meditations of a Hermit, by C. de Foucauld, ed. R. Bazin (London, 1930): pp. 166-8, 178, 184; *Letters from the Desert*, by C. de Foucauld, tr. B. Lucas (London, 1977): pp. 41-8, 85-6; *Memories of Charles de Foucauld, Explorer and Hermit, seen in his Letters*, ed. G. Gorrée (London, 1938): p. 44, 155-6; *Two Dancers in the Desert: The Life of Charles de Foucauld*, by C. Lepetit, tr. J. Griffiths (London & New York, 1981).

DEI RICCI, ST CATHERINE

Le lettere spirituali e familiari di S. Caterina de'Ricci, ed. C. Guasti (Prato, 1861); *St Catherine dei Ricci: Her Life, her Letters, her Community*, by F. M. Capes (London, 1905): pp. 184-7.

DELP, ALFRED

Im Angesicht des Todes, by Alfred Delp (Frankfurt am Main, 1965): p. 234; *Facing Death*, by A. Delp (London, 1956): p. 193; *Alfred Delp* (Berlin, 1954).

DE PAUL, ST VINCENT

Saint Vincent de Paul: Correspondance, entretiens, documents, ed. P. Coste, 14 vols (Paris, 1920-5); *Letters of Vincent de Paul*, ed. J. Leonard (London, 1937): p. 34-5, 150-2, 201-3, 307-10; *Monsieur Vincent*, by P. Coste, CM, 3 vols (London, 1934-5); *St Vincent de Paul*, by M. Purcell (London, 1963).

DE SALES, ST FRANCIS

Lettres de Saint François de Sales à des gens du monde, ed. E. Veuillot (Paris, 1865): pp. 118-9; *Oeuvres de Saint François de Sales*, ed. the Visitandines of Annecy, 26 vols (Annecy, 1911): Vol. 12, pp. 267-9; Vol. 17, p. 386-9; *St Francis of Sales*, by Margaret Trouncer (London, 1963).

DE TOURVILLE, HENRI

Piété Confiante, by H. de Tourville (Paris, n.d.): pp. 80-3; *Letters of Direction*, by the Abbé de Tourville (London, 1939).

DONNE, JOHN

Collected Works, ed. H. Alford, 6 vols (London, 1839); *The Life and Letters of John Donne*, ed. E. Gosse, 2 vols (London, 1899); *Poems*, ed. H. J. C. Grierson, 2 vols (Oxford, 1912); *John Donne: Complete Poetry and Selected Prose*, ed. J. Hayward (London, 1929): pp. 445-6, 454-6, 459-61, 471-4; *John Donne: A Life*, by R. C. Bald (Oxford, 1970).

DUCHESNE, BD PHILIPPINE

Mother Philippine Duchesne: 1769-1852, by Marjory Erskine (London, 1926): pp. 239-79.

ENGLISH MYSTIC, UNKNOWN

The Cloud of Unknowing and the Epistle of Privy Counselling, ed. P. Hodgson (London, 1944); *The Cloud of Unknowing and other treatises by a fourteenth-century mystic*, ed. J. McCann, OSB (London, 1924); *A Letter of Private Direction*, ed. & tr. J. Griffiths (Dublin & New York, 1983), pp. 17-8.

ERASMUS, DESIDERIUS

Opera Omnia (Amsterdam, 1969 ff); *Letters*, ed. P. S. Allen , 11 vols (Oxford, 1906-47); *Letters* (Toronto, 1969 ff); *Thomas More and Erasmus*, by E. E. Reynolds (London, 1965): p. 165; *Erasmus*, by R. H. Bainton (New York & London, 1969-70).

EUDES, ST JOHN

Lettres choisies, ed. C. Berthelot du Chesnay (Namur, 1958); *En tout la volonté de Dieu: S. Jean Eudes à travers ses lettres*, ed. C. Guillon (Paris, 1981): pp.68-9; *St John Eudes*, by D. Sargent (N.Y., 1949); *S. Jean Eudes*, by P. Herainbourg (Paris, 1960).

FENELON, FRANÇOIS

Oeuvres complètes de François Fénelon, 34 vols (Paris, 1820-30), Vol. II, p. 24, Vol. VI, pp. 236-9, 315-8; "Lettre à Louis XIV, ou Lettre secrète", in *Histoire des membres de l'Académie Française*, by Jean d'Alembert (Paris, 1787); *Fénelon:*

Letters, ed. J. McEwen, intr. T. Merton (London & New York, 1964); *Francis Fénelon, Study of a Personality* (New York, 1951).

FOX, GEORGE

The Journal of George Fox, ed. N. Penney (London, 1924): pp. 141, 265, 339-40; *Voice of the Lord*, by H. E. Wildes (Philadelphia, 1965).

FRY, ELIZABETH

Memoir of the Life of Elizabeth Fry with Extracts from her Journal and Letters, ed. two of her daughters, 2 vols (London, 1848): Vol. I, pp. 434-7, Vol. II, pp. 438-9; *Elizabeth Fry*, by J. Kent (London, 1962).

GERARD, JOHN

The Life of John Gerard of the Society of Jesus, by J. Morris (London, 1881): pp. 112-3, 417-25.

GREGORY THE GREAT, ST

Patrologia Latina (J. P. Migne), lxxv-lxxviii; lxxvii, col. 878; *Gregory the Great*, by F. H. Dudden, 2 vols (London, 1905); *Gregory the Great*, by P. Batiffol (London, 1929).

HERBERT, GEORGE

Works, 2 vols (London, 1835-6); *The Works of George Herbert*, ed. F. E. Hutcheson (Oxford, 1941): pp. 375-6; *George Herbert*, by M. Bottrall (London, 1954).

HOPKINS, GERARD MANLEY

The Letters of Gerard Manley Hopkins to Robert Bridges, ed. C. C. Abbott (London & New York, 1935): pp. 59-61, 62-5; *The Correspondence of Gerard Manley Hopkins and Richard Watson Dixon*, ed. C. C. Abbott (London & New York, 1935); *Further Letters of Gerard Manley Hopkins*, ed. C. C. Abbott, 2nd ed. (London, 1956), pp. 50-2; *Gerard Manley Hopkins: A Very Private Life*, by R. B. Martin (London & New York, 1991).

HOWARD, ST PHILIP

Memories of Missionary Priests, by Bishop Challoner, ed. J. H. Pollen (London, 1924): p. 108; *Catholic Record Society*, Vol. 21: pp. 315-7.

IGNATIUS OF ANTIOCH, ST

The Apostolic Fathers, by J. B. Lightfoot, Part II, 3 vols (London, 1885); LS, pp. 65-9; *St Ignatius and Christianity in Antioch*, by V. Corwin (Yale, 1960).

IGNATIUS LOYOLA, ST

Monumenta Ignatiana: Epistolae et Instructiones, series I, 12 vols (Madrid, 1903-14); *Saint Ignatius Loyola: The Pilgrim Years,* by J. Brodrick, SJ (London, 1956); *St Ignatius Loyola: Letters to Women,* ed. H. Rahner, SJ (New York & London, 1960); LS, pp. 170-2; *St Ignatius Loyola,* by H. Rahner, SJ (London, 1968).

JEROME, ST

Patrologia Latina, xxii, col. 562-4, ep. cvii; *Epistolae,* ed. J. Labourt, 8 vols (Paris, 1949-63); *Select Letters,* ed. F. A. Wright (Oxford, 1933); LS: pp. 82-4, 99-102; *The Letters of St Jerome,* vol. I, ed. T. C. Lawler, tr. C. C. Mierow (Westminster, nd. & London, 1963): pp. 139-41, 145-6, 164-6.

JOAN OF ARC, ST

Condamnation et Réhabilitation de Jeanne d'Arc dite la Pucelle, ed. Jules Quicherat, 5 vols (Paris, 1841-9): Vol. V, pp. 96-8, 123-7, 139-40, 147-8, 150-62; *The Trial of Joan of Arc,* ed. W. P. Barrett (London, 1931); *St Joan of Arc,* by R. Pernoud (London, 1961); *Joan of Arc,* by M. Warner (London, 1980).

JOGUES, ST ISAAC

Jesuit Relations, ed. R. G. Thwaites (London, 1897-1901), Vol. 39: p. 175.

JOHN OF THE CROSS, ST

The Complete Works of Saint John of the Cross, Doctor of the Church, ed. & tr. E. Allison Peers, new edition, 3 vols (London & New York, 1953): Vol. 3, pp. 255-8; *A Handbook to the Life and Times of St Teresa and St John of the Cross,* by E. Allison Peers (London, 1954); *Crucible of Love,* by E. W. T. Dicken (London, 1963).

KEBLE, JOHN

Letters of Spiritual Counsel and Guidance, by J. Keble, ed. R. J. Wilson (Oxford, 1870): pp. 6-7, 39-40, 154-7; *John Keble,* by G. Battiscombe (London, 1963).

KIERKEGAARD, SØREN

Samlede Verker, ed. A. B. Drachmann, J. L. Heiberg & H. O. Lange, 15 vols (Copenhagen, 1901-36); *Either/Or,* by S. Kierkegaard, ed. H. A. Johnson, tr. W. Lowrie, Vol. II (Princeton, 1944; New York, 1959): pp. 270-2, 350-6; *The Mind of Kierkegaard,* by J. Collins (Chicago & London, 1953-4).

KOLBE, MAXIMILIAN

Maxmilian Kolbe, by W. Nigg (Freiburg im Breisgau, 1980): pp. 54-5; *Saint of Auschwitz,* by D. Dewar (London, 1982).

LIGUORI, ST ALPHONSUS

Le Lettere di S. Alfonso de Liguori, ed. P. Kuntz, 3 vols (Rome, 1887); *Works of St Alphonsus de Liguori,* ed. E. Grimm (New York, 1891): p. 94; *Alphonsus Liguori, Saint of Bourbon Naples,* by Frederick Jones, CSSR, (Dublin, 1993); *Celebrating Eternity Now: A Study in the Theology of St Alphonsus Liguori,* by Hamish F. G. Swanston (New York, 1995).

MACDONALD, GEORGE

George Macdonald and his Wife, by Greville Macdonald, intro. G. K. Chesterton (London, 1924): pp. 108, 110-1, 117, 184, 184-5, 197-8, 222-3.

MORE, ST THOMAS

The Life and Illustrious Martyrdom of Sir Thomas More, by T. Stapleton (London, 1928): pp. 92, 101, 106, 111, 115; *The Correspondence of Sir Thomas More,* ed. E. F. Rogers (Princeton, 1947), p. 138; *St Thomas More,* by E. E. Reynolds (2nd ed., London, 1968); *Thomas More and Erasmus,* by E. E. Reynolds (London, 1965): pp. 37-9, 146-8; *Thomas More,* by A. Fox (London, 1982).

NEWMAN, JOHN HENRY

John Henry Newman: Letters and Diaries, ed. C. S. Dessain (London, 1961 ff); *The Life of John Henry, Cardinal Newman,* by W. Ward, 2 vols (London, 1912): Vol. II, pp. 287-9, 289-90, 376-7, 539, 556; *Newman, Prose and Poetry,* ed. G. Tillotson (London, 1957): pp. 794, 800; *Young Mr Newman,* by M. Ward (London, 1948); *John Henry Newman,* by C. S. Dessain (London, 1966).

PASCAL, BLAISE

Oeuvres complètes, ed. J. Chevalier (Paris, 1954): pp. 486-90, 511-3, 703-15; *Provincial Letters,* tr. A .J. Krailsheimer (Harmondsworth, 1967); *Blaise Pascal,* by E. Mortimer (London, 1959); *Pascal,* by J. H. Broome (London, 1965).

SOUTHWELL, ST ROBERT

Works by the Rev. Robert Southwell, ed. W. J. Walter (London, 1822): pp. 106, 109; *An Epistle of Comfort,* ed. M. Waugh (London, 1966): pp. 136-9, 167-9, 219-24; *Records of the English Province of the Society of Jesus,* ed. H. Foley, SJ, series I, pp. 339 ff; *The Life of Robert Southwell,* by Christopher Devlin, SJ (London & New York, 1956).

TEN BOOM, CORRIE

A Prisoner Yet, by Corrie ten Boom (London, 1954); *Prison Letters,* by Corrie ten Boom (London, 1975): pp. 33-6, 89-90.

TERESA OF AVILA, ST

The Letters of Saint Teresa of Avila, tr. & ed. E. Allison Peers (London, 1951):

2 vols, Vol. I, pp. 389-95, 408-13, 465-8, 468-71, Vol. II, pp. 543-6; *The Eagle and the Dove*, by E. Sackville-West (London, 1943); *Mother of Carmel*, by E. Allison Peers (London, 1945); *Crucible of Love*, by E. W. T. Dicken (London, 1963); *St Theresa of Avila*, by S. Clissold (London, 1978).

THERESE OF LISIEUX, ST

Lettres de Sainte Thérèse de Lisieux de l'Enfant Jésus, ed. A. Combes (Lisieux, 1948): pp. 9, 17, 31; *Letters of St Teresa of Lisieux*, ed. A. Combes (New York, 1948); *Thérèse: Saint of a Little Way*, by Frances Parkinson Keyes (New York & London, 1962); *St Teresa of Lisieux*, by J. Norbury (London, 1966).

VENARD, ST THEOPHANE

Bienheureux Théophane Vénard, ed. J. Guennou (Paris, 1960): p. 98; *Life of J. Théophane Vénard* by E. Vénard (London, 1888): pp. 57, 156-64, 170, 183.

VON HÜGEL, BARON FRIEDRICH

Selected Letters from Baron Friedrich von Hügel (London, 1927): pp. 230-2; *Letters from Baron Friedrich von Hügel to a Niece*, ed. G. Greene (London, 1928): pp. xlii-xliii, 26-33, 58-60, 85-8; *Baron von Hügel: Man of God*, ed. P. F. Chambers (London, 1945).

WEIL, SIMONE

Gravity and Grace, by S. Weil (London, 1952): pp. xii-xiv; *Simone Weil: A Life*, by S. Pétrement (London, 1977).

WESLEY, CHARLES

The Journal of the Rev. Charles Wesley, M.A., to which are appended selections from his correspondence and poetry, ed. T. Jackson, 2 vols (London, n.d. [1849]): Vol. I, p. 173; *Charles Wesley as Revealed in his Letters*, by F. Baker (London, 1948).

WESLEY, JOHN

Works, 3rd ed, 14 vols (London, 1829-31); *The Letters of the Rev. John Wesley, A.M.*, ed. J. Telford, 8 vols (London, 1931): Vol. V, pp. 350-1, Vol. VIII, p. 209, Vol. II, pp. 264-7, Vol. I, pp. 218-20; *The Young Mr Wesley*, by V. H. H. Green (London, 1961); *John Wesley*, Vol. I, by M. Schmidt (London, 1962); *John Wesley*, by V. H. H. Green (London, 1964); *The Burning Heart*, by A. S. Wood (London, 1967).

II. General

These works are referred to above by the abbreviations following them here.

Letters from the Saints: Early Renaissance and Reformation Periods from St Thomas Aquinas to Blessed Robert Southwell, ed. C. Williamson (New York & London, 1948): LSER.
The Papal Encyclicals in their Historical Context, ed. A. Fremantle (New York, 1956, 1963): PE.
Letters from the Saints, ed. A Benedictine of Stanbrook (London & New York, 1964): LS

III. ACKNOWLEDGEMENTS

The editor and publishers gratefully acknowledge the kind permission of the following to reprint and/or to adapt extracts from certain works: Burns & Oates for translations of letters by St Bernard of Clairvaux, St Robert Bellarmine, St Teresa of Avila, Alfred Delp, SJ, and Charles de Foucauld, and quotations from other publications listed in I and the anthology (LS) cited in II above; Routledge & Kegan Paul for an extract from *Gravity and Grace* by Simone Weil, translated by Emma Crawfurd; SCM Press for extracts from *Letters and Papers from Prison* by Dietrich Bonhoeffer; HarperCollins for an extract from *No Rusty Swords* by Dietrich Bonhoeffer; the Oxford University Press and the Society of Jesus for extracts from *The Letters of Gerard Manley Hopkins to Robert Bridges*, ed. C. C. Abbott, and *Further Letters of Gerard Manley Hopkins*, 2nd ed., ed. C. C. Abbott; Princeton University Press for extracts from *Either/Or*, vol. II, by S. Kierkegaard, ed. H. A. Johnson, tr. W. Lowrie; Christian Literature Crusade for extracts from *Prison Letters* and *A Prisoner Yet* by Corrie ten Boom.